GREATEST GAMES

HEARTS

MIKE SMITH

First published by Pitch Publishing, 2012

Pitch Publishing
A2 Yeoman Gate
Yeoman Way
Durrington
BN13 3QZ
www.pitchpublishing.co.uk

A CIP catalogue record is available for this book from the British Library

ISBN 978-1 90805 150 9

Typesetting and origination by Pitch Publishing.

Printed in Great Britain by TJ International.

CONTENTS

FOREWORD
BY JOHN ROBERTSON

MY PLAYING career spanned nearly two decades and I spent the majority of it wearing the maroon and white of Heart of Midlothian. You don't spend 17 years at a club without developing a deep affection for the club – an affection which has lasted to this day and will never leave.

When I joined Hearts as a 16-year-old in 1981, the club were lurching between the Premier and First Divisions. The club had little money to spend on players and it was partly as a result of this that the manager at the time, former Newcastle United and Scotland centre-half Bobby Moncur, gave me and other young players such as Gary Mackay and David Bowman an early chance in the first team.

Gary would make a record number of appearances in a maroon shirt, Davie went on to have a successful career with Coventry City then Dundee United and all three of us would go on to play for Scotland so I like to think we didn't let anyone down.

I look back on my time at Hearts with great pride. While Wallace Mercer may have saved the club from oblivion in 1981, it was Alex MacDonald and Sandy Jardine who helped establish Hearts as a Premier Division side and in a remarkably short space of time turned the Maroons from First Division also-rans to a side that was eight minutes away from becoming champions of Scotland.

Those of us who were at Dens Park that fateful day in May 1986 when Hearts needed just a point against Dundee to win the league – but lost 2-0 thereby enabling Celtic to snatch the title on goal difference – will never forget the scenes of heartache at the end. However, there was immense pride at being part of a club that had taken Scottish football by storm. The Hearts team of 1985/86 of which I was a part had earned the respect of the rest of Scottish football – and returned a feeling of pride to Gorgie Road.

I was part of the Hearts team that secured some notable results in Europe. European nights at Tynecastle are very special and I was involved in memorable games against Dnieper, Slavia Prague and Bayern Munich – all covered in this book – that will live long in the memory.

Of course, one can't spent so long at one club and not suffer disappointment. 1986 aside – there was also defeat to Aberdeen in the Scottish Cup final that year – there was heartache in the Scottish Cup semi-finals of 1988 when Hearts lost two goals in the final two minutes to Celtic; 1992 when Hearts lost in the semi-finals to an Airdrieonians side managed by Alex MacDonald; and in 1996 when Hearts lost the final 5-1 to Rangers.

Six months after that 5-1 loss, Hearts played Rangers in the Scottish League Cup final and showed just how much we had learned as a team under Jim Jefferies when we lost narrowly 4-3 – when I scored Hearts' equaliser at 2-2 I genuinely believed we were about to end our trophy drought.

However, the long wait for silverware finally ended on 16th May 1998 when Hearts gained revenge for the 1996 final by defeating Rangers 2-1 at Celtic Park to lift the Scottish Cup for the first time in 42 years – and the first major piece of silverware since 1962.

I was on the substitutes' bench that day and when I collected my winners' medal I clutched my heart – it was the proudest moment of my playing career and one I had waited a decade and a half to savour. It was a day Hearts fans would never forget.

This book is a look back at 50 of the greatest games by one of Scotland's famous clubs – Heart of Midlothian. From the club's first national trophy, the Scottish Cup in 1891 to the modern era this book will appeal to supporters of all ages who have a special place in their hearts for a truly special club.

John Robertson,
August 2012

ACKNOWLEDGEMENTS

THE CHALLENGE of writing about Hearts' 50 Greatest Games – around 100,000 words – has been immense. I've had plenty of jibes from fans of other clubs, notably Edinburgh's lesser team, about how I would find 50 games worth writing about. To my colleagues of the Hibernian persuasion, I merely utter the words William Hill Scottish Cup final 2012 and they quickly disappear…

Football is all about opinions and Hearts fans reading this book may argue with my list of games. Why wasn't such a game included? Why does such a game have a mention? One of the joys of watching football – apart from regular thrashings of Hibernian – is that such topics are open to healthy debate. The 50 games in this book are what I consider to be the greatest Hearts games in the club's long and proud history.

I could not have completed this book without the support of my family and I'm grateful for their support. I dedicate this book to my three grandchildren Jack, Hannah and Ava, and to the memory of my late father who encouraged my writing many years ago.

Thanks are due also to Davy Allan at the excellent London Hearts website www. londonhearts.com and the huge database of information that helped me research much of this book; to the good people at www.jambos.net, Gerry Cassidy at Planet Hearts and Brian McColl who runs the truly excellent Scottish Football Historical Archive www. scottish-football-historical-archive.com. I must also thank those who have encouraged me and massaged my oft-battered ego when it needed massaging the most. Namely, Gary Copland (the nicest Hibby I know), Lindsay Wright, Allan McKillop, Graham Herriot and Paul Kiddie at Hearts.

I also want to pay tribute to two people who have given me immeasurable support during what has been a difficult year for me. Namely, my mother Isabella – she's an Aberdeen fan but we all have our cross to bear – and the lovely Marion Hunter, who is my inspiration. Thanks also to John Robertson, a Hearts legend, for writing the foreword for this book and to Eric McCowat for the use of photographs.

Finally, and without wishing to resort to cliché mode, thank you for buying this book – you've made an old Jambo very happy!

Mike Smith,
August 2012

v **Dumbarton** 1-0
Scottish Cup Final
7th February 1891. Hampden

Hearts:	Dumbarton:
Fairbairn	McLeod
Adams	Watson
Goodfellow	Millar
Begbie	McMillan
McPherson	Boyle
Hill	Leitch-Keir
Taylor	Taylor
Mason	Galbraith
Russell	Mair
Scott	McNaught
Baird	Bell

Referee: T Park (Glasgow)

I N 17TH century Edinburgh, there stood a prison in the old city's Royal Mile alongside a hangman's scaffold. The prison was referred to as the Heart of Midlothian and it was demolished in 1817. The name lived on however and later that century a dance hall adopted the famous moniker. In 1874, a group of men who frequented the dance hall got together to establish a club to partake in the latest craze to sweep the country – association football. Therefore, Heart of Midlothian Football Club was formed – and a Scottish football institution was born.

A year later, Hearts became members of the Scottish Football Association as well as founder members of the Edinburgh Football Association. The club chose white with a maroon-shaped heart on the chest as its team colours and the first club captain was a gentleman called Tom Purdie.

Early games were played at East Meadows in the centre of Edinburgh, with the club based in West Crosscauseway in the city. Hearts were big enough to compete in the Scottish Cup in 1875 and their first competitive fixture in the national cup competition came against the 3rd Edinburgh Rifle Volunteers. The game ended goalless, as did the replay at East Meadows. Bizarrely, the SFA rules at the time meant both sides progressed to the next round where Hearts travelled to Coatbridge and lost 2-0 to Drumpellier.

These days, football is not played on Christmas Day but 137 years ago, it was. On Christmas Day 1875, Hearts played another Edinburgh club – Hibernians (who later dropped the letter s from their name). The game was played at East Meadows and, like so many other Edinburgh derbies since, ended in triumph for Hearts who won 1-0.

A shortage of players meant Hearts didn't play any competitive games for a few months but, in 1877, St Andrews FC was incorporated to Heart of Midlothian.

Hearts briefly adopted the colours of red, white and blue hoops and legend has it of the occasion when the strips were washed, the dye from the colours ran and red, white and blue became maroon – the colours Hearts have famously kept ever since!

In 1879, the continued growth of the club saw Hearts move their base to Powburn in the capital. By now, Hearts felt they had progressed enough to take on the force of the land in the 1870s – not Rangers, who were formed before Hearts, and not Celtic, who were still the best part of a decade away from being formed; it was Queen's Park who were by far the leading force in Scottish football. Indeed, Queen's had supplied the team for Scotland's first ever international match, a goalless draw with England in 1872.

In October 1880, Hearts faced Queen's Park in a challenge match but were given something of a reality check when they lost 8-1. However, the fact that more than 3,000 fans turned up at the Powderhall grounds for the game was proof, if proof were needed, that Heart of Midlothian Football Club was here to stay.

In 1881, Hearts moved to the emerging Edinburgh suburb of Gorgie and a playing field at what has since become Wardlaw Place. However, in a scenario that has been repeated regularly ever since, Hearts found their best players would leave for pastures new, in particular England where professional football was becoming the norm as opposed to the amateur status of most Scots teams.

In an effort to redress this situation, Hearts offered illegal payments to some of their players in a bid to retain their services and in 1884 Hearts were suspended from the Scottish Football Association following an inquiry after the Maroons' 11-1 thumping of Dunfermline Athletic in the Scottish Cup. The Fifers suspected something was amiss and protested to the SFA. Hearts were found to be guilty. They weren't the only club to be paying players – but they were among the first to be caught doing so. Hearts confessed and were readmitted to the SFA soon after.

In April 1886, Hearts moved to their present home at Tynecastle, with leading English side Bolton Wanderers having the honour of being Hearts' first opponents there.

In 1890, Hearts were among the founding members of the Scottish League. This new body meant there would be regular competitive fixtures on a national basis. Hearts' first two league fixtures were a 5-2 defeat by Rangers at Ibrox and a 5-0 defeat from Celtic at Tynecastle a week later. However, Hearts recovered from these early setbacks and at the end of October, they thrashed Vale of Leven 8-1 in front of 2,500 spectators at Tynecastle. This was only Hearts' second league win and enabled them to keep clear of the club in second bottom place of the new league – Celtic, who had been deducted four points for breaching Scottish League rules. The Gorgie men's next league game wasn't until the end of January 1891 when they lost 1-0 to Rangers at Tynecastle.

In between, Hearts made progress in the Scottish Cup. They thrashed Raith Rovers 7-2 at Tynecastle before being awarded a walkover against Burntisland Thistle who had to withdraw from the competition. Subsequent victories over Methlan Park (3-0); Ayr FC (4-3); Morton (5-1) and East Stirlingshire (3-1) saw Hearts in the semi-final where they faced Third Lanark Volunteers. The game was played at Third's Cathkin Park in Glasgow and Hearts produced one of their best performances of the season to win 4-1 and reach their first ever Scottish Cup final.

Their opponents in the final, just a week later on 7th February 1891, were Dumbarton. Nearly 11,000 fans – producing gate receipts in excess of £600 – were at Hampden Park for the occasion with a huge contingent from Edinburgh. The game kicked off in a frenzied atmosphere and it was Dumbarton who had the first chance when Galbraith was through on goal only to be stopped by a fine challenge from Hearts full-back George Goodfellow. Hearts then had a great chance to open the scoring only for Davie Russell to see his effort cleared off the line by Watson.

The early exchanges were keenly fought and play raged from end to end. Hearts keeper Jock Fairbairn then produced a brilliant save to deny Bell and it was reported the cheers from the Hearts supporters was akin to a goal being celebrated. The ever-dangerous Russell then went agonisingly close with a header and it seemed only a matter of time before a goal would be scored.

One duly arrived after 15 minutes. Jimmy Adams played a superb pass to George Scott who fed Willie Mason whose ferocious shot beat Dumbarton keeper McLeod all ends up to put Hearts a goal ahead, much to the delight of the Edinburgh supporters. Hearts took great encouragement from this and came close on several occasions to adding to their score but half-time arrived with Hearts leading by just a single goal.

However, at the start of the second half, Dumbarton came out with all guns blazing. Hearts' Fairbairn was now the busier of the two keepers and he had to be at his best to keep out efforts from McNaught and Bell. Hearts though, to their great credit, weathered the storm and 15 minutes into the second half, Dumbarton had still not managed to equalise.

Then, the hugely influential Johnny Hill appeared to be struggling from injury and Hearts pushed Baird into a more defensive role. Hill carried on gamely but this was an era that was decades before substitutions were permitted and it was a case of backs to the wall for the Maroons, although Scott did cause the Dumbarton defence some problems with his pace on the wing. It was from a cross by Scott that Mason very nearly scored a second goal for Hearts that would have surely clinched victory.

Dumbarton pressed harder as the game drew to its conclusion but the consensus was that the Sons of the Rock were a beaten side well before referee Tom Park – who was the president of the SFA – blew his whistle for the final time. The game ended Hearts 1 Dumbarton 0 and the victorious Maroons had won their first ever Scottish Cup. There were jubilant scenes as fans came on to the Hampden pitch to carry the Hearts players shoulder high from the field of play.

All the Hearts players were heroes but Jimmy Adams, John McPherson, Davie Russell and George Scott were the pick of a victorious team, although special mention had to be made for the unfortunate Johnny Hill who struggled on through the game despite being in obvious pain. His duty to the cause of his team was praiseworthy. Hearts' achievement was even more notable as Dumbarton had, until the final, been unbeaten that season and would go on to share the league championship with Rangers just a few weeks later.

After the game, Hearts dined at the Alexandra Hotel in Glasgow and SFA president Park – after doing such a fine job as referee that afternoon – presented the Scottish Cup to Hearts, saying it was fitting that Scotland's cup should finally go to Scotland's capital city. Hearts headed back to Edinburgh later that evening and were greeted by a huge crowd at the city's Caledonian railway station. Indeed, it was reported that the city's police officers had some difficulty restraining the thronging masses of Hearts supporters who could not contain their delight.

It was the breakthrough Hearts had waited nearly 20 years for and established the club as a major force in Scottish football. Four of the Scottish Cup-winning team – David Baird, Isaac Begbie, John McPherson and Johnny Hill – would play for Scotland in a 2-1 defeat to England two months later.

Whether the celebrations caught up with the players is not entirely clear but Hearts ended the season on something of a losing streak as they lost to Third Lanark, Dumbarton, Abercorn and Cambuslang all within a fortnight – and without even scoring a goal. Dumbarton took full revenge for their cup final defeat when they thrashed Hearts 4-0 at Tynecastle on 20th April on their way to sharing the league title.

Hearts ended the first ever Scottish League season in sixth place in the table – 15 points behind the joint champions, Dumbarton and Rangers. The three teams immediately below Hearts in the league table – Abercorn, St Mirren and Vale of Leven – had to apply for re-election to the league for the following season.

Hearts supporters though, weren't complaining. While they had seen their team dominate Edinburgh football by winning numerous local competitions, it had been suggested, particularly by those from the west of Scotland, that Hearts didn't have what it took to challenge for honours at national level. Rangers were beginning to be the dominant team in the land and with the recent formation of a club that would be their greatest rivals – Celtic, who were established in 1888 – there remained a firmly established opinion that it would be the Glasgow teams who would continue to dominate, just as Queen's Park had done since association football was formed in Scotland a couple of decades earlier. In 1891, Hearts had proved the "experts" wrong – and would do so again before the end of the decade and at the turn of the century.

Edinburgh's finest were here to stay and although success would prove sporadic over the coming century, when it did arrive it tasted sweet – as it did on that cold, windy February day when Hearts became Scottish Cup winners!

v Celtic 4-0
Scottish League Division One
16th February 1895. Tynecastle

Hearts:	Celtic:
Cox	McArthur
Battles	Dunbar
Mirk	Reynolds
Begbie	Thom
Hall	Kelly
Hogg	Cassidy
McLaren	Campbell
Chambers	Blessington
Michael	McCann
Walker	Divers
Scott	Macmahon

Referee: M Dickson (Wishaw)

HEARTS' SCOTTISH Cup triumph of 1891 firmly established them as one of Scotland's leading football clubs and progress continued at a steady, rather than spectacular rate. The following season, Hearts finished third in Division One at the end of the second season of the Scottish League, just three points behind champions Dumbarton, who didn't need to share the championship this time around.

Hearts racked up some impressive results including an early season defeat of Dumbarton, 3-1 at Tynecastle in front of over 7,000 spectators, although I should point out the Maroons paid the price for this three weeks later when they were hammered 5-1 in the reverse fixture at Dumbarton.

Hearts though, were a free-scoring team. They put six goals past Vale of Leven at Tynecastle and scored ten goals at Clyde in a 10-3 win. The Glasgow men must have dreaded the prospect of heading to Tynecastle in November as Hearts began their defence of the Scottish Cup but they performed much better as Hearts led 3-1 when, with just three minutes left, the referee abandoned the game due to bad light. Hearts took their anger out on the visitors when the game was replayed the following week and coasted to an 8-0 win. Hearts eventually relinquished their hold on the trophy when they lost 3-2 to Renton after two drawn games.

Hearts, however, enjoyed a fine season and in April 1892 hosted a glamour friendly with FA Cup holders West Bromwich Albion. The game attracted a huge crowd of more than 12,000 to Tynecastle – despite the rather unseasonable snow showers! The presence of such a large number of fans necessitated a police presence but there was no repeat of the largely reported unsavoury scenes at the Scottish Cup final between Celtic and Queen's Park nine days earlier.

The large-numbered and well-behaved Tynecastle crowd were rewarded with a 2-0 win for the Maroons with some of them declaring Hearts were now world champions! The Maroons seemed to take inspiration from such a result and defeated Rangers 3-2 at Tynecastle a few days later. Hearts were reduced to ten men when home defender George Goodfellow was sent off but the player he made a rather crude tackle against – McCreadie – also had to leave the field because of his injury.

In the days when Queen Victoria sat on the throne, substitutes were not even considered in football so both sides played on with ten men apiece after a rather unfortunate ending to the game. Hearts were now just a point behind league leaders Dumbarton but the Maroons then drew with Leith Athletic before losing to Third Lanark and so hopes of a league title were dashed on the final day of the season – not the last time such a scenario would happen to Edinburgh's finest.

The 1893/94 season saw Hearts go one better and finish runners-up to Celtic in the league. Hearts won 3-2 at Celtic Park in March 1894 to move seven points behind The Hoops, having played two games fewer, but a 4-2 defeat at Tynecastle by city neighbours St Bernards on the first Saturday in April proved costly. Hearts let slip a 2-1 lead as the team from the Stockbridge area of Edinburgh came storming back.

The Maroons ended the league season by defeating Dumbarton 2-1 at Tynecastle but they finished three points behind Celtic who secured the first of what would prove to be many league titles. It was scant consolation that Hearts would defeat the new league champions 2-1 in a friendly at Tynecastle in the middle of May.

Hearts' famous victory over West Bromwich Albion the previous season saw no shortage of invitations from other English sides for 'challenge matches' and Hearts enjoyed victories over Sunderland, Bury and Blackburn Rovers this season – all of whom were no slouches south of the border. While disappointed in missing out on the league, Hearts at least had some silverware to show off after they defeated Leith Athletic 4-2 in the East of Scotland Shield Final at Edinburgh's Logie Green in May.

When 1894/95 began, Hearts were many people's tip for bringing the Scottish League flag to the east of the country for the first time. The club brought in several new players for the season and they began the league campaign with a 6-3 win over Third Lanark at Tynecastle.

In fact, Hearts made an incredible start, winning their first 11 games to storm to the top of the league. These included home and away victories over old adversaries Dumbarton, a 1-0 win over Rangers at Ibrox and a 2-0 win at champions Celtic in front of a huge crowd of over 20,000 in Glasgow. Those in maroon who had travelled through from Edinburgh could scarcely contain their delight at the end of the game. This win would surely prove wrong those sceptics who said Hearts would not be good enough to be champions.

Hearts' first league defeat of the season came on 1st December when Clyde won 4-2 at Tynecastle – something of a shock when one considered Hearts' recent record against the Glasgow side.

By the time champions Celtic headed for Tynecastle in February 1895, Hearts were already eight points clear of second-placed Rangers and the consensus was that a win for Hearts would secure their first league championship. More than 8,000 people headed to Tynecastle for the eagerly awaited clash, with the Maroons favourites given their astonishing form in the league. Celtic had a few players such as Doyle, Maley and Madden missing through injury and illness and this looked like the ideal opportunity for Hearts to triumph.

However, there had been heavy snow and freezing temperatures in Edinburgh that week and it was doubtful if the Tynecastle pitch was playable. Certainly, by today's standards it's probable the game would have been called off the day before but footballers in the Victorian era were a hardy bunch! Hearts covered the pitch with sand, straw and sawdust and when the game kicked off the players struggled to keep their balance.

However, it was Hearts who adapted far better to the conditions, which was hardly surprising given it was their pitch. The conditions were a factor when Hearts took the lead early in the game. Celtic's Reynolds slipped, allowing Hearts' Johnny Walker to gleefully open the scoring. The Hearts forward line was causing a nervous looking Celtic rearguard all manner of problems with Walker the tormentor in chief.

Thomas Chambers added a second midway through the first half before Walker added a third goal with a rasping shot that gave Celtic keeper McArthur no chance. Hearts led 3-0 at half-time and the game was effectively over as a contest – as was the league championship.

This was confirmed when Celtic restarted the game with only ten men as Kelly didn't appear and it was inevitably one-way traffic towards the Celtic goal, where McArthur produced a string of brilliant saves. At times, it looked like the Celtic custodian was playing Hearts on his own but he was helpless to prevent Willie Michael adding a fourth goal for Hearts to complete the scoring.

Despite the conditions and playing against ten men for the second half, it was an impressive performance from Hearts and the home support weren't slow in showing their appreciation. Sportingly, the Tynecastle crowd also offered warm applause to the Celtic team and goalkeeper McArthur in particular. Without his heroics, Hearts may well have reached double figures and he was applauded as he left the field somewhat beleaguered. It is difficult to envisage this happening today!

Hearts' attacking prowess did indeed take them to double figures the following week when they entertained non-league side Linthouse. More than 3,000 spectators headed to Tynecastle to witness what was a complete mismatch. Hearts thrashed their hapless opponents 11-0. The game was over by half-time, by which point the home side were already five goals to the good. The local newspaper reported the game was "a farce, with no interest of any kind attached to the result".

Friendly matches arranged between league fixtures was commonplace at the time and while one could understand that Hearts wanted to maintain their momentum after thrashing Celtic, it's doubtful if the mismatch with Linthouse proved to be of any great purpose – certainly not for those supporters who parted with hard-earned cash to watch the game!

Johnny Walker's two goals against Celtic was just part of a major contribution by the forward that season. The 20-year-old from Coatbridge was one of Hearts' leading players and there was huge disappointment when he signed for Liverpool in 1898. He would return to Scotland four years later and enjoy spells at Rangers and Morton. However, the great man couldn't find the net when Hearts played city rivals St Bernards in the semi-final of the Scottish Cup in March 1895.

A huge crowd of more than 14,000 attended the game at Tynecastle and a tense game ended goalless. The replay at Logie Green in Scotland's capital city a week later attracted an even larger attendance as 18,000 packed into the ground. Again, Johnny

Walker and his fellow forwards could not find the net and St Bernards won 1-0 to claim a cup final place.

Despite their Scottish Cup disappointment – and a rare defeat in the league to Clyde – Hearts regained their form and defeated Dundee 4-0 before gaining revenge on St Bernards with a 3-0 win at Logie Green to clinch their first ever league title. The Maroons finished the season five points clear of the team they deposed as champions, Celtic, and lost just two league games all season – both to Clyde. They scored 50 goals in 18 league games and it was evident, even early in the season, that Hearts were streets ahead of every other team in Scotland.

At the end of the season, Hearts were keen to continue the celebrations and yet another challenge match with English opposition was arranged. However, this just wasn't any English team – this was newly crowned English league champions Sunderland. The game was arranged for 27th April 1895 and more than 12,000 fans headed to Tynecastle for what was billed as the 'world championship decider'.

Sunderland showed just why they were England's best team and went in at the interval two goals ahead. However, Hearts fought back in the second half and scored through two goals from Bob McLaren and one from Willie Taylor. Sadly, their efforts weren't rewarded as Sunderland ran out 5-3 winners to claim the unofficial world championship but the occasion was a memorable one and marked Hearts' standing in not only Scottish but also British football. Little more than 20 years after being established, Heart of Midlothian had not only won the Scottish Cup but were now champions of Scotland – and very nearly champions of the world!

Hearts ended the 1894/95 season by winning the Edinburgh League and defeating Leith Athletic 3-1 in the final of the Rosebery Charity Cup to complete an impressive trophy collection. Davie Russell and Johnny Walker represented Scotland that season, Walker against Ireland and Russell against Ireland and England.

It had been a magnificent season for Hearts. However, those who followed the Maroons would soon realise that disappointment is never far away from Edinburgh's oldest and finest football team – as the following season, 1895/96 would prove when Hearts relinquished their league title. Nonetheless, there would still be a major trophy at Tynecastle in 1896...

v Hibernian 3-1
Scottish Cup Final
14th March 1896. Logie Green

Hearts:	Hibernian:
Fairbairn	McCall
McCartney	Robertson
Mirk	McFarlane
Begbie	Breslin
Russell	Neil
Hogg	Murphy
McLaren	Murray
Baird	Kennedy
Michael	Groves
King	Smith
Walker	O'Neill

Referee: W McLeod (Cowstairs)

HEARTS SUPPORTERS, unsurprisingly, savoured the summer of 1895. Their team were newly crowned champions of Scotland. They already knew their team was by far and away the best in Edinburgh and to emphasise this, Hearts arranged two friendly games at the beginning of the 1895/96 season against their city rivals.

Not unsurprisingly, Hearts defeated Hibernian 5-3 at Tynecastle on 3rd August – Alex King scoring a hat-trick – and followed this up a week later with a 4-1 win over capital rivals St Bernards, also at Tynecastle. Critics today often cite the repetitive nature of the Scottish Premier League with four games against opponents each season. It's interesting to note that Hearts' friendly victory over Hibernian would be the first of eight games against the Green and Whites during the 1895/96 season.

Hearts began the defence of their league championship in Paisley – and it was a start few people expected as St Mirren won 2-1 in front of a crowd of around 4,000 on a baking hot August afternoon. *The Scotsman* newspaper expressed an element of surprise that so many people chose to attend a football match rather than head for the beach and enjoy the scorching weather. Football, although rapidly growing in popularity, was still a wee bit away from being the raison d'etre it is for many people today!

Those Hearts supporters present probably had wished they had headed further along the west coast as their team suffered a rare and unexpected loss. When Hearts won the league championship the season before, they had lost to just one team – Clyde. The Maroons rectified this by winning 2-1 at Shawfield on 24th August, but a week later lost 2-1 to Rangers at Tynecastle. Hearts had now lost as many games after three fixtures as they had done during the entire 1894/95 league season and supporters could not help but feel these were ominous signs.

However, in September, Hearts at last hit top form and thrashed league leaders Celtic 5-0 at Celtic Park with Alex King hitting another hat-trick. Ironically, Hearts' hammering of the Hoops meant Hibernian hit the top of the league but Hearts, after their indifferent start, were just three points behind.

After local victories over St Bernards and Hibernian – more than 17,000 people came to Tynecastle to witness a thrilling 4-3 win over the Hibees – Hearts adopted a 'we didn't forget' attitude against the only team to beat them in the league the previous season and hammered hapless Clyde 9-1 at Tynecastle with Davie Baird claiming four goals. *The Scotsman* newspaper stated "it was a somewhat one-sided game" – a contender for understatement of the year!

Hearts were now joint top of the league with Celtic and fans were dreaming of another league championship win. However, calamity struck the following week at Dundee. Goalkeeper Jock Fairbairn suffered a hand injury meaning he was unable to play and his replacement, Gardner, didn't enjoy the best of afternoons. Dundee won 5-0, Hearts dropped to fourth place in the league table and for the first time in months, questions were being asked about Hearts' capability to be league champions.

Hearts answered those questions in emphatic fashion a week later when they thrashed Dumbarton 9-2 at Boghead. Jock Fairbairn was back in goal and Davie Baird, as he had done earlier in the season against Clyde, scored four goals. The Maroons then avenged recent reversals by defeating St Mirren 5-1 and Dundee 2-0, both at Tynecastle, and Hearts were back at the top of the league – but not for long.

Three successive defeats – 4-1 to Celtic at Tynecastle, 5-4 at Third Lanark and, alarmingly, 7-2 to Rangers at Ibrox – took the wind right out of the sails of the Tynecastle championship challenge. Hearts were now six points behind league leaders Celtic and were seldom in contention for the league title again.

Hearts knew their indifferent form was unlikely to land them a successive league flag so they turned to the Scottish Cup for salvation. In their opening tie in January 1896, the Maroons blasted 12 goals past non-league Blantyre before coasting past Ayr FC and Arbroath to reach the semi-finals once more. As had been the case the previous season, Hearts were drawn against Edinburgh rivals St Bernards and a solitary goal from Willie Michael three minutes from the end of the game sent the Hearts fans in the 16,000 crowd at Tynecastle into raptures. Their team may have been out of the running for the league championship but another Scottish Cup final appearance beckoned. Moreover, Hearts' opponents in the final were none other than a certain other team from Scotland's capital city – Hibernian!

The final made history as the only Scottish Cup final to be held outside Glasgow. Perish the thought of that happening today! More than 16,000 fans packed into St Bernards' ground at Logie Green in Edinburgh on 14th March 1896 to witness the historic event. The location for the final caused something of a controversy. In a move dripping in irony given the circumstances 110 years later when Hearts and Hibs had to play their Scottish Cup semi-final at Hampden Park, Glasgow, many supporters of both Edinburgh teams were less than enamoured with the showpiece game of the season being played outside Glasgow for the first – and subsequently last – time.

Many people wanted the final switched to Glasgow and either Ibrox or Hampden Park. However, the Scottish Football Association were determined the game would be played in Edinburgh at Logie Green. As author William Reid later wrote in his

1925 book *The Story of Hearts*: "The man in the street was in no hurry to die at one shilling admission" – an obvious reference to fears that St Bernards' ground was ill-equipped to hold such a major game and there was genuine fear for the safety of the spectators. In the end, just over 16,000 people turned up – the expected crowd was around 20,000 – and there was little crowd incident of note.

History relates to the fact that Hibernian may have counted themselves fortunate to be in the final at all. Renton, who they defeated in the semi-final, protested that one of the Hibs players was ineligible and sought an interim interdict from the Court of Session looking for the game to be replayed. Their request was thrown out – although given the way the final transpired, Hibs may well have wondered why they fought the decision.

Before an expectant crowd at Logie Green, the Hibs team were the first to take to the field followed soon after by Hearts and there was a rousing reception for both sides from the huge all-Edinburgh crowd. It was Hearts who settled quicker and there were just three minutes played when the league champions took a sensational lead.

Hibs' Robertson handled the ball on the goal line and referee McLeod had no hesitation in awarding a penalty to Hearts. Davie Baird's powerful spot kick struck the flailing legs of Hibs keeper McCall but the ball spun into the net to give Hearts an early lead.

Stung by this early setback, Hibs flooded men forward with Groves, the former Aston Villa forward, causing the Hearts defence problems. However, Hearts goalkeeper Jock Fairbairn, ably assisted by defenders Bob McCartney and Isaac Begbie, was equal to anything Groves and his colleagues could throw at him and Hearts defended stoutly. At the other end of the field, Johnny Walker and Alex King were causing the Hibs defence – and centre-half Murphy in particular – problems of their own.

Midway through the first half Hearts could and indeed should have doubled their lead when Hibs goalkeeper McCall left his goal unguarded but Bob McLaren couldn't direct the ball into the goal. Hearts had further chances to score through the ever-dangerous King and Johnny Walker, but half-time arrived with the score still at just 1-0 to Hearts.

The Hearts supporters in the huge crowd, while pleased their team were ahead and had dominated the game, were nonetheless wary of the fact the lead was so slender. Even more than a century ago, Hearts supporters could take nothing for granted!

Sure enough, it was Hibs who began the second half in determined fashion and Jock Fairbairn was called into action more often than was comfortable for the Hearts support. For the first few minutes of the second half, Hearts were pinned in their own half as Hibs pressed hard for the equaliser. However, with the Green and Whites becoming more desperate, they were caught by a classic sucker punch.

Johnny Walker broke free at great pace and linked up with Alex King. From the goal line near the corner of the field, King fired in a great effort which Hibs keeper McCall got his fingers to but could not prevent from crossing the line. That made it 2-0 to Hearts and it looked like the end for Hibs' Scottish Cup challenge.

It was indeed all over a few minutes from the end, when Willie Michael headed home a third goal and Hearts fans celebrated in some style with hats, sticks and handkerchiefs being thrown wildly in the air – much to the disgust of the Hibs contingent! They did see their team score a late consolation through O'Neill, but minutes later referee McLeod signalled the end of the game – and Hearts had secured their second Scottish Cup triumph in five years. It had been a thrilling game, particularly in the second half when play raged from end to end.

Hearts celebrated a famous victory. However, in a scenario that would be repeated in years to come, there was a cloud to this silver lining. Alex King, an impressive goalscorer who scored Hearts' crucial second goal in the cup final, signed for Celtic a few weeks after and a depressing trait of Hearts losing their best players soon after winning silverware began.

After what had been a disappointing season in the league, Hearts ended 1895/96 with a flourish. A week after the Scottish Cup triumph, Hearts beat Hibs again, 1-0 at Easter Road in the Edinburgh League. A month later, in the return fixture at Tynecastle, the Maroons thrashed their city rivals 7-1.

As they had done when they won the Scottish Cup in 1891, Hearts arranged a challenge match with the English FA Cup winners at the end of April. Unlike the event five years before when they lost to Sunderland, this time Hearts were victorious as they defeated Sheffield Wednesday 3-0 at Tynecastle.

Hearts finished fourth in Division One at the season's end, eight points behind champions Celtic. Many felt the Maroons had given up their league title all too easily but they at least ended the season with more silverware in the Tynecastle trophy room.

Hearts would win the Scottish Cup again in 1901 when they defeated Celtic 4-3 in a thrilling final at Ibrox – the great Bobby Walker opening the scoring for Hearts – and in 1906 when they defeated Third Lanark 1-0, once more at Ibrox in front of a huge crowd of over 30,000.

Hearts seemed to be enjoying Scottish Cup success in five-year cycles and they were, by now, one of Scotland's leading football clubs. One hoped that club officials took a long hard look at the Scottish Cup in 1906 as it sat proudly in the Tynecastle boardroom. For it would be fully half a century before the famous trophy would reside again in the west end of Edinburgh.

Moreover, less than a decade after the 1906 triumph, more important matters had to be considered – and Heart of Midlothian FC were to lead by example…

v St Mirren 5-0
Scottish League Division One
12th September 1914. Tynecastle

Hearts:	St Mirren:
Boyd	O'Hagan
Crossan	Todd
Currie	A Reid
Briggs	McGrory
Scott	R Reid
Nellies	Davidson
Low	Sowerby
Wilson	Brannick
Gracie	Clark
Graham	Hutchison
Speedie	Brown

Referee: J Dickson (Glasgow)

BY THE summer of 1914, Hearts, while remaining one of Scotland's top football clubs, had not quite maintained the regular challenge for honours their supporters had hoped for. The Maroons lifted the Scottish Cup in 1906, defeating Third Lanark 1-0 in the final at Ibrox Park in Glasgow, but eight years had passed without a national trophy.

Indeed, Hearts had not even come close to challenging for the league championship, with the club finishing 9th, 11th, 11th, 12th and 14th in the five years that followed the cup triumph. However, two successive third-placed finishes in the league – in seasons 1912/13 and 1913/14 – gave hope Hearts were ready to rise again.

John McCartney, who took over as Hearts manager in 1910, was steadily building a new team but he wasn't afraid of making decisions that might prove unpopular. In February 1914, in a move that astounded the football world, Hearts sold forward Percy Dawson to top English club Blackburn Rovers for what was, at the time, a world record transfer fee of £2,500. Scottish football was shocked and Hearts supporters found it difficult to comprehend. Dawson had cost the club just £100 when he signed from North Shields Athletic in 1911 and he would score over 100 goals in just over three years at Tynecastle, including four goals in one game against St Bernards in April 1911 and four against St Mirren in November 1913.

The loss of Dawson was a considerable one but manager McCartney used some of the huge transfer fee to bring in players who he believed would push Hearts from league title contenders to champions. He brought players such as Archie Boyd, James Frew, Tom Gracie, Robert Malcolm, George Bryden and Jock Wilson to Gorgie with Gracie scoring on his debut in a 2-0 win over champions Celtic at Tynecastle in August 1914.

This game was played in front of Hearts' brand new grandstand – the present day structure that, in 1914 cost nearly £13,000 to build, a sum that placed the club under severe financial pressure. Some things, it seems, never change!

Hearts made a superb start to the 1914/15 league campaign and after the opening four games were top of the league alongside Rangers. The visit of St Mirren to Tynecastle on 12th September 1914 was against the backdrop of the outbreak of war in Europe a month earlier. More than 10,000 fans headed to Tynecastle on a cold early autumn day and recruiting officers from the British Army were out in force urging men to join up and fight for their country. Posters of "Lord Kitchener Needs You" were on just about every street corner and it's fair to say football was used by the powers that be as a tool for signing up able-bodied men.

As a club, Hearts were only too aware of their obligation to their country. Nonetheless, with football carrying on and the Maroons sitting top of the league, the visit of fourth from bottom St Mirren was an ideal chance for John McCartney's men to maintain their status as league leaders.

Hearts started the game well and the expectant home crowd urged them on for an early goal. And they got it when a superb cross from James Low was brilliantly fired home by forward Harry Graham to give Hearts the early lead they wanted. Strangely though, the Maroons seemed to lose their way somewhat and the game threatened to turn into a scrappy affair with defences – unusually for this era – well on top.

However, just when it seemed the Paisley Saints would hold out to half-time just the one goal behind, the impressive Low showed great skill in skipping past St Mirren's full-back Reid to give Tom Gracie the easiest of chances and double Hearts' lead. With Hearts two goals ahead at the interval, not many in the 10,500 crowd gave St Mirren much chance of saving the game.

However, Hearts huffed and puffed for a spell in the second half. St Mirren seemed determined to fight back and they had clearly identified Low as Hearts' danger man with the result being that the Tynecastle winger was a marked man. There were just ten minutes left for play when, with the score still at 2-0 to the home side, Hearts' James Speedie got the better of Saints full-back Todd and delivered a fine cross for Tom Gracie who fired an unstoppable shot past goalkeeper O'Hagan.

The third goal put the result beyond doubt and Hearts appeared to relax and play some sparkling football, the sort of football everyone knew this Hearts team was capable of playing. Two minutes later, Speedie himself produced great skill to get clear of the trailing Saints defence and fired in a magnificent effort for Hearts' fourth goal.

The home support was thrilled to see their heroes play such great football at last and they were rewarded with a fifth Hearts goal six minutes from time when Nellies completed the scoring with a fine effort. The final score of Hearts 5 St Mirren 0 may have slightly flattered the home side, but the final ten minutes saw Hearts at their very best and demonstrated why many people were tipping them to win the league. Fate, however, decreed otherwise.

Hearts continued their fine run of form and a week later, they defeated Rangers 2-1 at Ibrox. Victories over Ayr United and Aberdeen followed and defeat at Dumbarton was their first of the league season. By Christmas, the army recruitment campaign was increasing momentum as the war intensified. Hearts' Jimmy Speedie joined

Tynecastle team-mates George Sinclair and Neil Moreland – who were already army reservists – in volunteering for action.

The government of the day then made enlistment to the armed forces compulsory – although the profession of footballer was exempt. This created a lot of anger and, it's fair to say, feelings of guilt among some football players who believed it was simply wrong to carry on playing football while others were giving their lives for their country.

When Sir George McCrae created a new battalion in Edinburgh, the 16th Royal Scots, no fewer than 13 Hearts players joined Sir George's regiment. The full story of this heroic deed is told in Jack Alexander's excellent book *The McCrae Battalion*. As well as 13 Hearts players, more than 600 Hearts supporters, taking their lead from the players they idolised, also signed up for the 16th Scots which now had more than 1,300 fighting men.

Those players left at Tynecastle continued the good form the full-strength Hearts team had begun and when Hearts earned a point following a hard fought draw with Celtic in Glasgow in January 1915, it seemed the league championship would be Tynecastle bound for the first time in nearly 20 years.

However, Hearts' fitness coach James Dickson suffered mental health problems and a depleted Hearts team began to lose steam. On 20th February 1915, in front of over 23,000 spectators at Tynecastle, Hearts lost an epic game to Rangers by 4-3 and Celtic closed in on the Maroons. Hearts were then held to draws by Hibernian and Airdrieonians before successive away defeats to Morton and St Mirren finally ended their hopes of the league title. Hearts finished season 1914/15 as runners-up to Celtic in the league, finishing four points adrift of the Glasgow club.

It had been a valiant effort and most people believed Hearts would have been league champions but for the outbreak of war. Many more footballers from around the country signed up to serve their country but Heart of Midlothian was among the first to have the nucleus of their first team sign up together. The Great War as it became known – although I have to say I have never understood how such death and destruction and ruining of lives could be called 'great' – ended in 1918. Of the Hearts players who signed up, seven made the ultimate sacrifice.

James Speedie, one of the first Hearts players to sign up for his country, died in September 1915 in France. A month later Tom Gracie died in a military hospital from leukaemia. In July 1916, Ernie Ellis, Harry Wattie and Duncan Currie were killed. Then a further month progressed and James Boyd was also killed. In 1917, John Allan became the seventh Hearts player to die in the war.

The club has never forgotten the heroic actions of these courageous men and the many Hearts supporters who suffered the same fate. Every November, on Remembrance Sunday, Heart of Midlothian Football Club has a service which, until the recent tram works in Edinburgh, was held at the Haymarket Memorial in the capital city's west end. Those who gave the ultimate sacrifice for their country are remembered with dignified silence. It is an incredibly moving ceremony and the message every year is clear – we will never forget.

Football continued to be played during the Great War but, given the fact seven of what may well have turned out to be Hearts' greatest team up to that point in their history gave their lives for their king and country – and more were seriously injured

– it's no surprise the history books show Hearts struggled after coming so close to winning the league in 1915. They finished fifth in the league the season after, before the effects of war took its toll.

Hearts ended the 1916/17 season in 14th position and it would be nearly 20 years until Hearts recovered sufficiently to mount another serious challenge for the championship.

The Maroons did finish in third place in the league at the end of 1920/21, the highlight of which was a 5-1 win over Hibs in August 1920.

Hearts also reached the semi-final of the Scottish Cup and were many people's favourites to defeat Partick Thistle. However, the teams played out two goalless draws and a third game was required to decide who would progress to the final to meet Rangers. The third game, like the first two, was played at Ibrox Stadium and it was the Jags who celebrated with a 2-0 win, much to the disappointment of the Hearts supporters in the 33,000 crowd. It was little consolation that Hearts lost to the eventual winners – Thistle defeating Rangers 1-0 in the final at Celtic Park.

Hearts also attained a third-placed finish in the league in 1925/26 and two successive fourth-placed finishes in 1928 and 1929. Hearts again finished third in the league at the end of the 1932/33 season and, like 1921, reached the semi-final of the Scottish Cup. And, like 1921, they had to replay the game after a goalless first tie. However, Celtic won the midweek replay so Hearts' hopes of glory were dashed once more.

In the summer of 1935, Hearts appointed David Pratt as manager. Pratt, a former Celtic player, had been manager of English side Notts County and the Hearts board of directors looked to his experience to bring silverware to Tynecastle for the first time in 30 years. The memory of those players who gave the ultimate sacrifice for their country two decades earlier deserved no less.

v Hibernian 8-3
Scottish League Division One
21st September 1935. Tynecastle

Hearts:	Hibernian:
Harkness	Culley
Anderson	Souter
J Munro	Urquhart
Massie	Wilson
Reid	Watson
Miller	Egan
A Munro	Walls
Walker	Brady
McCulloch	Black
Black	Smith
Wipfler	Anderson

Referee: J Horsburgh (Bonnyrigg)

HEARTS' NEW manager David Pratt wasted little time in bringing in new players to Tynecastle following his arrival in Gorgie in the summer of 1935. Englishman Charlie Wipfler arrived from Bristol Rovers and could play in both outside-left and outside-right positions. Inside-left Andy Black was brought in from junior football and during the 1935/36 season, manager Pratt handed first-team debuts to Black and Johnny Harvey.

Hearts began the season with their traditional A team versus B team match at Tynecastle at the end of July 1935. A trial match it may have been, but nonetheless, it did attract 20,000 spectators. It was a sign of the team's progress that Hearts' five Scottish internationals were awarded their 'caps' from the Scottish Football Association prior to kick-off, to great acclaim from the huge crowd.

There were nearly 10,000 more to see Hearts kick off their league campaign with a 2-0 win over Partick Thistle at Tynecastle ten days later – with new signing Charlie Wipfler getting his name on the score-sheet. However, Hearts' early season form brought a mixed bag of results, including defeats by Airdrieonians and Queen of the South, draws with Dunfermline Athletic and Queen's Park and a thumping win over Dundee at Dens Park.

David Pratt's side were fifth in the league table, four points behind leaders Celtic, when city rivals Hibs headed to Gorgie at the end of September. Hibs had had an awful start to the season and sat second bottom of the league without a league win to their name thus far. More than 27,000 spectators headed to Tynecastle on a dull September afternoon and while the Maroons were favourites, no one expected what was to follow.

Inside-forward Tommy Walker would, in later years, become Hearts' most successful manager of all time. In 1935, he was the darling of the fans, Hearts' most important player and one of the most skilful players in Scotland. Just five minutes had been played and Hearts were already two goals ahead – both scored by Walker, the man they said had dancing feet. His first effort in the second minute was a fine effort that should perhaps have been cleared by Hibs defender Watson, and Culley in the Hibs goal was left helpless as Walker prodded the ball home. The second effort, after just five minutes, was a forceful shot that Walker placed with precision beyond the Hibs goalkeeper and Hearts found themselves two goals ahead in the opening minutes.

Hibs were shocked and Hearts looked hungry and eager to add to their tally. They did so in the 20th minute, when Andy Black, whose lightning pace at inside-left troubled the visiting defence all afternoon, raced past the static looking Hibs defence to drive the ball past Culley to make it 3-0 to Hearts.

The home side were rampant and just before half-time they scored again. Munro delivered a fine cross into the Hibs penalty box where Black leapt majestically to power home a magnificent header to leave Culley helpless and put Hearts four goals ahead at the interval. It had been a marvellous first half from the home side and it was difficult to see a Hibs side, already suffering from a lack of confidence given their position in the league, doing anything to save the game – particularly as Hearts began the second half in exactly the same way they began the first.

In the 48th minute, the industrious Andy Black delivered a fine pass to Charlie Wipfler and the Englishman made no mistake with a fine finish to score Hearts' fifth goal. Shortly afterwards, Wipfler turned provider and he delivered a deft cross which Alex Munro headed home. Astonishingly, with 40 minutes still to play, Hearts were six goals ahead against their Edinburgh rivals. The fans could scarcely believe it, yet still roared for more.

Inevitably, however, Hearts took their foot off the pedal and showed their city neighbours some mercy. Perhaps too much mercy, as Hibs scored three goals in succession through Walls, Black and Brady and with the score now reading 6-3 to Hearts it was yet another example – littered throughout this great club's history – of Hearts never doing anything easy!

However, the enigmatic Charlie Wipfler then produced a moment of sublime skill to tease and turn the Hibs defenders before firing home. That snuffed out any inkling of a Hibs comeback and Hearts' Dave McCulloch put the icing on the cake near the end with a simple finish to complete the scoring at a remarkable Hearts 8 Hibs 3.

It was a record score in an Edinburgh derby and, to date, neither Hearts nor Hibs have managed to put eight goals past each other since (Hibs came close in 1973 but I won't dwell on that…).

Such a brilliant result didn't do much for Hearts' league position as they remained in fifth place, still four points behind leaders Celtic who had defeated arch-rivals Rangers at Ibrox that same afternoon. Seven days later, Hearts lost 2-1 at Celtic. However, the Maroons had shown they were to be considered as serious league title contenders.

If only the team could have found a level of consistency. After the loss at Celtic Park, Hearts defeated Third Lanark, lost to Motherwell and drew with Rangers. You will note, dear reader, this is a theme that persists throughout this book. There were, however, plenty of positive signs for Hearts throughout the 1935/36 season.

Tommy Walker had produced a sublime performance against Hibs and big things were predicted for the 20-year-old from Livingston Station. He had already played for Scotland, against Wales at the age of 19 in 1934, and he would become a Scotland regular until the outbreak of the Second World War in 1939.

His most famous appearance in the dark blue of his country came at Wembley Stadium in 1936 as Scotland faced the 'auld enemy' England. With the Scots trailing 1-0, they were awarded a penalty that young Walker elected to take. As he was about to shoot for goal, the wind blew the ball from the penalty spot so he had to replace it and try again. The wind blew it away for a second time so Walker had to show nerves of steel as he tried for a third time to take the penalty. He belied his youthfulness by calmly steering the ball home to equalise and earn the Scots a well-deserved draw.

Walker became an important player on the pitch for Hearts and in years to come would become an even more important figure off it. After the end of the Second World War, Walker returned to Tynecastle but Chelsea put in a bid of £8,000 for the forward, a huge sum of money at that time.

With football, as with society in general, facing austere times in the immediate aftermath of the war, Hearts could not afford to turn down such a huge offer and Walker headed for Stamford Bridge in September 1946. Thankfully, he returned home just two years later, initially as a player, but was then appointed assistant manager.

In November 1935, Hearts arranged a testimonial game for right-half Alex Massie, as part of his transfer to Aston Villa. The fans knew Massie as the Ace of Hearts and Villa were prepared to part with the huge sum of £6,000 for his services. The testimonial game saw Yugoslav club Belgrade Sports Club come to Tynecastle. It was an innovative move and more than 12,000 spectators turned up to witness Hearts win 4-2.

Hearts were so delighted with the success of the game they arranged another fixture against continental opposition a month later when Austria Vienna came to Tynecastle as part of their British tour. The Austrians were a crack outfit having won most of the honours in their own country but they were no match for Hearts, who won 3-0. Fifty-three years later, the two clubs would meet again in European competition.

Hearts would end the league campaign of 1935/36 in fifth place, albeit 19 points behind champions Celtic. Hopes of success in the Scottish Cup disappeared after the first round with a 2-0 loss away to Third Lanark on a bitter Wednesday afternoon at the end of January. That word inconsistency again. There were encouraging signs, though. As well as Tommy Walker, Alex Massie and Andy Anderson played for Scotland, Anderson also featuring in that 1-1 draw with England at Wembley.

Hearts continued to improve, even if against the backdrop of dark clouds of another war covering much of Europe at that time. The Maroons were runners-up in the league to Celtic in 1938 and were scoring goals galore in 1938/39, finishing just two short of a century of goals in the league with a fourth-placed finish.

In the Scottish Cup, Hearts scored an incredible 28 goals in their two opening rounds of the Scottish Cup. They defeated Penicuik Athletic 14-2 at Tynecastle before thrashing Elgin City 14-1 also at Tynecastle in the next round. Yes, both their opponents had non-league status but it was a testament to Hearts' goalscoring prowess at the time.

The Maroons fancied their chances of winning the Scottish Cup, particularly as the holders East Fife had suffered a shock home defeat to Second Division side Montrose. However, Hearts were drawn against Celtic in the next round and after a 2-2 draw at Tynecastle – watched by nearly 50,000 fans – the Gorgie men lost the replay at Celtic Park 2-1 with a controversial winner for the home team coming five minutes from the end of the game.

It appeared the ball had not crossed the line and several Hearts players protested vehemently to the referee. It said it all about one particular Hearts player that he returned to the halfway line without protest and waited for his angry team-mates to join him. That summed up the class of Tommy Walker.

Hearts were third in the league after making a decent start to the 1939/40 season when league football was abandoned due the outbreak of the Second World War. Those who had survived the ravages of the Great War were aghast at the country going into conflict once more, but the defeat of Adolf Hitler and his Nazi Party would take six years and the loss of millions of lives across Europe. Some things are more important than football.

Hearts, like most other clubs, would continue to play football during the Second World War but there were no league or Scottish Cup games – such an organised format would have played into enemy hands. However, the seeds of future success were being sown when Hearts appointed David McLean as manager on 1st August 1941. McLean saw youth as the way forward as the club struggled with financial constraints and, as during the Great War, the majority of its players fight for their country.

This time, conscription into the armed forces for football players was enforced. Most clubs had 'guest' players turning out for them depending on who was stationed where, when they were back on the shores of this country – and McLean turned towards young players trying to make their mark in the game as the end of the conflict came into sight.

His signing of 18-year-old forward Alfie Conn in June 1944 would herald the beginning of a new and brighter era for this famous club. An era that would bring unprecedented success.

6 v East Fife 6-1

Scottish League Cup
9th October 1948. Tynecastle

Hearts:	East Fife:
Brown	Niven
Parker	Laird
McKenzie	Stewart
Cox	Philip
Dougan	Finlay
Laing	Aitken
Sloan	Adams
Conn	Fleming
Wardhaugh	Morris
Bauld	Brown
Williams	Duncan

Referee: D Kerr (Glasgow)

ACERTAIN Danish brewery may have been associated with a team from the east end of Edinburgh just a few short years ago, but more than six decades back there was something special brewing on the other side of Scotland's capital city.

The years following the Second World War were a boom time as far as football in Scotland and the UK as a whole was concerned. The word austerity is oft used these days, particularly by politicians, but in the immediate aftermath of the war, Britain remained a country of rationing and struggling to make ends meet. The country's working class turned to football for its saviour and in the post-war years, crowds flocked back to football grounds across the country, starved of competitive games as they were during the war when league football was abandoned and wartime games, while satisfactory in their own right, weren't quite the real deal.

Hearts, like almost every other club, set about a rebuilding programme after the war and they were extremely fortunate to have a manager who had a keen eye for good footballers, particularly young players who would be the future of the club. David McLean took over the reins of Hearts manager during the war, in August 1941, when his first match in charge was a 1-0 defeat by Arsenal in a challenge match at Tynecastle. More than 20,000 fans attended that match, happy to get a brief respite from the war, but the country had more pressing needs. When the war ended, McLean was like every other manager in British football and faced a rebuilding exercise. Clearly, this would take some time.

Two months into the 1948/49 season, after an inauspicious start to the league campaign – Hearts sat bottom of the table after the first six matches – McLean played three players of outstanding talent together for the first time. Alfie Conn, Jimmy

Wardhaugh and Willie Bauld would become known as the "Terrible Trio" although few Hearts fans thought, on that cold October day, that their collective appearance would be the start of something special.

Conn and Wardhaugh had already made their Hearts debuts as teenagers – Conn in a wartime game against Dumbarton in 1944 and Wardhaugh in a 3-2 win against Celtic in Glasgow in a league game in 1946 – but this was to be the first time they would be joined by the precocious talent that was centre-forward Willie Bauld in the first team.

Hearts' opponents were East Fife in the Scottish League Cup, a competition that was still in its infancy as the Scottish League had sought to cash in on football's huge popularity after the war by creating their own cup competition, to add to that of the long established Scottish Cup.

1948 was a period well before regular European competition had been thought of and at that time, the League Cup saw teams playing in sections of four. Hearts were drawn in a section containing East Fife, Partick Thistle and Queen of the South. The team from Methil were one of the best teams in Scotland – ten years earlier, they made history by becoming the only Second Division team to win the Scottish Cup, defeating Kilmarnock in the final at Hampden. A decade on and East Fife, managed by Scot Symon who would later go on to manage Rangers, were the proud holders of the new League Cup, having defeated Falkirk in a replayed final in 1947.

In September 1948, Hearts drew their first sectional game when Partick Thistle held the Maroons to a 2-2 draw at Tynecastle. Hearts then lost 4-0 to East Fife at Methil and manager David McLean knew changes had to be made. Hearts were struggling and the vicious circle of bad results affecting confidence therefore inducing more bad results was in full swing. There was no money to spend on new players – some things never change in Gorgie – so the manager had to rely on the younger players he had brought to Tynecastle in the years immediately after the war.

After losing the return fixture with Partick Thistle 3-1, McLean made five changes to the Hearts team that lost that game all too easily – including a first-team start for centre-forward Willie Bauld – for the visit of East Fife a week later. Little did anyone realise history was about to be made.

Having lost heavily to the Fifers three weeks earlier, Hearts began the game as underdogs but with the youthful Bauld making his presence felt, there was a freshness and vigour about Hearts' play that had not been seen for some time. With Tommy Sloan and Archie Williams supporting the "trio" in attack, the Maroons threatened to score every time they went forward, with Bauld looking particularly dangerous.

The 21-year-old coal miner from Newtongrange took just 14 minutes to score his first goal for the first team after good work from Alfie Conn had carved open the East Fife defence. The men from Methil equalised, somewhat against the run of play, after 27 minutes through Morris and the goal gave the Black and Golds the belief they were in the ascendancy and ready to carry on where they left off three weeks earlier. The goal seemed to dent Hearts' confidence and well into the second half, the game remained in the balance – until Willie Bauld and Alfie Conn took charge.

After 64 minutes, Bauld headed powerfully past East Fife keeper Niven to put Hearts in front and eight minutes later Conn drove home Hearts' third. Two minutes later, Bauld completed his hat-trick, much to the delight of the Tynecastle faithful. At

4-1 to the hosts, there was no way back for the cup holders now. Hearts were rampant going forward and just two minutes later Davie Laing converted a penalty. Four goals in just 12 minutes destroyed East Fife and was a prelude of what was to come from an emerging Hearts side over the next decade. Conn completed the scoring ten minutes from the end and the game ended Hearts 6 East Fife 1.

The majority of the crowd of more than 24,000 at Tynecastle roared their approval at the end of the game. This was the best Hearts had played all season and, as well as the "Terrible Trio" making an immediate impact, Hearts looked assured in defence with Bobby Dougan commanding at centre-half and full-backs Tam McKenzie and Bobby Parker keeping what was previously a free-scoring East Fife forward line at bay.

It was, above all, a youthful Hearts team. McKenzie, at 25 years of age, was the oldest player in the side. Willie Bauld was 21, Alfie Conn 22 and Jimmy Wardhaugh was still in his teenage years. The average age of the team that mauled the Fifers was 22 and it gave battle-scarred Hearts supporters genuine hope that they had a team that would develop into one of the country's finest. Their hope wasn't misplaced – more youngsters would come through thanks to David McLean's successful youth policy and arguably Hearts' finest ever side would eventually take the country by storm.

Incredibly, the following week, Willie Bauld hit another hat-trick as Hearts ended their League Cup campaign with a 4-0 win at Queen of the South. Sadly, ten goals in two games were not enough to prevent the Maroons from exiting the competition, their earlier abysmal form costing them dear.

When league business resumed after the sectional stages of the League Cup had been completed, Hearts defeated Rangers 2-0 in front of more than 40,000 fans at Tynecastle – Wardhaugh and Conn the scorers – and hopes rose that here, at last, was the dawn of a new age for the Maroons.

However, Hearts yielded just two points from their following four games. After a 3-3 draw with an impressive Clyde team at Shawfield, Hearts faced another Glasgow team, Partick Thistle, at Tynecastle. The Jags enhanced their reputation for being the big unpredictables of Scottish football by pulling off a 3-1 win in front of over 26,000 expectant fans in Gorgie. Worse was to follow the following week, when Falkirk raced into a three-goal lead after 35 minutes at Brockville and while Hearts pulled two goals back early in the second half, the Bairns went on to win 5-3.

Perhaps youth contributed to the inconsistency that would continue to blight this Hearts side for the remainder of season 1948/49. Just before Christmas, Hearts put four goals past East Fife and five past Albion Rovers. The Fifers must, by this time, have been sick of the sight of their maroon-shirted foes although they did exact a fair measure of revenge on the final day of the season when they trounced Hearts 5-1 at Bayview.

On New Year's Day 1949, more than 45,000 fans first-footed Tynecastle for the traditional New Year's Day derby game with Hibernian. Hearts were two goals ahead after 20 minutes and led by this score until 17 minutes from the end when Hibs' Lawrie Reilly pulled one back before the Easter Road side hit an equaliser with just four minutes left on the clock. As the home support struggled to contain their frustration at losing a two-goal lead, their new hero would soon put a smile back on their faces. Great play by Willie Bauld set up Alfie Conn to score the winner in the last minute to secure a fine 3-2 win over an emerging Hibs team.

Despite this, inconsistency continued to dog Hearts and two 4-2 defeats at Tynecastle on consecutive Saturdays – to Dundee in the quarter-final of the Scottish Cup and Morton in the league – highlighted the fact that David McLean still had work to do to build the team he wanted. There were definite signs though, that optimism in Gorgie was not misplaced. On 2nd April 1949, Hearts defeated Albion Rovers 7-1 at Tynecastle with Willie Bauld hitting a hat-trick and Jimmy Wardhaugh and Alfie Conn also getting on the score-sheet.

Hearts ended 1948/49 in eighth place in Division One but the fans knew the emergence of Conn, Bauld and Wardhaugh as part of a strike force that would become the most potent in the land would mean an exciting future for their team.

As what would transpire to be the most successful decade in the history of Heart of Midlothian Football club began, Hearts' progress continued apace with a third-place finish in Division One at the end of season 1949/50. The "Terrible Trio" would hit over 60 league goals between them that season and results included a 6-2 win over Clyde; a 4-1 win over Aberdeen; a 4-2 win over Celtic; and a 9-0 hammering of Falkirk at Tynecastle in November. This performance against a team who held something of an Indian sign over Hearts was quite sublime and while the Bairns played the second half with just ten men as a result of an injury to their inside-right Reid, Hearts showed no mercy and could well have doubled the nine goals they did score. It was a clear indication that Hearts were emerging as a powerful force in Scottish football.

No one at Tynecastle was in any doubt this was the beginning of a new era, an exciting team playing wonderful, flowing football. The trophy room at Tynecastle, having lain empty since 1906, was about to become highly populated…

v Motherwell 4-2

Scottish League Cup Final
23rd October 1954. Hampden

Hearts:	Motherwell:
Duff	Weir
Parker	Kilmarnock
McKenzie	McSeveney
Mackay	Cox
Glidden	Paton
Cumming	Redpath
Souness	Hunter
Conn	Aitken
Bauld	Bain
Wardhaugh	Humphries
Urquhart	Williams

Referee: J Mowat (Rutherglen)

DURING THE 1950s, post-war Britain began to show signs of prosperity. Prime Minister Harold Macmillan told the nation in 1957 "we had never had it so good". As far as supporters of Heart of Midlothian FC were concerned, the PM was correct!

At the start of the decade, Hearts began to flourish. Three successive fourth-placed finishes and a second-placed finish in the First Division in 1954 – Hearts ending as runners-up to champions Celtic – as well as two semi-final appearances in the Scottish Cup hinted that good times lay ahead, a theory that proved spectacularly correct in the 1954/55 season.

By now, the man who had laid the foundations of this fine young Hearts side, David McLean, had sadly passed away. The man who took over as manager was already a Hearts legend as a player – McLean's assistant Tommy Walker. Hearts fans from before the Second World War remembered Walker as a brilliant player who was the star of the Hearts team of the late 1930s. Walker left Tynecastle for Chelsea for a fee of £6,000 in 1946 – a phenomenal sum at the time – only to return to Tynecastle two years later as a player-assistant manager.

When McLean died in 1951, Walker was his natural successor and he seemed at least equally adept at spotting talented players as his predecessor. His most notable signing, in April 1952, was a right-half from Midlothian junior side Newtongrange Star. Seventeen-year-old Dave Mackay would develop into one of Hearts' – and Scotland's – most famous players.

In finishing runners-up to Celtic in the league championship in season 1953/54, Hearts produced some wonderful football. Mackay was given his debut against Clyde at Tynecastle in November 1953 and while Hearts lost 2-1 that day, there was much to admire from Mackay's play.

When Celtic visited Gorgie in February 1954, there were more than 47,000 packed into Tynecastle and most were thrilled to see the home team emerge 3-2 victors to open up an eight-point lead over Celtic at the top of the league table. Naturally, hopes were high Hearts would become champions of Scotland for the first time this century, but the more pragmatic among the Hearts support – and there can be none more pragmatic than supporters of Heart of Midlothian given what we've gone through over the years – pointed to the fact Celtic had three games in hand.

When Hearts lost 4-2 at Raith Rovers and 1-0 at Aberdeen, their lead over Celtic was down to three points. When the Hoops caught up with games and Hearts lost 2-1 at Partick Thistle on a Monday evening in April, the writing was on the wall for the Maroons' title challenge. However, it had been a valiant effort from Tommy Walker's young team and lessons were learnt.

Suffice to say much was expected of Hearts in season 1954/55. Walker added goalkeeper Willie Duff and outside-left Ian Crawford to the first-team pool and they would prove to be vital components of this exciting Hearts team. Hearts started the season in brilliant fashion when they romped through their League Cup section, defeating league champions Celtic home and away. The tie against Falkirk at Brockville was notable not just for Hearts winning 6-2 but for Dave Mackay scoring his first goal for the club he adored. The "Terrible Trio" scored the other goals that day – two each for Jimmy Wardhaugh and Willie Bauld and one from Alfie Conn.

After defeating St. Johnstone 7-0 on aggregate in the quarter-finals and Airdrieonians 4-1 at Easter Road in the semi-finals, Hearts secured their first ever League Cup final appearance. Their opponents were a team who had achieved League Cup and Scottish Cup success in the early 1950s – Motherwell. A crowd of more than 55,000 headed to Hampden Park on 23rd October 1954 – eventually, as many hadn't realised there was an early kick-off in case extra time was required and Hampden didn't have floodlights then – to witness an epic cup final.

The League Cup may have been a relative newcomer to Scottish football but in its eight short years of existence, its importance had grown substantially. This may have explained a rather nervous start to the final by the Maroons with centre-half Freddie Glidden not looking his usual assured self at the back in the early stages. However, once the nerves had settled, Hearts began to find their way and Glidden soon had the Motherwell danger man Bain metaphorically in his back pocket.

Ten minutes had been played when Hearts took the lead. Motherwell's Paton looked to intercept a ball played towards Hearts' Jim Souness – but slipped at a crucial moment on the greasy Hampden surface. The Hearts winger had all the time in the world to deliver the perfect cross to the perfect centre-forward – King Willie Bauld duly headed home.

Six minutes later, Hearts doubled their lead with a goal that showed the King was as skilful with his feet as he was with his head. Collecting a pass from Alfie Conn, Bauld switched the ball from one foot to the other, which got the trailing Motherwell defenders in a tangle before he finished sublimely with a shot past the despairing Weir in the Motherwell goal. Hearts were two goals ahead before a quarter of the game was over and the maroon-clad fans on the huge Hampden terracings were already planning their celebrations. However, a common theme in this book is that Hearts rarely do things easily!

Five minutes before half-time, Conn fouled Humphries and Redpath converted the subsequent penalty to bring Motherwell back into the game – but not for long.

Just before the half-time whistle, the impressive Jim Souness delivered yet another fine cross into the Motherwell penalty box. This time, it wasn't the imposing figure of Willie Bauld who provided the finish – it was another of the Trio, Jimmy Wardhaugh, who steered the ball home to make it 3-1 Hearts at the interval.

Rather predictably, a Motherwell side desperate to get back into the game dominated the second half. Hearts were on the back foot but it was a scenario made for Dave Mackay. The right-half was immense as he organised Hearts' rearguard action and when Motherwell did break through, they found Hearts keeper Willie Duff in inspirational form.

Motherwell's frustrations grew as the game headed to its conclusion. With just three minutes left, Hearts ended any lingering doubts when Bauld, despite sustaining a thigh injury in the second half, completed a memorable cup final hat-trick by heading home a pass from Wardhaugh. Although Bain scored for Motherwell just before the end, when the final whistle blew, Hearts had won a superb final 4-2 – and collected their first major silverware for close to half a century. *The Daily Record* commented that Motherwell didn't get the breaks but didn't deserve them as ball after ball was speculatively banged upfield while Hearts, on the other hand, "never deviated from their plan of ground football with man-to-man passing".

Hearts headed back to Edinburgh for a weekend of celebrations and they paraded the League Cup trophy through the streets of Scotland's capital city. Silverware had been a long time coming for the club – 48 years to be precise, since Hearts' triumph in the 1906 Scottish Cup final – but this famous victory was the prelude for one of the most remarkable periods in the history of Heart of Midlothian FC.

In the league campaign of 1954/55, Hearts ended in a somewhat disappointing fourth place in the table. They began the season brightly enough – an astonishing 5-4 victory over Partick Thistle at Tynecastle in front of over 30,000 fans in the opening game – followed by a thrilling 3-2 win over Hibs at Easter Road. However, Hearts then lost at Dundee and at Pittodrie where league leaders Aberdeen won a tight game 1-0. This left the Maroons eight points behind the Dons and it was a gap they would not close.

As well as the League Cup triumph, Hearts enjoyed two thumping wins over Hibs – in addition to the early season victory in Leith. The New Year's Day derby at Tynecastle saw a joyous start to 1955 for Hearts. A huge crowd of 49,000 squeezed into Tynecastle to see Hearts score four second-half goals in a 5-1 win over their great rivals. A little over a month later, Hibs were back at Tynecastle – this time on Scottish Cup business.

It wasn't quite a 5-1 scoreline this time around – it was 5-0 to Edinburgh's finest, with the "Terrible Trio" carving out the goals between them, with two for Wardhaugh, two for Bauld with Alfie Conn settling for just the single. To record two magnificent victories over a Hibs team that included their renowned "Famous Five" forward line of Turnbull, Reilly, Ormond, Johnstone and Smith, was a quite brilliant achievement for this young Hearts team and the fans licked their lips in anticipation of their heroes lifting the Scottish Cup for the first time in 49 years.

Sixth-round opponents Buckie Thistle, from the Highland League, were duly sent packing 6-0 – the Maroons finishing off their part-time opponents by half-time when Tommy Walker's side were already 5-0 ahead – before Hearts faced their biggest cup challenge yet in the quarter-final, league champions elect Aberdeen.

Another huge crowd of over 48,000 headed for Tynecastle to witness another tight game that ended a goal each so a replay at Pittodrie was required. Over 41,000 were inside the ground with several thousand more locked outside – a scenario that would be repeated on a somewhat smaller scale 30 years later. Sadly, Hearts reserved one of their poorest performances of the season for the replay in the Granite City and lost 2-0, meaning hopes of a long-awaited Scottish Cup triumph were banished for another year – but only a year. Hearts gained an element of revenge on the Dons three days later when a Willie Bauld double secured a 2-0 win in a league game at Tynecastle.

Hearts' season petered out somewhat after their Scottish Cup exit. There were defeats to Rangers, East Fife and Celtic although Tommy Walker's men did finish the season on a traditional note – they defeated Hibs 4-3 in the final of the East of Scotland Shield at Easter Road. The Maroons finished in fourth place in the league, ten points behind champions Aberdeen. That 2-0 victory over the Dons at Tynecastle in March was proof – if proof was needed – of what might have been had Hearts had the consistency required to be champions. However, this was only a matter of time.

Hearts' League Cup triumph was the highlight of the season and heralded the start of a new period for the boys in maroon. A period that would become known as the golden age for Edinburgh's oldest and finest football club. The League Cup adorned the Tynecastle boardroom but if the critics thought that would be as much as this Hearts side would win then there was that old adage that was never truer – you ain't seen nothing yet!

v Celtic 3-1
Scottish Cup Final
21st April 1956. Hampden

Hearts:	Celtic:
Duff	Beattie
Kirk	Meechan
McKenzie	Fallon
Mackay	Smith
Glidden	Evans
Cumming	Peacock
Young	Craig
Conn	Haughney
Bauld	Mochan
Wardhaugh	Fernie
Crawford	Tully

Referee: RH Davidson (Airdrie)

AS JUBILANT as Hearts supporters were at seeing their team lift silverware for the first time in 48 years, there were still pangs of disappointment that their heroes could only finish fourth in the league and were knocked out at the quarter-final stage of the Scottish Cup. However, Hearts manager Tommy Walker continued to add to this exciting young side and in the summer of 1955 brought two players to Tynecastle, who would, in time, become legends in Gorgie.

Like Dave Mackay, Alex Young arrived from Newtongrange Star and the forward, although a different kind of player, was seen by many as the long-term successor to Willie Bauld. If Bauld were the King of Hearts, Alex Young would be the Prince, the heir apparent. The irony was Young would make such an impact he would leave Tynecastle before the man he was meant to succeed.

Tommy Walker also brought in Johnny Hamilton, a winger of some repute from Lesmahgow Juniors, as the manager contemplated the fact most Hearts fans didn't want to admit – the "Terrible Trio" of Conn, Bauld and Wardhaugh would not be around forever. Seven years had now passed since they first played together and it had been more than a decade since Alfie Conn had made his Hearts debut. Tommy Walker though, was one of the most forward-thinking men in Scottish football.

Hearts began the 1955/56 season in emphatic style by breezing through their section as they began their defence of the League Cup by winning five of the six sectional games. However, they met league champions Aberdeen in a two-legged quarter-final and the Dons, as they had done in the previous season's Scottish Cup, triumphed over the Maroons. Alarmingly, the Pittodrie men put nine goals past Hearts over the two games and nobody needed to tell Tommy Walker about Hearts' defensive frailties. That said, by the time 1956 began, Hearts were very much in the mix for the league title with defending champions Aberdeen and Rangers.

However, having lifted the League Cup the season before, many observers believed Hearts' best chance of winning more silverware lay in the Scottish Cup – five decades after they last lifted the famous old trophy. After comfortably disposing of Second Division Forfar Athletic and First Division basement side Stirling Albion in the early rounds, both at Tynecastle, Hearts were given another home draw for the quarter-final – Rangers. Yet again, Willie Bauld was the inspiration and the forward netted twice as Hearts thrashed the would-be league champions 4-0 in front of over 47,000 fans at Tynecastle. Raith Rovers proved stiffer opponents in the semi-final and Hearts required a replay to see off the Fifers to reach their first Scottish Cup final since 1906.

Their opponents in the final were Celtic, having a disappointing season by their standards. Already out of contention for the league title, Celtic saw the Scottish Cup as their only hope of success. An astonishing crowd of over 133,000 headed for Hampden Park on 21st April 1956.

Hearts fancied their chances but, as always, Tommy Walker wanted his players to let their feet do the talking. Celtic suffered a blow when their commanding centre-half Jock Stein and forward Bobby Collins were ruled out of the final because of injury.

Hearts, having triumphed at Hampden 18 months before, knew what was expected of them in a major cup final. However, they started in a similar fashion to the way they had started the League Cup final against Motherwell. Whether it was the occasion with the huge crowd packed into Hampden or the strong wind that swirled around the vast bowl, something seemed to be affecting the Maroons' play in the early stages.

Hearts looked edgy, almost in awe of Celtic's physical strength. After ten minutes, a misjudgement from Hearts' Tam McKenzie let Celtic's Craig sweep the ball forward but thankfully, for the Maroons, his colleague Haughney blazed the ball high over the bar. After 17 minutes, Jimmy Wardhaugh delivered a brilliant pass to Ian Crawford who took too much time to fire in a shot that was deflected by goalkeeper Beattie.

However, after 20 minutes, Hearts did go ahead after a well-constructed move. Willie Bauld, clearly identified by Celtic as Hearts' main threat, passed inside to Alfie Conn. The senior member of the Trio sent the ball forward to Ian Crawford who fired in an effort that Beattie got fingers to – but he could not prevent the ball crossing the line. Hearts were ahead and although Celtic's Mochan had a powerful header that was just inches past the post, it was Edinburgh's finest who had the advantage at half-time.

No one, however, exemplified Hearts' will to win more than captain John Cumming. The fearless centre-half received a gash on his forehead after clashing with Celtic's Fernie that saw the Hearts man leave the field with blood pouring from his wound. The incident happened just before half-time and it looked certain Hearts would be reduced to ten men, the 1950s being a time before substitutions were part of football.

After what had been a cagey first half, manager Tommy Walker knew his team could play better. Hearts started the second half without Cumming but the players responded to Walker's words just three minutes after the interval.

Like the first goal, Willie Bauld was involved in the build-up. The King, not normally renowned for his pace, nonetheless forced his way past the Celtic full-back Evans down the left wing and delivered a fine cross. Alex Young got his blonde head to the ball and directed it into the path of Crawford who duly despatched the ball beyond Beattie to put Hearts two goals ahead.

The massed ranks of the Hearts support at Hampden danced for joy – or rather, they would have done had there been any room to move. Were 50 years of hurt about to end? Not so fast – this is Hearts I'm talking about. Seven minutes later, Hearts keeper Willie Duff, who didn't appreciate the close attention of Celtic's Haughney, spilled a Charlie Tully free kick and Haughney prodded the ball home to bring the Celts back into the game.

At that stage, Celtic believed they would make their numerical advantage count and go on to force an equaliser – until they looked towards the touchline. For there, incredibly, was the sight of a stitched-up John Cumming preparing to re-enter the fray. If the Glasgow side thought they would exploit a weakness in the Hearts defence by directing play to the bloodied centre-half, they were hugely mistaken.

No sooner had the big man came back on the field than Celtic launched a long ball in his direction. Cumming – the original lion heart – leapt majestically and headed clear. One could almost see Celtic's despair. For the next 25 minutes, they threw everything they had at Hearts but Dave Mackay, Freddie Glidden and Captain Courageous Cumming thwarted the Celts' challenge at every opportunity.

With just ten minutes left and Celtic running out of ideas, another goal duly arrived – for Hearts. Again, Bauld was the provider when he set up Conn and the Hearts marksman didn't miss to end the scoring at 3-1 for Hearts.

Half a century after they had last lifted the Scottish Cup, the finest Hearts team of a generation had done it again. They were worthy winners and the celebrations that followed in Edinburgh lasted several days. There was any number of Hearts heroes that day. Two-goal Ian Crawford; goal taker turned goal maker for the day Willie Bauld; goalkeeper Willie Duff who kept Celtic out in the second half in particular; Dave Mackay and Freddie Glidden who worked tirelessly. However, the rest of that victorious Hearts side would tell you whom they had to thank for bringing the Scottish Cup back to Edinburgh for the first time in half a century – John Cumming. Bloodied, battered and dazed he may have been, but when he returned to the field of play in the second half it turned the tide – which had been flowing Celtic's way after their goal – back in Hearts' favour.

It was an act of courage no one at Tynecastle would ever forget and confirmed that this Hearts side, as well as having great skill and style and playing swashbuckling football, had a spirit no one else in Scotland could touch. A spirit that brought the Scottish Cup back to Tynecastle.

In the league Hearts had spent much of the season in pursuit of Rangers and defending champions Aberdeen. However, Hearts' old foe – inconsistency – was a frequent unwanted visitor.

Hearts began the 1955/56 league campaign with a thumping 4-0 win over Dundee at Tynecastle but succumbed to the law of averages when they lost 1-0 to Hibs thanks to a goal five minutes from the end at Easter Road a fortnight later. Six weeks before Christmas, the unlikely league leaders were Queen of the South and when Hearts headed for Ibrox, they were seeking a win that might have ended Rangers' title challenge, as they were already five points behind the Palmerston Park club.

However, Hearts had one of their off-days in Govan and despite taking the lead through Alex Young, they lost 4-1. This was a turning point in the league season as Queens also lost that day and Rangers were very much back in the chase for the championship.

Hearts then recorded two 5-1 wins over Clyde and Dunfermline Athletic before an impressive 3-0 win over defending champions Aberdeen at Tynecastle. However, Tommy Walker's men then dropped points to Raith Rovers and Hibs. On 17th March 1956 – a little over four weeks before their Scottish Cup final date with Celtic – Hearts entertained Rangers at Tynecastle in a top of the table clash. A win for the Maroons would see them leapfrog Rangers at the top of the league and this encouraged more than 50,000 fans to head to Tynecastle for a game the whole country wanted to see.

Unsurprisingly, for a game with so much at stake, it was a tense affair with no goals until 20 minutes from the end when Hubbard scored for Rangers. That looked like the end of Hearts' title dreams but the Maroons were built of stern stuff and Willie Bauld scored an equaliser five minutes later. The game ended 1-1 and the league championship was still up for grabs.

After Hearts qualified for the Scottish Cup final, their league form dipped at the most inopportune time. Defeats to Partick Thistle and Aberdeen were followed by a draw against Clyde and Hearts' title hopes had slipped away. They disappeared completely when they lost to Kilmarnock and Motherwell. In the end, the Maroons didn't even finish as runners-up to Rangers in the league – Aberdeen pipped them at the post – and they were the length of Princes Street behind the Ibrox men as they ended up seven points adrift.

Nonetheless, it had been another memorable season. The Scottish League Cup triumph in 1954 was a landmark occasion in the club's history. However, the Scottish Cup was the one Hearts really had their eye on as far as cup competitions were concerned. A week short of 50 years after their last triumph in the famous old competition, Hearts had brought the cup back to Tynecastle. The 1950s was an era when people weren't prone to showing emotion but there were a few lumps in the throat when Hearts paraded the Scottish Cup along Gorgie Road that memorable April evening in 1956. Tommy Walker's team of heroes had now lifted both cup competitions.

The biggest prize in Scottish football – the league championship – was next.

v Celtic 5-3
Scottish League Division One
14th March 1958. Tynecastle

Hearts:	Celtic:
Marshall	Beattie
Kirk	Donnelly
Thomson	Fallon
Mackay	Fernie
Milne	Evans
Bowman	Peacock
Blackwood	Collins
Murray	Smith
Young	McPhail
Wardhaugh	Wilson
Crawford	Byrne

Referee: W Massie (Dundee)

WITH THE League Cup and now Scottish Cup gracing the Tynecastle boardroom as Hearts' greatest team progressed through the 1950s, there remained one prize to be won that was the most coveted of all in Scottish football – the league championship.

The season after Hearts had lifted the Scottish Cup in 1956 saw the Maroons play some sparkling football – but, ultimately, end up with nothing to show for their efforts. Although they ran champions Rangers close – missing out on the league flag by just two points after Rangers won what most people felt was the title decider at Tynecastle on the third last Saturday of the league season – the Maroons also lost to Rangers in the Scottish Cup and, to the crushing disappointment of Hearts fans everywhere, went out at the sectional stage of the League Cup, this in spite of defeating Hibernian home and away (including 6-1 at Tynecastle) as Partick Thistle won the section.

Hearts fans had now almost become accustomed to seeing their team win trophies and manager Tommy Walker vowed his team would not disappoint when 1957/58 kicked off. To say Walker kept his promise is perhaps the understatement of the century as Hearts went on to enjoy one of the most incredible seasons in Scottish football history.

Half-back Billy Higgins – signed from Rangers – and forward Danny Paton, signed from the seemingly never-ending pool of talent that was Midlothian junior side Newtongrange Star, were welcome additions to the Hearts first-team squad and the Maroons began the league campaign by hitting an astonishing 25 goals in their opening four games.

Dundee were beaten 6-0 on the opening day at Tynecastle; this was followed by a 7-2 trouncing of Airdrieonians at Broomfield – Hearts were five goals ahead at half-time after playing some breathtaking football in the opening 45 minutes when Jimmy Wardhaugh scored a hat-trick – a 3-1 win over Hibernian at Tynecastle, before East Fife were hit for nine goals without reply in Gorgie.

Willie Bauld and Alfie Conn may have had their first-team appearances restricted due to injury but Jimmy Wardhaugh was still banging in the goals and he was joined by an exciting array of dynamic Hearts players such as Alex Young, Jimmy Murray and Dave Mackay.

A memorable 3-2 win over defending league champions Rangers at Ibrox in October – when Tommy Walker's men came roaring back from two goals down after half an hour – signalled Hearts' intent and opened up a nine-point gap between them and the Ibrox side. Rangers had slumped to joint second bottom place in the league after a poor start to the season and while they would recover, the points difference was something the Light Blues would never make up.

There was no stopping Hearts as the goals flowed in and the points racked up. 8-0 against Queen's Park; 9-1 against Falkirk where Alex Young scored four goals; 7-2 against Third Lanark. Hearts were not only banging in the goals left, right and centre but the defence, superbly marshalled by Iron Man John Cumming was doing its job too. Tommy Walker's men looked unstoppable.

By the time Celtic came to Tynecastle on the evening of 14th March 1958, Hearts were already an incredible 16 points clear at the top of the league at a time when there were just two points for a win – and had already scored more than 100 league goals. For Celtic – and, ironically, Rangers – their Friday evening visit was their last chance saloon for hopes of catching the marauding Maroons.

More than 35,000 fans packed into Tynecastle under the floodlights and if there were those who thought Hearts might be showing signs of title nerves after labouring somewhat to a 3-1 win over Queen of the South on the preceding Monday, they were very quickly proved wrong. In the opening seconds, Alex Young had an effort that flew just over the crossbar and after just three minutes, Hearts took the lead.

Young began the move and passed to Bobby Blackwood whose cross was inch perfect for Jimmy Wardhaugh. The veteran forward hit a 20-yard effort with his left foot that the Celtic keeper Beattie could only parry – and Ian Crawford said thank you very much as he tapped the ball into the net to give Hearts an early lead. Three minutes later, incredibly, the Maroons doubled their lead when the hard-working Blackwood collected a superb pass from the man who would be called "The Golden Vision" – Young – to slot the ball past Beattie for 2-0.

Hearts looked in easy street but they suffered a blow a few minutes later when Dave Mackay took a kick on his thigh and had to limp off in obvious pain. With no substitutes in those days, Hearts carried on a man short and Celtic's Byrne pulled a goal back on the half-hour.

Tough guy Mackay returned to the field but he was clearly struggling, even when the second half resumed with Hearts leading by 2-1. However, despite his injury, Mackay was instrumental in Hearts restoring their two-goal advantage just a minute into the second half. His header was collected by Young who squared the ball across goal for Ian Crawford to drive past Beattie.

Shortly after, Celtic missed a glorious chance to get back into the game when McPhail's effort on goal trundled past the post and seven minutes into the second half, it looked like game over when yet another sublime pass from Young found Blackwood who sent a left-foot cross to the head of Jimmy Murray. The man who would go on to score Scotland's first ever goal at a World Cup finals that summer headed powerfully past Beattie to put Hearts 4-1 ahead. However, Celtic weren't throwing in the towel just yet.

Five minutes later, Collins hit a well-struck penalty past Gordon Marshall to make it 4-2 and the Hoops sensed a comeback was on, a feeling endorsed when a defensive lapse by Hearts let in Smith to make it 4-3 with still 25 minutes left.

Hearts fans anxiously checked their watches, but the Maroons withstood some Celtic pressure and were soon back on top. It was still anyone's game with 14 minutes left, when Jimmy Murray drove forward and lashed the ball past Beattie to end the scoring at Hearts 5 Celtic 3. In fact, Hearts should have had a sixth goal when they were awarded a penalty with 11 minutes left, after Young's long-range effort was handled in the penalty box by Evans. However, Jimmy Milne blasted the spot kick high over the bar. Nonetheless, Hearts won a tumultuous match, one of many in a tumultuous season.

The only team Hearts didn't beat in this remarkable season was Clyde. Hearts' only defeat in the league came at Shawfield in November 1957, when the home side won 2-1. A week after the Celtic spectacle in March, the Bully Wee visited Tynecastle and looked like repeating their victory earlier in the season when they led by the same score with just a couple of minutes left to play.

However, Hearts – who missed the injured Dave Mackay for this game – equalised with seconds left, when Ian Crawford fired in an effort that came off the Clyde player Coyle. The Maroons duly clinched the league championship a month later with a 3-2 win at St Mirren and ended the season an incredible 13 points clear of second-placed Rangers.

Hearts scored 132 goals in their charge to the title – a British record for top-flight football that will surely never be equalled.

Such was Hearts' dominance that many people had the Maroons down for a league and cup double, something unheard of outside the Old Firm at that time. Hearts began their Scottish Cup campaign at Bayview and, given the Maroons had mauled East Fife 9-0 at Tynecastle earlier in the season, few gave the men from Methil much of a chance. However, it took a late goal from Bobby Blackwood to secure a 2-1 win, while in the next round Hearts were given a scare from Second Division Albion Rovers who threatened a brief comeback in the second half at Tynecastle before Hearts ran out 4-1 winners.

Hearts then got the draw they wanted for the quarter-final – Hibs at Tynecastle. Just over 41,000 fans were at the Gorgie ground for the game on the first day in March and most expected a win for the home side. Hibs had been struggling this season but, taking a leaf out of Hearts' book, they turned to youth and gave a debut to 17-year-old striker Joe Baker.

Urged on by an expectant home support, Hearts took the lead early on through Johnny Hamilton and the fans waited for their team to send their city rivals – without a Scottish Cup triumph since 1902 – spinning from the competition. However, young Baker hadn't read the script and he equalised two minutes later before giving the Hibees the lead just before the half-hour mark.

Jimmy Wardhaugh equalised for Hearts in the second half, but young Baker wasn't letting Hearts' reputation as the best team in the land bother him in any way and he scored two more goals to give Hibs a 4-2 lead before Hearts' Jimmy Murray pulled one back a minute before the end. However, this was too little too late for the home team and there was huge disappointment for the Hearts supporters – while four-goal Baker wrote himself into the Hibs history books.

It was a triple whammy for Hearts – to lose to a team they would normally have beaten easily that season was bad enough; when the defeat comes in the Scottish Cup to end your dreams of going to Hampden was worse; but when the defeat comes from your greatest rivals and on your home turf, then it's very difficult to take. One wonders what might have happened if Willie Bauld had not been injured and sat on the sidelines.

Hearts were 15 points clear at the top of the league at the time and it wasn't just fans of the maroon persuasion who were disappointed the double could not be concluded.

Nevertheless, Hearts' incredible performances in the league campaign made history. This was undoubtedly Hearts' greatest ever team. One that made records that will never be broken. As the fabulous decade that was the 1950s drew to a close, there would be one last hurrah for these hugely talented Hearts players.

Inevitably, such talent would attract suitors from elsewhere. Inevitably, the club could not refuse the tempting offers that would soon come their way. Scouts from other clubs came to Tynecastle in their droves to watch this quite brilliant Hearts team. Never, in Scottish football history, had there been a team that had played such breathtaking, attacking football.

Alas, there would soon be changes made at Tynecastle that the fans found difficult to swallow. In 1958 though, the glory was put into the club's famous anthem – Hearts, Hearts, Glorious Hearts!

v Partick Thistle 5-1
Scottish League Cup Final
25th October 1958. Hampden

Hearts:	Partick Thistle:
Marshall	Ledgerwood
Kirk	Hogan
Thomson	Donlevy
Mackay	Mathers
Glidden	Davidson
Cumming	Wright
Hamilton	Mackenzie
Murray	Thomson
Bauld	Smith
Wardhaugh	McParland
Crawford	Ewing

Referee: RH Davidson (Airdrie)

I ONCE READ about a survey in some medical journal or other that stated there were more people in Edinburgh who had problems associated with heart disease than in the whole of Sweden. While accepting this was a comment on the dietary habits of those of us lucky enough to live and work in Scotland's beautiful capital city, stress was also a factor and I did wonder if anyone had asked those conducting the survey how many people in Sweden followed Heart of Midlothian FC.

Even when Hearts were the dominant force in Scottish football – and there has surely been no team who dominated Scottish football the way Hearts' record-breaking league championship team of 1958 did – there were those aficionados of the Gorgie club who pondered in the summer of 1958 just how Hearts would follow that.

A question that was sure to be on the lips of manager Tommy Walker. There were no new significant arrivals at Tynecastle that summer and that, perhaps, was a rare error of judgement by the great man. The rest of Scottish football, while admiring what the Maroons achieved in that remarkable season of 1957/58, would be determined they would not be put to the sword by the marauding Maroons again.

It didn't take long for this to become evident. Hearts began the 1958/59 season with a League Cup section game at Ibrox – and a Rangers team eager to bring the champions down a peg or two, cantered to a 3-0 win in front of over 63,000 fans. The Govan side were three goals ahead at half-time and that first half was a warning to Hearts that resting on one's laurels simply wasn't an option.

The Maroons duly learnt their lesson and won their remaining five League Cup section games – including defeating Rangers 2-1 in the return fixture at Tynecastle. Thus, Hearts qualified for the quarter-final and romped past Second Division Ayr United on an 8-2 aggregate, that meant a semi-final clash with their defeated opponents' fierce rivals, Kilmarnock.

The game at Easter Road attracted a huge crowd of over 41,500 and after a strangely nervous looking opening half hour, Hearts opened the scoring through George Thomson and went on to win 3-0 to book their place in their second League Cup final in four years. In fact, it was almost four years to the day they defeated Motherwell 4-2 to end their near five decades without silverware that Hearts faced Partick Thistle in the 1958 final at Hampden.

Yet again, Hearts supporters headed west in huge numbers. *The Scotsman* reported "something like 60,000 spectators, 11 of them wearing red and yellow, saw Heart of Midlothian prove themselves Scotland's most accomplished football team at Hampden Park on Saturday". And so it proved.

Thistle had been affected by injuries and a Hearts team, now used to winning silverware and relishing the big occasion, went for the jugular straight from kick-off. With just five minutes played, Hearts' Jimmy Murray raced down the right wing with the Thistle defenders claiming in vain for offside. Murray's effort on goal was deflected and Willie Bauld, despite looking offside himself, duly accepted the gift to give Hearts an early lead.

Referee Bobby Davidson ignored the protests from the Thistle players and they were angry again seven minutes later, when they appealed for a free kick when Hearts' Dave Mackay tackled Thomson only for the referee to wave play on.

By today's standards, there is no doubt a free kick would have been awarded and Mackay's name would have gone into the referee's book. However, football was a much tougher game six decades ago and Hearts' Bobby Kirk swept forward a long pass towards Jimmy Murray on the right wing. Murray showed great control and as Thistle's Davidson made to tackle, Murray slipped the ball past the defender as if he weren't there before finishing off the chance with his usual deadly accuracy. Hearts were two goals ahead with less than 15 minutes gone and it was already an uphill task for the men from Firhill.

To their credit, Thistle tried manfully to fight back fuelled, no doubt, by a sense of injustice, but Hearts stood firm and just before the half-hour mark, increased their lead further. From a corner by Ian Crawford, Murray – who seemed to be everywhere on the Hampden field – hooked the ball across the penalty box where Willie Bauld was on hand to stroke it past Ledgerwood and put Hearts three goals ahead.

The huge Hearts support celebrated on the Hampden slopes as if their team had now done enough to bring the cup back to Gorgie. The more cautious among them – and, believe me dear reader, it pays to be a cautious Hearts fan – felt the game wasn't quite over yet.

However, it was just ten minutes later when Hearts scored a fourth goal. That man Jimmy Murray found himself with plenty of space 20 yards from the Thistle goal – again, the Thistle players appealed in vain for an offside decision – and he let fly with a left-foot shot that struck a post before rolling over the line to give the league champions an unassailable lead. Remarkably, Hearts went in at the interval 4-0 ahead and the Scottish League officials were already looking out the maroon and white ribbons to put on the trophy.

Like the league campaign of the previous season, one wondered how Hearts could top that when the game restarted. Willie Bauld almost answered that teaser at the start of the second half, when Jimmy Wardhaugh picked him out with a sublime pass, but the striker uncharacteristically fluffed his shot and the chance was gone.

Moments later, another goal did arrive. However, this time it was Thistle who pulled one back after McKenzie raced down the right wing before delivering a fine cross for Smith to head past Hearts goalkeeper Gordon Marshall. For a few moments, Hearts looked shaken as Thistle came forward in search of the goal that would make a real game of this cup final.

McParland, who would in later years go on to manage Partick Thistle to a famous League Cup win over Celtic, thundered in an effort from 20 yards that cannoned off the crossbar with Marshall helpless. This, however, seemed to be the wake-up call Hearts needed.

Inspired by Dave Mackay and John Cumming, Hearts simply rolled up their sleeves and regained control of a match they had totally dominated up until Thistle had scored. Cumming, in particular, was immense and his brilliant use of the ball was an inspiration to his team-mates.

With 25 minutes left, Hearts utilised their irritation at the temerity of their Glasgow opponents to score a goal, by restoring their four-goal advantage with the best goal of the afternoon. Mackay, Bauld, Jimmy Murray and Johnny Hamilton all combined in a beautiful, flowing move that saw Murray nonchalantly back-heel the ball into the path of Hamilton. He then drove in an effort from around 15 yards that veered away from the outstretched hand of Thistle keeper Ledgerwood to end the scoring at Hearts 5 Partick Thistle 1.

The jubilant Hearts fans lapped up every minute of their latest triumph and departed Hampden for the capital city in high spirits. Afterwards, Hearts captain Dave Mackay spoke of his team's target for the season – the treble of League Cup, Scottish Cup and league championship, something that, in 1958, had never been achieved before.

Four days later, Hearts thrashed Raith Rovers 5-0 at Starks Park to open up a three-point gap at the top of the First Division and it seemed Mackay's claims weren't as fanciful as some people thought. Hearts' next away game also saw the Maroons hit five goals without reply at Queen of the South. However, sandwiched in between those 5-0 routs was a 2-0 home defeat by Motherwell – and signs Hearts weren't quite the invincible force many believed.

Hearts then entered a curious spell when they blew hot and cold. A 5-1 trouncing of Aberdeen at Tynecastle was followed a week later by a 5-0 hammering at the hands of Rangers at Ibrox – Hearts were five goals behind after barely half an hour – and this was a result that took the Gers to the top of the league. It's fair to say that this thrashing took the wind out the sails of Hearts' bid to retain their league title.

The Maroons then dropped points to Celtic and Dunfermline Athletic before, whisper it, Hibs won at Tynecastle. When lowly Stirling Albion won 4-1 at Tynecastle at the end of January 1959, the alarm bells rang loudly in Gorgie. Hearts had slipped to fourth in the league table, six points behind Rangers and hopes of retaining the championship began to fade.

However, it was typical of Hearts to set off on an unbeaten run of eight games. In April, hope was rekindled that Hearts would retain their league title when they defeated Rangers 2-0 at Tynecastle. When the Gers surprisingly lost on the final day of the league season at home to Aberdeen, the championship – which in January had seemed a forlorn hope – was there for the taking for Hearts. However, a 2-1 defeat at Celtic Park, of all places – after Hearts had taken the lead – meant Rangers won the flag.

The 1958/59 season saw Hearts make their debut in the European Cup. For much of the 1950s, football authorities in Scotland and England were opposed to this new competition – it's difficult to believe this now, given the stature of today's Uefa Champions League competition.

As champions of Scotland, Hearts took their bow in Europe's premier football competition and were paired with Belgian champions Standard Liege in the first round. Back in the 1950s, there were no group stages in the European Cup and it was a straight knockout format. Which is precisely what happened to Hearts – they were delivered a knockout punch in the first leg in Belgium when they lost 5-1.

The result didn't stop more than 37,000 fans heading to Tynecastle for the return leg six days later and after a goalless first half, Willie Bauld gave the briefest glimmer of hope for the home fans when he scored ten minutes into the second period. Three minutes later, Liege equalised on the night and although Bauld restored Hearts' lead five minutes later, the game ended 2-1 to Hearts on the night – meaning the Maroons were eliminated on a 6-3 aggregate.

It had been a chastening experience for Hearts and their supporters who began to look at European football in a different light. If a team that had dominated Scottish football the way Hearts had done the previous season could be taken apart so easily by a team that weren't quite one of the leading lights in Europe, then what did that say about Scottish football?

As well as pipping Hearts to the league title, Rangers also denied the Maroons a Scottish Cup success by winning 3-2 at Ibrox in a second round tie on Valentine's Day – cue the plethora of "heartbreaker" headlines in the newspapers the following day.

Despite Hearts' disappointment in the league and the European and Scottish Cups, it is still worth remembering the 1958/59 season for another piece of silverware in the Tynecastle trophy room. Hearts were developing something of a love affair with the League Cup – as they were to prove again a year later…

v Third Lanark 2-1

Scottish League Cup Final
24th October 1959. Hampden

Hearts:	Third Lanark:
Marshall	Robertson
Kirk	Lewis
Thomson	Brown
Bowman	Reilly
Cumming	McCallum
Higgins	Cunningham
Smith	McInnes
Crawford	Craig
Young	D Hilley
Blackwood	Gray
Hamilton	I Hilley

Referee: T Wharton (Glasgow)

THE 1960s was to prove to be a decade that changed the world. Hearts supporters, having enjoyed unprecedented success in the 1950s, didn't particularly want their world to change.

Nonetheless, as a new decade approached, Hearts' world was changing. The all-conquering team of the 1950s was beginning to split up. However, Tommy Walker was still manager and approaching a decade in the job. Hearts had followed up their record-breaking league championship-winning season of 1957/58 by being runners-up to Rangers – losing their title by two points – at the end of season 1958/59.

In addition, some of the players who had become legends in Gorgie were moving on. Most notably, Dave Mackay left Hearts for English giants Tottenham Hotspur in March 1959 for a fee of £30,000. Mackay was a Hearts man through and through and many fans were dismayed at the club accepting what they thought was a pittance from a club that wasn't short of a penny or two.

Many observers believed Hearts would not recover from the loss of one of the greatest players ever to wear maroon and with Alfie Conn already away to pastures new, Jimmy Wardhaugh about to take his leave and Willie Bauld nearing the end of his career, some predicted Hearts' time as the dominant force in Scottish football was nearing its end. However, Tommy Walker wasn't quite finished yet.

At the start of the 1959/60 season, Walker pulled off another masterstroke. In a move that astounded Scottish football, Walker signed one of the greatest players ever to play for Edinburgh's other team – Hibernian. Gordon Smith was one of the celebrated "Famous Five" Hibs forward line that had dominated Scottish football – briefly – nearly a decade before. Even at 35 years of age, Smith was still impressively fit and it was something of a surprise when Hibs released him on a free transfer.

Hearts began the final League Cup competition of the 1950s at Rugby Park where more than 16,000 fans turned up to see if Kilmarnock could dent the aspirations of the cup holders. They threatened to in a goalless first half, but then the Maroons turned on the style in the second period and cantered to a 4-0 win.

To say Hearts loved the League Cup is a bit like saying they are Edinburgh's big team and Tommy Walker's side breezed through the sectional stage. While Aberdeen snatched a 2-2 draw at Tynecastle in the next game – Hearts stormed back from being two goals down in the opening 12 minutes – the Gorgie boys then won their next four games, including the return fixture with Kilmarnock at Tynecastle that marked the debut of Gordon Smith. All this meant Hearts had already qualified for the knockout stages by the time Stirling Albion held them to a 2-2 draw in the final section game at Tynecastle.

Hearts were then paired with an impressive Motherwell side in the two-legged quarter-final and over 32,000 fans packed into Fir Park to witness the first leg. A youngster called Ian St John equalised for the home team to cancel out Bobby Blackwood's opener for Hearts and the teams reconvened at Tynecastle a week later for the second leg. Another huge crowd – 44,000 – witnessed a rampant Hearts destroy Motherwell under the floodlights with Blackwood and Alex Young both scoring twice as the Maroons won 6-2 on the night to progress to yet another League Cup semi-final, 7-3 on aggregate.

St John scored both Motherwell's goals that evening and it was clear the young forward had a big future; a thought confirmed when he signed for Liverpool in 1961 for £37,500, a huge fee at the time.

When the semi-final draw was made, fortune smiled on Hearts when they were paired with the competition's surprise package – Second Division side Cowdenbeath. The semi-final was played, inevitably, at Easter Road and with Cowden struggling in the lower league, no one gave the Fifers a chance against a Hearts team who were yet again scoring goals galore.

However, few in the crowd of over 27,000 had predicted Cowdenbeath would cause as many problems for Hearts as they did in the opening half-hour. Hearts twice took the lead only for the part-timers to equalise on both occasions and it could be argued Hearts were a tad fortunate to be 4-2 ahead at half-time. In the second half however, Tommy Walker's side cut loose and with Ian Crawford scoring four goals on the night, Hearts eventually cruised to an astonishing 9-3 win to book their place in the final.

Hearts' opponents were Third Lanark, who had made an impressive start to the season and headed for the Hampden Park showdown in second place in the First Division, just two points behind the joint leaders – Hearts and Rangers. This was egg on the face for those who chose to demean cup finals that didn't include Celtic or Rangers – the League Cup final of 1959 was contested between second and third in the league!

Just under 58,000 fans headed to Hampden Park – for Hearts supporters the trip to the national stadium was by now such a well-worn path they could have found their way there blindfolded. A year earlier, Hearts had taken just five minutes to take the lead in the League Cup final against Partick Thistle. The 1959 final had an even earlier goal – but it didn't follow the expected script. Just two minutes had gone, when

Hearts goalkeeper Gordon Marshall, blinded by the autumn sun at the King's Park end of Hampden, made an uncharacteristic error of judgement on a through pass from Thirds' McInnes. The keeper fumbled the ball, which allowed Gray to strike home to give the Cathkin Park side an early and unexpected lead.

Strangely, the goal seemed to have more of an influence on Third Lanark's thinking than Hearts'. Rather than be buoyed by their start to the game, Thirds retreated into their collective shell and seemed content to let Hearts do the attacking. The Maroons swarmed forward and at times, it seemed they were camped in Thirds' half. Johnny Hamilton and Ian Crawford both had excellent chances to net Hearts' equaliser but they were thwarted by the brilliance of the Thirds goalkeeper Robertson.

With Hearts' Alex Young being man-marked, it was left to Blackwood to provide the danger and he combined well with Crawford and Hamilton. Such was Hearts' pressure, it was fully half an hour after they scored until Third Lanark threatened again when Craig fired in an effort that Marshall, keen to atone for his earlier error, did well to save.

For the remainder of the first half, Hearts continued to pound the Third Lanark goal, but it seemed to be one of those days when nothing was going to get past Thirds' small, but extremely agile goalkeeper. It seemed at times as if Robertson was playing Hearts on his own. As the teams headed to the dressing room for half-time, it seemed incredulous that Third Lanark were still one goal ahead.

The second half resumed where the first had left off – with Hearts on the attack. It surely seemed just a matter of time before Tommy Walker's side would equalise and it appeared they had done so in the 52nd minute. Following yet another Hearts attack, Alex Young powered in a header that seemed a goal all the way. Hearts fans were about to celebrate only to see the ball hit the bottom of the post – and bounce into the grateful arms of keeper Robertson. Young held his head in his hands as did many of his team-mates and the groans from the Hampden terracings from an anguished Hearts support told their own story.

Even the weather had taken a turn for the worse, with the rain now teeming down. However, Hearts finally made the breakthrough six minutes later. The ebullient Johnny Hamilton set off on one of his famous runs. With the Thirds defence trailing in his wake, Hamilton looked up and from fully 25 yards unleashed a spectacular shot that not even Robertson could prevent swishing the Hampden net and Hearts were on level terms at last.

It had taken the Maroons nearly an hour to score the equaliser – but they took only another two minutes to go in front. Gordon Marshall launched the ball downfield and, with wind assistance, Young got the better of Thirds defender McInnes and their heroic goalkeeper Robertson to stroke the ball into an empty net to put Hearts 2-1 ahead.

Hearts weren't the kind of team to settle for a 2-1 scoreline and they continued to swarm forward. It wasn't just the usual forward runs from Hamilton, Jimmy Murray and Ian Crawford. George Thomson, Andy Bowman – whose son Davie would play for Hearts a little over 20 years later – and youngster Billy Higgins also helped their attacking colleagues as Hearts sought the third goal that would finish off Thirds.

As if that wasn't enough, Third Lanark were also tormented by a player who was renowned for his time playing for Edinburgh's other team – Gordon Smith. The elder statesman of this Hearts team showed he still had class and not inconsiderable style as he strolled through the game with comparative ease. At one point in the second half, the former Hibby produced a highly impressive display of keepy-uppy and danced round Thirds player Brown. It was a sublime piece of skill from a player who, despite being part of the Easter Road team that won the league title in 1951, had never won a cup medal while at Hibernian.

It brought great cheers from the admiring Hearts support and summed up the afternoon – Third Lanark worked hard and tried manfully to compete with the League Cup holders but it was Hearts who had the style and panache. There was no further scoring and Hearts had won the League Cup for the third time in five years – and collected their fifth piece of major silverware since 1954.

Despite the closeness of the score, Hearts were streets ahead of their Glasgow opponents. In fact, many Hearts fans thought their side had played better in the 1959 final than they had when they hammered Partick Thistle 5-1 a year before. Against Third Lanark, Hearts played what would later become known as "total football" with players dovetailing into a formation that left Third Lanark helpless.

True, some of the Cathkin Park players were part-time professionals and there was little doubt Hearts' superior fitness told as the final drew to its conclusion. In this respect, Thirds' tactics of trying to hold on to their second-minute lead backfired on them – it was a huge ask of their players to defend against a relentless Hearts onslaught.

As is often the case in football, Hearts faced Third Lanark again just four days later on league business at Tynecastle. This time Hearts didn't struggle for goals and cruised to a 6-2 win to open up a two-point lead at the top of the First Division. Interestingly, the local newspaper report on the game contained a footnote stating Third Lanark had posted a small financial profit. Eight years later, this famous football club would fold because of financial difficulties.

Hearts, however, had other things on their mind. With one piece of silverware already secured, they went in search of the major prize of season 1959/60 – the league championship…

v Hibernian 5-1

Scottish League Division One
1st January 1960. Easter Road

Hearts:	Hibernian:
Marshall	Wren
Kirk	Grant
Thomson	McClelland
Cumming	Young
Milne	Plenderleith
Bowman	Baxter
Smith	McLeod
Young	Johnstone
Bauld	Baker
Blackwood	Preston
Hamilton	Ormond

Referee: RH Davidson (Airdrie)

HEARTS MADE a decent start to the league campaign of season 1959/60 even though points were dropped to Hibs – that man Joe Baker again proving to be a thorn in Hearts' side by scoring twice in a 2-2 draw at Tynecastle – and Stirling Albion. In between those games, Tommy Walker's men had won a thrilling game at Celtic Park 4-3, Bobby Blackwood scoring the winner two minutes from the end.

On Halloween, Hearts travelled to Ibrox to face the team that had taken their league title from them six months earlier. The Maroons were majestic that day and defeated Rangers 2-0 to open up a four-point gap at the top of the league. This was Hearts' second win in Glasgow in a week – seven days earlier they lifted the League Cup for a third time, successfully defending their trophy with a 2-1 win over Third Lanark in the final, as described in the previous chapter.

Hearts then hit something of a blip when they drew with Clyde and lost to St Mirren and Motherwell in successive games but they remained top of the league when they faced Hibernian at Easter Road for the traditional New Year's Day Edinburgh derby. Given the Hibees had drawn at Tynecastle earlier in the season, the trip to Leith looked a tricky one.

A huge crowd of more than 54,000 packed the sloping terraces of Easter Road for the Ne'er Day spectacle.

Hibs themselves had designs on the league championship even though they were seven points behind their great rivals – they saw this as an opportunity to reduce the deficit. And it was the home team who began the game the livelier with Baker and Ormond looking dangerous. However, as they so often did at that time, Hearts responded to being put under early pressure by opening the scoring after seven minutes. Bobby Blackwood got his head to a fine free kick from Jimmy Milne and directed the ball to Willie Bauld. The King may have been approaching the end of his reign at Tynecastle but there was still no better header of a ball. His effort beat Hibs keeper Wren but smacked off the post. Thankfully for Hearts, there was Alex Young – the Prince – to touch home the rebound and give Hearts the lead.

A minute later, Hibs' Baker took the ball round Hearts keeper Gordon Marshall and stroked it into the net for what appeared to be the equaliser. However, the home supporters' joy was short-lived when it was chalked off for offside. Three minutes later, Hibs thought they would have the chance to equalise from the penalty spot when George Thomson appeared to foul Baker – but the referee waved play on.

In the 17th minute Wren pushed a superb effort from Willie Bauld over the bar. From the resultant corner, taken by Gordon Smith, Hibs defender Plenderleith, under pressure from Young, headed the ball into his own net and Hearts were two goals ahead.

Hibs pushed men forward in an effort to get back into the game and when Baker hit the crossbar, one could sense this just wasn't going to be their day.

Hearts began the second half in superb fashion, pinning their city rivals into their own half. There was the remarkable sight of centre-half John Cumming playing like a centre-forward and he had three superb efforts on goal, each brilliantly saved by the Hibs keeper. Eight minutes into the second period, Hearts' pressure paid off when Gordon Smith played in Young who passed to Bauld. The forward saw his shot on goal saved by the overworked Wren who could only parry the ball to a grateful Young who scored his second and Hearts' third.

In the 66th minute, Johnstone pulled a goal back for Hibs but any hope of a comeback for the home team disappeared 60 seconds later when Young set off on a mazy run before firing in a brilliant shot from 20 yards to complete his hat-trick and restore Hearts' three-goal advantage.

Five minutes later came the moment Hibs fans were dreading. It pained them to see their former hero Gordon Smith in maroon and white colours. Their pain became excruciating when Smith thumped home a volley from the edge of the penalty box to complete the scoring – and misery for the home support – at Hibernian 1 Hearts 5.

After the game, the *Daily Record* football reporter "Waverley" suggested John Cumming was the best player in Britain. The following day, Hearts defeated Celtic 3-1 at Tynecastle – two games in 24 hours was no problem for our hardy football players five decades ago – and people asked who could stop Hearts winning the league championship now. The answer was no one.

There was a never say die spirit about this Hearts team and they simply refused to accept defeat. After the victory over Celtic, Hearts travelled across the River Forth for the short trip to Dunfermline. The "Pars Athletic" may have been fighting against the threat of relegation, but manager Andy Dickson was building a team that would go on to lift the Scottish Cup a year later. The home side went two goals ahead with 20 minutes remaining, but George Thomson pulled a goal back ten minutes from the end before Young scored the equaliser in injury time.

After defeating Stirling Albion 4-0, Hearts then dropped more points when they were held to draws by Ayr United and Motherwell and questions were asked by the cynics if this Hearts team – unlike the all-conquering side of two years before –

had the winning mentality to go on and take the championship. However, closest challengers Rangers were held to a goalless draw at home to Dundee as both sides displayed signs of nerves.

When Rangers came to Tynecastle on 5th March 1960, it was billed by many as the title decider. Forty-five thousand fans had similar thoughts and a scrappy encounter remained goalless until seven minutes from the end when Hearts' Cumming scored, before Young immediately added a second goal with just six minutes left on the clock.

There was jubilation among the home support on the Tynecastle terracing as they realised their favourites had now moved eight points ahead of the Glasgow giants. In fact, it was Kilmarnock who were now Hearts' nearest challengers and when Tommy Walker's men lost at Rugby Park a fortnight later, Gorgie nerves began to jangle once more. However, Hearts then recorded comprehensive wins over Aberdeen (3-0) and Clyde (5-2) meaning if the Maroons defeated St Mirren, they would win the championship.

While the team was not quite as dominant as the 1958 side, Hearts duly secured the title with a 4-4 draw at St Mirren in April 1960 – Kilmarnock and Rangers fought out a 1-1 draw at Rugby Park that same afternoon meaning a single point was all that was necessary for Hearts in Paisley. Fittingly, Willie Bauld's last-minute equaliser earned a point – and Hearts' second league title in two years.

They were worthy champions and Hearts completed the season with a 2-2 draw at Kirkcaldy against a Raith Rovers team that included future Heart Willie Wallace and a 20-year-old Jim Baxter. Hearts then embarked on a close-season tour in the United States where they recorded a 4-0 win over Manchester United. The start of the 1960s was indeed swinging for Heart of Midlothian!

Sadly, this would be the last occasion Hearts would be league champions. By the end of 1960, Hearts had sold the Golden Vision that was Alex Young to Everton for £42,000. Jimmy Wardhaugh had left Tynecastle for Dunfermline Athletic in November 1959 while Alfie Conn had also crossed the River Forth for Raith Rovers in 1958. The last of the "Terrible Trio" – Willie Bauld – would find his appearances in a maroon jersey becoming more infrequent as the 1960s began and he retired in 1962.

The season after lifting the league championship in 1960, Hearts finished in seventh place in the First Division – their lowest league placing since 1949. Injuries to key players such as Jimmy Murray, Jimmy Milne and Andy Bowman didn't help and it was asking a lot of 36-year-old Gordon Smith to produce his undoubted class and style week in, week out.

At the end of the 1960/61 season, Smith left Tynecastle for Dundee. Astonishingly, a year later, he was celebrating another league championship success with the Dark Blues, thereby becoming the only player in Scottish football history to win the league title with three different clubs – Hibernian in 1950 and 1951, Hearts in 1960 and Dundee in 1962 – and none of them being the Old Firm!

Hearts began 1960/61 unimpressively, losing two of their League Cup section games meaning they were involved in a play-off with Clyde to ensure progress to the knockout stages. Given the Maroons had thrashed the Bully Wee 6-2 at Tynecastle just two weeks earlier, one might have thought this would not present a problem. However, this is Hearts we're talking about.

The play-off game was played at a neutral venue – Celtic Park – and Hearts lost 2-1, bitter disappointment for the cup holders. Although Hearts lifted the League Cup once more in 1962, the downward spiral had started.

At least Hearts began the defence of their league championship impressively – a 3-1 win over St Johnstone followed by a 4-1 hammering of Hibs at Easter Road but then, mysteriously, their form slumped remarkably. The League Cup play-off defeat seemed to affect morale and Hearts went on a run of ten league games without a victory.

When they faced Raith Rovers at Tynecastle at the end of November, the league champions were fifth from bottom of the First Division. Perhaps they were somewhat distracted by their second appearance in the European Cup. As with their previous appearance in 1958, Hearts were paired with dangerous opponents – Portuguese champions Benfica.

The first leg was played at Tynecastle where Benfica showed their class by leading 2-0 with just a few minutes to go. As many of the Hearts fans in the 29,000 crowd began to head for the exits, Alex Young scored a late counter for the home side meaning there was still a flicker of hope the Maroons could turn it around in Portugal. Reality, though, dictated this was never going to happen and Hearts lost the second leg 3-0 to crash out 5-1 on aggregate. Forty-six years would pass before Hearts got another chance to play in European football's premier competition.

With Hearts struggling in the league, hopes of silverware in the first half of 1961 turned to the Scottish Cup. Hearts hammered non-league Tarff Rovers 9-0 at Tynecastle in the first round before winning an altogether more difficult tie at Rugby Park, defeating Kilmarnock 2-1.

After Partick Thistle were beaten 2-1 at Firhill, the Maroons faced St Mirren at Tynecastle in the quarter-final. Despite dominating the game, Hearts missed chance after chance. Inevitably, St Mirren scored the only goal of the game and the majority of the 34,000 crowd felt the bitter taste of disappointment once more.

The glorious era that was the 1950s was now a fading memory and while the 1960s started promisingly, by the end of this decade Hearts were but a shadow of the team that had dominated Scottish football ten years previously. Great advances were made in technology and by the end of the 1960s, man was landing on the moon. Hearts, though, seemed stuck in reverse gear. Worryingly, no one seemed to know how to drive the club forward again.

Thankfully, there were no such thoughts on New Year's Day 1960 when Hearts – and Alex Young and Gordon Smith, in particular – were the most unwelcome first foots Hibs could have asked for!

v **Kilmarnock** 1-0

Scottish League Cup Final
27th October 1962. Hampden

Hearts:	Kilmarnock:
Marshall	McLaughlan
Polland	Richmond
Holt	Watson
Cumming	O'Connor
Barry	McGrory
Higgins	Beattie
Wallace	Brown
Paton	Black
Davidson	Kerr
W. Hamilton	McInally
J Hamilton	McIlroy

Referee: T Wharton (Glasgow)

WHEN FOOTBALL resumed after the Second World War, there were those who were sceptical about the new League Cup competition. Many observers opined the new tournament was just a gimmick cashing in on football's popularity, which had never been higher. It's fair to say Hearts supporters loved it, having seen their heroes lift the cup three times since its inception in 1946.

When the draw was made for the sectional stage of the 1962/63 competition, it was doubtful if Hearts could have had a tougher group. Section A saw them grouped with both Dundee clubs and Celtic. Dundee now had Gordon Smith in their ranks, having left Tynecastle for Dens Park. The Dark Blues had their finest ever team at this point with skilful players such as Andy Penman and Ian Ure. Smith added much needed experience to this team and they won the Scottish League championship for the only time in their history at the end of 1961/62.

Despite Hearts' impressive record in the League Cup – as well as their three triumphs, the Maroons lost the 1961 final to Rangers after a replay – there were those who doubted if an evolving Hearts team would make it past the group stages. Many of the players who played their part in Hearts' dominance of Scottish football in the latter half of the 1950s such as Dave Mackay, Alex Young and the "Terrible Trio" were now no longer at Tynecastle.

Manager Tommy Walker was rebuilding his team and made a significant signing for the 1962/63 season when he bought inside-forward Willie Hamilton from Middlesbrough for the princely sum of £5,000. The term used nowadays for teams undergoing this process is "transitional" and it certainly looked that way when Hearts lost their opening game in the League Cup, 3-1 away to Celtic. However, they then defeated both Dundee clubs and when Celtic came to Gorgie for the return game at Tynecastle, Hearts' chances of qualifying from the section were very much alive.

More than 31,000 spectators watched Hearts race into a three-goal lead, including two goals from centre-forward Willie Wallace. However, this being Hearts, things are never straightforward and Celtic stormed back into the game with goals from Murdoch and Hughes, the latter being near the end of the game, thus ensuring an uncomfortable final three minutes for Hearts supporters. Hearts hung on for a memorable 3-2 win and, after losing their next game at Tannadice, defeated Dundee in their final group game to progress to a two-legged quarter-final meeting with Morton.

In the first leg at Cappielow, a Norrie Davidson double added to an own goal put Hearts in easy street and they duly completed the job in the return leg at Tynecastle 3-1 to go through 6-1 on aggregate. This meant a semi-final clash with St Johnstone at Easter Road where a Willie Wallace hat-trick helped Tommy Walker's men to a 4-0 win – and a fifth League Cup final appearance in eight years.

Their opponents in the final were Kilmarnock who were in the process of building a fine team of their own. A crowd of 51,280 headed to Hampden Park on 27th October 1962 to see if the Ayrshire team could break their League Cup duck – or if Hearts could win the trophy for a fourth time.

There was a pre-match blow for Killie when the hugely influential Davie Sneddon was ruled out with injury. However, this didn't seem to affect them too much in the early stages when they dominated play.

Hearts made a nervous start. In the opening minutes, keeper Gordon Marshall tangled with Killie forward Black and John Cumming cleared the danger. Black threatened again shortly after and it seemed the Hearts players were struggling with the heavy Hampden pitch. It took the Maroons some time to make an impression with Davidson creating Hearts' first real chance with a rasping 20-yard shot which Killie keeper McLaughlan tipped over.

This encouraged Tommy Walker's men and the enigmatic Willie Hamilton began to revel in the huge space that Hampden had to offer. In the 27th minute, Hamilton produced a piece of magic befitting a major cup final. Collecting a long ball from Willie Wallace, Hamilton deftly controlled the ball, skipped past Killie defender Jackie McGrory and raced in on goal. He looked up and delivered a glorious pass into the penalty box where Davidson thrashed the ball past McLaughlan to give Hearts the lead.

It was a brilliant goal, created by the magic of Hamilton and finished by the guile of Davidson. Against the run of play, it may have been, but it transformed the game and Hamilton tormented the Killie defence thereafter, although Gordon Marshall had to save brilliantly from Frank Beattie, while Davie Holt made a crucial tackle on McIlroy following a slip from Roy Barry just before half-time.

Killie's Jackie McInally – father of future Celtic and Bayern Munich player Alan – was injured during that first half. This was the era before substitutes, so McInally limped bravely on. Hearts took advantage, dominated much of the second half, and could – indeed should – have added to the one goal they had. Then, with just seconds remaining and the Hearts fans whistling at referee Tom Wharton, urging him to blow for full time, Kilmarnock launched one last desperate attack.

Richmond floated a free kick into the Hearts penalty box. Frank Beattie rose above everyone to head the ball past the flailing arms of Gordon Marshall and into the net. It appeared Kilmarnock had tied the game at the death. Blue and white shirted players forgot their tiredness and danced for joy. Hearts players slumped to the sodden Hampden pitch.

However, referee Wharton was not signalling towards the centre circle. He was giving a free kick to Hearts. The official had spotted an infringement that no one else appeared to have noticed. Furious Killie players urged the official to consult his linesman, which, to his credit, he did. Nevertheless, his decision remained the same. Free kick to Hearts. Wharton believed Beattie had handled the ball as the cross came in.

Seconds later, Wharton blew his whistle for the end of the game. Hearts had won the Scottish League Cup for the fourth time in eight years, their seventh major trophy since 1954. Triumphant Hearts headed back to the capital for a night of celebration. Willie Hamilton was the toast of Edinburgh. Hamilton was a natural ball player, although he was affected by injury throughout his colourful career. Manager Tommy Walker knew how important Hamilton was to the team even if his penchant for hugging the ball when it might have been better passing to team-mates was sometimes infuriating! Sadly, however, Hamilton and his Hearts team-mates would taste no more success in the maroon jersey.

The Maroons made a decent enough start to the league campaign of 1962/63 and were top of the league after scoring 20 goals in their opening five league games – which included a 4-0 drubbing of Hibs at Easter Road where Danny Paton scored a hat-trick. When Airdrieonians were thrashed 6-1 at Tynecastle the following week and four goals were scored against Partick Thistle at Firhill the week after that, Hearts fans were dreaming of a season similar to that of five years before when Hearts demolished almost every team they played. However, Hearts then drew with Dunfermline Athletic and Kilmarnock and Rangers took over at the top of the league.

Three days after lifting the League Cup at Hampden, Hearts travelled to Falkirk to face a Bairns team who were second bottom of the league and who had won just one league game all season. The more seasoned Hearts fans can tell what's coming here. The Maroons gave the distinct impression they had partied a tad too much after winning the League Cup and were awful. Falkirk took an early lead they never looked like relinquishing.

Hearts' Roy Barry then achieved something akin to notoriety when he was sent off with 20 minutes remaining after protesting too much about a penalty being awarded to the home team. Barry was so incensed by the decision he continued to argue after he had been booked and was consequently booked again.

After all the hoo-ha, Falkirk missed the penalty but when Barry left the field so did Hearts' chances of salvaging a draw, a fact confirmed when Falkirk scored a second goal in stoppage time. It was Hearts' first defeat of the season and left a bad taste in the mouth. Barry was the first Hearts player to be ordered off since the Second World War and manager Tommy Walker – a stickler for discipline – was furious.

Hearts then drew with Aberdeen and Clyde but were still just a couple of points behind league leaders Rangers. Three weeks before Christmas, the Maroons staged what was billed as a "glamour friendly" with opposition from what was then called the Soviet Union. Moscow Torpedo came to Gorgie on a cold Thursday night in December as part of their British tour. They had already beaten Rangers at Ibrox and more than 20,000 came to Tynecastle to see them. However, Hearts produced a breathtaking display of football and ran out 6-0 winners with Willie Hamilton the star of the show.

When Hearts drew with Dundee United on 15th December, little did anyone know it would be the Maroons' last league game for nearly three months. The winter of 1962/63 was so severe it led to Scottish football being almost completely shut down for weeks. Hearts did manage a Scottish Cup tie in January when they defeated Second Division side Forfar Athletic 3-1 in front of 2,900 hardy souls at Station Park, but their opponents in the next round nearly two months later were tougher opposition. The Maroons suffered a 3-1 defeat at Celtic Park, thus ending hopes of adding the Scottish Cup to the League Cup in the Tynecastle boardroom.

Hearts' hopes of winning the league championship were undoubtedly affected by the impact of the severe winter and they had to play six games in 18 days in March in an effort to reduce the backlog of fixtures. One of those was a 3-2 defeat by League Cup foes Kilmarnock at Tynecastle but Hearts had to play for an hour with ten men when goalkeeper Gordon Marshall had to go off injured. Defender Roy Barry went in goal but couldn't prevent defeat.

An impressive Rangers team were top of the league and when they visited Tynecastle at the end of March, they faced a Hearts team hit by injury. Rangers ran out 5-0 winners and Hearts slumped to sixth in the league. A week later Hearts were hammered 7-3 at St Mirren. A season that had begun with Hearts at the top of the table and winning the League Cup, ended in disappointment with a huge backlog of postponed games taking their toll.

Hearts finished the season by playing six games in three weeks as the season ended on 18th May and there were just 5,665 fans at the final game at Tynecastle to see Hearts defeat Dunfermline Athletic 2-0. It seemed an eternity since Hearts' League Cup triumph but the bitter row over Kilmarnock's "goal that never was" rumbled on for some time afterwards. And bitter, dejected Kilmarnock would return to haunt Hearts soon after – on the final day of the 1964/65 league season when Hearts needed to avoid losing the game by two goals to prevent handing the Ayrshire men the league title on a plate. Hearts were champions designate – until, inevitably, Killie won 2-0 to snatch the championship from the Tynecastle trophy room and blag it back to Rugby Park.

However, no one foresaw this at the Scottish League Cup final of 1962 as Hearts triumphed yet again. Although no one envisaged it then, it would be nearly 36 long years before Hearts would win a major trophy again…

v Dundee United 6-5

Scottish Cup Second Round
17th February 1968. Tannadice

Hearts:	Dundee United:
Garland	Mackay
Sneddon	Miller
Mann	Cameron
E Thomson	Smith
A Thomson	Neilson
Miller	Gillespie
Ford	Seeman
Townsend	Hainey
Moller	Mitchell
Irvine	Rolland
Traynor	Wilson

Referee: RH Davidson (Airdrie)

AFTER HEARTS, Aberdeen and Hibernian had dominated Scottish football in the 1950s, the late 1960s was a period undoubtedly dominated by the Old Firm of Celtic and Rangers. Celtic were, of course, champions of Europe in 1967 and Rangers had also reached a European final in the same season – the Cup Winners' Cup final.

However, excitement and high drama were not the exclusive property of the men from Parkhead and Ibrox. An exciting Dunfermline Athletic team were carrying on the good work started by Jock Stein before he left for Celtic and, from the north-east, Aberdeen were about to emerge as a force to be reckoned with once more.

The Hearts team of 1967 – a period declared by many as "the summer of love" – was about to undergo further surgery. Hearts had finished in 11th place in the league at the end of the 1966/67 season – their lowest placing in the league since 1927. Even allowing for the hugely successful Celtic team of the time and a highly impressive Rangers side, the malaise that had set in at Tynecastle in such a short time alarmed many.

The devastating loss of the league title on the final day of of season 1964/65 and the departure of manager Tommy Walker in September 1966 were blows the club was clearly struggling to recover from. Walker's replacement as manager, Johnny Harvey, tried manfully to stem the tide and brought much needed fresh blood to Tynecastle with full-backs Arthur Mann and Ian Sneddon being given their chance in the first team while forward Rene Moller was recruited from Danish side FC Randers.

Although money, as ever, was tight, Harvey prised £15,000 from the Tynecastle coffers to sign another forward, Jim Irvine, from Middlesbrough. While Hearts had the supremely talented Donald Ford up front, it was clear too much was being asked of the West Lothian man and support was badly needed.

Hearts' love affair with the League Cup was now a distant memory and they exited the 1967 competition at the group stage – as they had done every season since they last won the trophy in 1962. Hearts began the league season in quite awful fashion. A 4-1 defeat from Hibs at Tynecastle – where the visitors' Pat Quinn scored a hat-trick – had Hearts fans collectively shaking their heads.

Equally worrying for the Tynecastle hierarchy was the attendance for the game – less than 21,000 for an Edinburgh derby was a sad reflection on the disaffection affecting the club and its supporters. Johnny Harvey did manage to rally his troops and Hearts did win five games in a row during the late autumn, but it remained the fact you were never quite sure what you were going to get from this Hearts team – as was witnessed in a 6-3 thrashing from Clyde at Shawfield in January 1968.

At least Hearts got a decent draw in the Scottish Cup – Second Division side Brechin City at Tynecastle – but the game was tied at 1-1 with half an hour to go and the home fans weren't slow in showing their anger. Hearts then scored three goals as the part-time visitors tired but the game seemed symptomatic of Hearts' season.

When the draw for the second round gave Hearts a trip to Dundee United, there were few eyebrows raised. While it was an all-First Division clash, both clubs were struggling in the league. United, under the leadership of long-serving manager Jerry Kerr, were very much regarded as the second side in the city of jam and jute. The Dark Blues of Dundee had been league champions only six years previously at the start of the decade and had earned a reputation of being one of the most feared sides in Scotland. The team from Tannadice, however, had been playing Second Division football a little over a decade before and had made little impression since returning to the top flight.

In any case, this particular game was overshadowed by the Dundee v Rangers tie, which, remarkably, was being played the same day some 400 yards along the road (Tannadice Street in Dundee, of course, houses both Tannadice and Dens Park)! The only concession made by United was to kick off their game an hour earlier at 2pm. A crowd of 9,021 braved the snow and ice on a wintry February afternoon and the teams did their best to keep warm on the pitch that had barely passed an inspection minutes before kick-off.

It was Johnny Harvey's side who seemed to adapt more quickly to the tricky conditions and, with less than 20 minutes of the game played, the Maroons were two goals ahead. Striker Donald Ford, very much the jewel in the Tynecastle crown, slipped the ball past United keeper Mackay to put the Edinburgh side in front and, shortly after, Danish star Rene Moller added a second. If Hearts thought they were in for an easy afternoon, however, they were soon made to think otherwise. After 21 minutes, captain Eddie Thomson's attempted pass back seemed to stick in the snow and former Rangers and Scotland star Davie Wilson pounced to pull one back for United.

The Tannadice team had their tails up and centre-forward Rolland stroked the ball past the startled Hearts goalkeeper Kenny Garland to give United a deserved equaliser five minutes later. United, with young Mitchell and the more experienced Gillespie causing havoc every time they came forward, kept up the pressure.

With the first half barely two-thirds over, controversy raged. United's Mitchell seemed to use a hand as he burst through a porous Hearts defence and looked suspiciously offside in any case. As the Hearts defenders stood and waited for a referee's whistle that would never blow, Mitchell ran on and slotted the ball past Garland to make it 3-2 to United. There was bedlam around the stadium and some angry Hearts supporters began throwing missiles on to the park. When Mitchell scored again for United to make it 4-2 after 37 minutes, there were more angry scenes amongst the contingent from Edinburgh, but their collective mood was pacified somewhat when Eddie Thomson made up for his earlier mistake by pulling the score back to 4-3 just before the interval.

The half-time break gave players and supporters alike a chance to draw breath and with a goal being scored every six and a half minutes, it seemed there was little time to feel the icy blast of the Tayside winter! Within the first few minutes of the second half, this rollercoaster of a cup-tie took another turn. United were awarded a penalty for a foul on Seeman but when the number seven took the kick himself his shot was brilliantly saved by goalkeeper Garland. Suitably encouraged, Hearts raced up the park where the enigmatic Moller displayed his more skilful facet with an angled shot past keeper Mackay to level the scores at 4-4 – and there were still more than 35 minutes to play!

Before an hour was played, United were back in front once more when Hainey fired in an effort from 20 yards that eluded the grasp of Hearts keeper Garland. It was now 5-4 to the home team and Hearts swarmed forward in search of the equaliser. With 15 minutes left, Tommy Traynor had a goalbound effort handled on the line by Cameron. Hearts captain George Miller assumed responsibility for the penalty and fired the ball past Mackay to make it 5-5. Surely, this would be the end of the scoring and the sides would need to reconvene at Tynecastle for a replay? Not a bit of it!

With just four minutes to go, there was to be yet another twist in this astonishing tale, and an ironic one at that. Former United hero Jim Irvine, now sporting the maroon of Hearts, intercepted a throw-in from his old colleague Gillespie and ran virtually unopposed into the United penalty box where he dispatched the ball past Mackay with great aplomb. It was 6-5 to Hearts and the travelling support from Edinburgh could hardly contain their delight. The final whistle sounded soon after and Hearts were into the next round. Dejected Dundee United players trooped sadly off the snow covered park and it was little consolation to them that they had just taken part in one of the most remarkable games in the history of the Scottish Cup.

Hearts' reward for that memorable victory was a quarter-final trip to Ibrox to face a powerful Rangers side that had duly completed the business down the road at Dens Park. Jim Irvine was again the Maroons' hero as he scored in a 1-1 draw, a result that went against all expectations – as did Hearts' victory in the replay. In front of more than 44,000 fans at a packed Tynecastle, Hearts and Rangers played out a 'blood and thunder' cup-tie that remained goalless until four minutes from the end. Hearts' Tommy Traynor picked out Donald Ford with a fine pass. Ford took the ball round Rangers defender McKinnon before hitting a shot low into the net to give Hearts a sensational winner. The noise that erupted at Tynecastle when the ball hit the net had not reached such decibel levels for ten years.

Hearts' opponents in the semi-final were Morton and the Maroons needed extra time in a Hampden replay to overcome the Greenock side and reach the final where their opponents were Dunfermline Athletic. It was typical of the Hearts team of the time that the form they showed in defeating Dundee United and Rangers didn't accompany them to Hampden on 27th April 1968. It was a poor game, played in less than April-like conditions. Moreover, there was huge disappointment as the Maroons lost the final 3-1.

Four decades ago, the Scottish Cup final wasn't covered live on television and for the 1968 final a near full programme of league fixtures was played on cup final day (marketing was a word that hadn't quite yet reached the hallowed corridors of power of the Scottish Football Association). A crowd of just over 56,000 meant Hampden was less than half full, although the fact Rangers were entertaining Aberdeen in front of 45,000 spectators in Glasgow's south side probably didn't help matters. In the balance of fairness, the officials realised the error of their ways and the 1968 Scottish Cup final was the last to be played at the same time as a full league programme – although it was to be another nine years before live television coverage was introduced.

Hearts' final league game of the season came just two days after the cup final on a chilly April evening in Greenock. Typically, Hearts lost 1-0 and ended the season in 12th place in Division One having lost exactly half of their 34 league games. Hearts fans didn't need anyone to tell them a Scottish Cup final appearance was merely papering over the cracks.

Players came and players went at Tynecastle but the fact was the team was slipping further into mediocrity – and fans demanded the slide be arrested.

It is doubtful, though, if any of the players who took part in that cup tie at Tannadice in February 1968 would ever experience anything like it again. For all the players, officials and supporters who were in one half of Tannadice Street that day, it was a game they would never forget.

v Celtic 2-0

Scottish League Division One
8th November 1969. Celtic Park

Hearts:	Celtic:
Cruickshank	Fallon
Clunie	Craig
Oliver	Gemmell
MacDonald	Murdoch
Anderson	McNeill
Thomson	Brogan
Jensen	Johnstone
Moller	Dalglish
Ford	Hughes
Brown	Macari
Lynch	Callaghan

Referee: B Padden (Ardrossan)

HEARTS' STEADY slide from a team that had dominated Scottish football in the 1950s to mid-table mediocrity a decade later was perhaps accelerated by the emergence of one of the finest teams in Scottish football history – the Celtic side of the late 1960s.

Jock Stein had made a name for himself as a manager at the beginning of the decade when he led Dunfermline Athletic to Scottish Cup glory in 1961 – ironically, the Pars defeated Celtic, the team Stein once played for, in the final – before he headed for a brief spell in charge of Hibs. Cynical Hearts fans may suggest Stein soon saw the error of his ways and didn't hang about long at Easter Road, but it's reasonable to suggest he couldn't resist the offer of managing a Celtic team that had been bereft of success in the 1950s and early part of the 1960s.

Stein was to rectify that in some fashion when he built a team of local players and would lead them to nine successive league championships – and, famously, the European Cup in 1967, becoming the first British side to do so. In 1969, Celtic had won their fourth league title in a row, as well as the Scottish Cup and League Cup. No one could touch them in Scotland, not even Rangers who finished five points behind their great rivals in the league. Hearts, meanwhile were 18 points behind in eighth place, below teams such as Airdrieonians and St Johnstone although I feel it's my duty to point out the Maroons were still four places above Edinburgh's other team in the First Division.

Hearts manager Johnny Harvey tried manfully to arrest the team's slide but with a lack of cash and Celtic so far ahead of everyone else, it was an unenviable task. He turned to junior football in the spring of 1969 and brought in outside-left Andy Lynch from Kirkintilloch Rob Roy while he paid Highland League side Ross County £10,000 for winger Neil Murray. Youngsters such as full-back Peter Oliver and centre-forward Eric Carruthers would also be given their chance but it's fair to say the majority of Hearts fans weren't overly optimistic as season 1969/70 got underway – particularly as Hearts lost a pre-season friendly at Carlisle United 5-0 in July.

The season proper got going, as usual, with the sectional stage of the League Cup and memories of that remarkable Scottish Cup tie described in the previous chapter came flooding back as Hearts began with a 3-2 win over Dundee United at Tannadice, the visitors coming from two goals down to triumph. However, Harvey's men then failed to score against St Mirren (twice) and Morton and inevitably exited the competition at the group stage. Clearly, Hearts had fallen out of love with the League Cup.

Hearts began the league campaign with a 1-0 loss to Morton at Tynecastle – the winner coming from youngster Joe Harper, who would later make a name for himself at Aberdeen, Everton and Hibs. It didn't take a brilliant mind to suggest where Hearts' problems lay – scoring goals. For those Hearts fans brought up on a diet of the "Terrible Trio" a decade and more before, this was particularly hard to take.

However, Hearts then scored three against St Johnstone and defeated old adversaries Kilmarnock 4-1 at Tynecastle, where Norwegian Roald Jensen and Donald Ford scored twice each. Any hopes the fans may have had that the answer had been found to the lack of firepower were immediately dashed, however, when Hearts failed to score in their next three games.

Come November 1969, there was an odd look to the top of the First Division. Celtic had, uncharacteristically, already lost two games in the league and Dundee United and Dunfermline Athletic sat at the top of the table. Even odder was the sight of Hibernian in third place.

With the champions already playing catch-up, few gave a shot-shy Hearts team much of a chance when they headed to Celtic Park on 8th November 1969. Johnny Harvey looked again to the forward partnership of Moller and Ford while his opposite number brought in a couple of the so-called "quality street" kids from Celtic's youth system – 20-year-old Lou Macari and 18-year-old Kenny Dalglish.

Unusually, given Hearts' record in the east end of Glasgow, it was to be an afternoon when everything went right for the Gorgie boys. Celtic's stuttering start to the season seemed to reflect their performance and they seemed unsure right from kick-off. Perhaps Jock Stein's men had their minds on their European Cup tie with Benfica four days later. However, this would be something of an injustice to a Hearts team who outplayed and – remarkably given Celtic's status at the time – outclassed the home team.

The game began with Celtic dominating possession but the champions didn't seem to know what to do with the ball when they had it. Hearts looked strong in defence, with centre-half Alan Anderson a dominant figure. His defensive partner was Alan MacDonald, one of the last players to be signed by Tommy Walker. MacDonald was a solid defender and he and Anderson gave Celtic's diminutive winger Jimmy Johnstone no freedom to display his undoubted skills.

However, don't think this was a backs-to-the-wall performance from Johnny Harvey's team – far from it. Hearts had their own answer to "Jinky" Johnstone – Danish winger Rene Moller. The man signed from Danish side FC Randers danced and dribbled his way through the Celtic defence almost at will. The home side were unaccustomed to visiting teams attacking in such a style and they clearly had no answer to Moller.

Midway through the first half, Moller's impressive footwork set up Donald Ford who fired in a shot past keeper Fallon to give Hearts the lead. Or so we thought. Referee Padden, for reasons known only to him, chalked the goal off and Hearts fans in the 32,600 crowd could only think "here we go again". However, it was only a temporary reprieve for the champions. Hearts were now dominating the game – all they needed was a goal.

Just after the half-hour mark, Hearts' other Scandinavian import, Roald Jensen, took delivery of a pass from Ford. The Norwegian raced forward but was closely shepherded by Celtic full-back Gemmell away from goal. From about a yard in from the touchline, Jensen managed to defy the odds and fire in a ferocious shot that swung beyond Fallon and into the net to give Hearts a lead they fully deserved. It was a goal of breathtaking magnificence. *The Glasgow Herald*'s William Hunter wrote that Jensen's attempt at goal came "along a line which does not exist in any formal geometry". It was a goal that stunned those inside Celtic Park – and Hearts were not finished yet.

Three minutes before half-time, Ford found himself with time and space to shoot at Fallon. Twice, the Celtic keeper denied the Hearts man with brilliant saves but the third time the ball rebounded to him, Ford made no mistake and his effort lashed into the net to double Hearts' advantage. Hearts went in at the interval full value for their two-goal lead. Seldom had Celtic been so outplayed in any game, let alone on their own patch. Some boos emanated from the home support, not used to seeing their usually all-conquering team – champions of Europe just two years earlier and who would reach the European Cup final again this season – taken apart in such a fashion.

In the second half, Celtic reacted to what must have been a few choice words from Jock Stein and youngster Dalglish forced a fine save from Jim Cruickshank. However, it was Hearts who tightened their grip on the game. Not even moving Jimmy Johnstone to the other wing changed anything – it just meant Hearts' impressive full-back Peter Oliver took care of him, rather than Eddie Thomson who had done such a sterling job in the first half.

Although it was mostly Celtic in the second period, it was Hearts who came closest to scoring. Moller, who had tormented the Celtic defence all afternoon, contrived to miss an open goal from just five yards out. At the death, Ford was denied by a brilliant save from Fallon. Had Hearts taken all their chances they could well have scored five goals on an astonishing afternoon. The gamed ended Celtic 0 Hearts 2.

It had been a brilliant performance by Hearts, one most unexpected but nonetheless welcome. Full-backs Dave Clunie and Peter Oliver let nothing past them; the aforementioned Anderson and MacDonald were immense and covered every blade of grass at Celtic Park. It had been Hearts' best performance for some time and the fans wanted to believe their team could mount a serious challenge for the league. After their famous victory at Celtic Park, Hearts remained in eighth place in the league – although just four points behind some other team from Scotland's capital city whose name temporarily escapes me, but who were now top of the league.

Hearts then drew with Aberdeen and lost at Dundee. However, when Rangers came to Tynecastle at the beginning of December, hopes rose again when Jim Brown gave Hearts the lead in the opening minute. Sadly, the Maroons lost 2-1 and dropped to tenth place in the league.

Hearts began the new decade that was the 1970s with an unbeaten run of ten league games that had brought them to fourth in the table. This run was ended when Hearts lost to Partick Thistle at Firhill thanks to a winning goal from a youngster who would come to Hearts' aid 13 years later – striker Jimmy Bone. At the end of March, Hearts tried to repeat their Celtic Park success at the other side of Glasgow but were three goals down to Rangers with half an hour remaining. However, two goals in the last ten minutes from Ernie Winchester and Jim Irvine had the Rangers nerves jangling and the home side were relieved to hear the final whistle.

Hearts ended the season in fourth place in the First Division, their best placing since that infamous last-day finish five years earlier when they lost the title to Kilmarnock. At least optimism was calling in on Gorgie Road – if only Hearts could achieve a level of consistency.

Given their impressive showings against both halves of the Old Firm, there were those tipping Hearts as dark horses for the Scottish Cup, although this particular horse almost fell spectacularly at the first fence when it took a last-minute goal from George Fleming to salvage a draw at Second Division side Montrose and a goal three minutes from time from the same player in the replay to take Hearts through to the next round – where they lost 2-0 at Kilmarnock.

The 1970s would prove to be a decade to forget for Hearts supporters. A record defeat in the Edinburgh derby, two relegations and the club standing on the edge of a financial precipice would ensue. Something no one envisaged in November 1969 when Rene Moller tore league champions and soon to be European Cup finalists Celtic apart!

16 v Aberdeen 3-2

Scottish League Division One
27th November 1971. Pittodrie

Hearts:	Aberdeen:
Cruickshank	Clark
Sneddon	G Murray
Kay	Hermiston
Brown	S Murray
Anderson	McMillan
Thomson	M Buchan
Townsend	Forrest
Renton	Robb
Ford	Harper
Winchester	Willoughby
T Murray	Graham

Referee: T Marshall (Glasgow)

"SEE THIS nonsense?" asked the old fella standing next to me on the crumbling Tynecastle terracing one day in April 1971. "It's just a gimmick. Fitba's fitba. There's nae place fur all this commercial rubbish."

Rubbish was an oft-used word that spring evening as Wolverhampton Wanderers put Hearts to the sword in the newly-created Texaco Cup by winning the first leg of the final 3-1. It was the changing face of football and while the muttering Jambo chewed on his pipe and reflected on Willie Bauld doing a shift down a Midlothian coal mine hours before turning out for Hearts 20 years earlier, the next generation of Hearts fans in the 1970s were being weaned on a diet of Texaco Cup games, one of the first football tournaments in Britain to be sponsored. Commercialism had indeed arrived, but while the Texaco Cup was an early form of a British Cup, it was a poor consolation for those clubs not good enough to compete in European competition.

Back in the decade of long hair, tank-tops and Gorgie Boys with laced up boots and corduroys, we cast envious glances across Edinburgh where Hibernian were pitting their wits against the likes of Juventus and Liverpool in the Uefa Cup. Hearts were sliding down the slippery slope at an alarming rate as the 1970s began, so we made the most out of our achievement of reaching the final of the Texaco Cup in 1971. Defeat by Wolverhampton Wanderers was hard to take, particularly as Hearts typically won the second leg 1-0 down in the West Midlands. At this juncture, thoughts of Hearts actually playing, far less competing, in Europe were a million miles away.

In comparison to the Tynecastle experience we have today, the Tynecastle experience of 1971 could have been from a different planet. Four decades ago, there were just two divisions in Scottish football. The patently obvious First and Second Divisions – despite the Texaco Cup, sponsorship was still some distance from the hallowed corridors of the Scottish League.

In 1971, Hearts were on a downward spiral, although no one at the time realised what lay at the bottom. Eleven years had passed since Hearts had last won the Scottish League championship – an honour that hasn't been bestowed on Hearts since, although they've come mighty close on a couple of occasions.

By 1971, Hearts were no longer challengers for any domestic honours. That well-versed football cliche, mid-table mediocrity, may well have been penned for Hearts, as each season saw the boys in maroon ensconced in the middle of the league. This invariably meant when Hearts were knocked out of the Scottish Cup, their season was over and meaningless end of the season league games against the likes of Arbroath and East Fife saw sparse crowds at Tynecastle, the wide-open spaces on the crumbling terraces telling their own story.

I was nine years old in 1971 and had already endured three years of being a Hearts fan. When my parents divorced, I was taken from my home in Cumbernauld to live in Aberdeen, 130 miles away from Gorgie Road, but the way Hearts were playing at the time this wasn't necessarily a bad thing. My visits to Tynecastle were few and far between at this time; my father had wanted me to be a Falkirk fan but his intention backfired somewhat on an October day in 1968 when he took me to my first game – Falkirk against Hearts at Brockville. I was bitten by the Jambo bug.

Consequently, my father never really supported the idea of me supporting Hearts – but once bitten etc. However, it did mean that when Hearts visited Aberdeen this would be the highlight of my season. My father would travel up from his home in Cumbernauld and take me to Pittodrie. Being an Aberdonian, he was keen to show his support for his hometown team – as I was for the boys in maroon.

Hearts had made a decent start to the 1971/72 league season – something that could not be said for the majority of the decade. Four weeks before Christmas, they headed to Pittodrie in third place in the league having lost just twice in 12 games. Those in maroon heading north with unaccustomed optimism knew that while those statistics were impressive, they weren't as impressive as those of Hearts' opponents that afternoon. For Aberdeen were top of the league, unbeaten all season having not lost at Pittodrie for 18 months.

The Dons, managed by Jimmy Bonthrone, who had taken over when Eddie Turnbull returned to his first love Hibernian in the summer, had set Scottish football alight. With a forward line containing Joe Harper, Davie Robb and youngster Arthur Graham, the men from the Granite City had scored an impressive 36 goals in just 12 games.

More than 20,000 fans headed for Pittodrie on a dank November afternoon. Forty years ago, there was still an open terrace at Pittodrie – as there was at most Scottish football grounds. At the back of the terracing adjacent to the pitch was a giant gas tank that loomed over the ground. At the top of the terrace stood the half-time scoreboard with a yellow clock. Hearts fans, as ever, headed north confident, despite the home team's record.

It wasn't a complete surprise that Aberdeen dominated the first half. Harper and Forrest came close to opening the scoring and Hearts were indebted to goalkeeper Jim Cruickshank, who was in fine form, to keep the highest scoring team in Scotland at bay. Hearts, however, weren't sitting back and Derek Renton fired in an effort which smacked off the crossbar. It appeared Aberdeen's frustration at failing to break through the Hearts defence was boiling over. Robb was booked just before half-time for a crude foul on Jim Townsend. Half-time arrived with a somewhat surprising goalless scoreline – but with hackles raised.

The second half began in the same manner as the first – with Aberdeen in the ascendancy. It seemed just a matter of time before the opening goal and it duly came ten minutes into the second half – but not at the end the home crowd expected. Great work by Hearts' Tommy Murray took him beyond his Aberdeen namesake George before he passed to Donald Ford who fired in a great goal from an acute angle. Tommy Murray was capable of such sublime skill – he once sat on the ball at Ibrox before crossing to make a Hearts goal.

The home side were stunned and the crowd were angered minutes later when their side was awarded a penalty – only for the referee to change his mind and award an indirect free kick instead, which came to nothing. With 20 minutes left, Aberdeen replaced Graham with veteran Miller – and the impact was immediate. With the Hearts defence keeping their collective eyes on the substitute, Willoughby steered the ball beyond a trailing Hearts defence to allow Harper to equalise.

It was anyone's game now and Ford set off on a great run with a chance to put Hearts back in front but home keeper Clark saved well. With 15 minutes left, an already controversial game erupted once more when Aberdeen took the lead. There was more than a suspicion of offside when Robb latched on to a long through ball and danced away from the Hearts defence. Robb finished with aplomb but the Hearts players were furious, to the extent Jim Townsend was sent off as he doth protest too much. With Townsend, seemed to go Hearts' hopes of getting anything from the game. We reckoned, however, without Donald Ford.

There were just four minutes to go when Ford eluded his marker in the Aberdeen defence to head past a startled Clark and level the score. Those Hearts fans who remained in the ground roared their delight – which would turn to ecstasy in injury time.

Aberdeen's defenders looked shell-shocked, which may well have contributed to Ford having the freedom of Union Street to place another header beyond Clark to snatch a sensational winner for Hearts. Aberdeen 2 Heart of Midlothian 3 was the final score. Hearts fans danced on the terracing. The home support shuffled out, not quite believing what they had seen. Aberdeen's unbeaten run and proud home record had been smashed to pieces. Ironically, the last team to beat Aberdeen at Pittodrie was Hearts in April 1970.

Hearts fans returned south convinced their team would go on to challenge for their first league championship for 12 years. Rangers were struggling that season and many thought the race for the league flag was a two-horse affair between Aberdeen and Jock Stein's Celtic. Moreover, Hearts had now achieved something no one else had done that season – beaten Aberdeen.

The following Saturday, Hearts were involved in another five-goal thriller when they defeated Dundee United 3-2 at Tynecastle. However, Hearts fans know what happens when optimism gets the better of them – the following week, Hearts travelled to Brockville to face a Falkirk team containing Alex Ferguson and Andy Roxburgh – and were beaten 2-0, former Hearts stalwart George Miller rubbing salt into the wounds by scoring one of the goals.

Hearts took that defeat badly – they didn't win any of their next seven games. At the end of January, any flicker of title aspirations were well and truly snuffed out when the team capitulated to a 6-0 drubbing at Ibrox – this coming a week after a 5-2 defeat at Tynecastle by Dundee. Hearts' league season was over and although they finished the season in sixth place they were 21 points behind champions Celtic, in the days when there were only two points awarded for a win. Incidentally, Aberdeen finished runners-up, ten points behind the champions.

Hearts fans sought salvation in the Scottish Cup and the early signs were promising when a very good St Johnstone team – at the time managed by Willie Ormond, who would go on to manage Scotland and Hearts – were beaten 2-0 at Tynecastle. Clydebank were thrashed 4-0 in Gorgie in the next round before Hearts faced Celtic at Celtic Park in the quarter-final.

Derek Renton scored a last-minute goal that gave Hearts a 1-1 draw and therefore secured a replay at Tynecastle. The game, on 27th March 1972, attracted an attendance of just over 40,000 – the last time a crowd of such size would be in Gorgie. A Lou Macari goal was enough to take Celtic through and more crushing disappointment ensued for the maroon legions.

It was a disappointing end to a season that, at one stage, promised so much. The triumph at Pittodrie in November 1971 was one of the highlights of the season; particularly in the style it was achieved. Ten-man Hearts simply refused to accept defeat and used their perceived injustice at the dismissal of Jim Townsend to spur them on to a memorable victory.

I left Pittodrie that day with my father with mixed emotions. I was thrilled my team had won and in such a way that caused considerable angst to the home support. Living in Aberdeen, I knew what awaited me at school on Monday morning had Donald Ford not stepped in with glorious and impeccable timing. However, I knew my father would drop me off at home before driving back to his home in Cumbernauld. I felt a little cheated at not being able to share the joy of victory with anyone.

It was, however, a great day to be a Jambo living in the Granite City.

v Celtic 4-1
Scottish League Division One
29th April 1972. Tynecastle

Hearts:	Celtic:
Garland	Williams
Sneddon	Craig
Clunie	Brogan
Thomson	Murdoch
Anderson	McNeill
Wood	Connelly
Murray	Hood
Brown	Hay
Ford	Deans
Renton	Macari
Lynch	Dalglish

Referee: J Paterson (Bothwell)

I MENTIONED in the last chapter that Hearts finished the 1971/72 season in sixth place in the league table – albeit they were 21 points behind champions Celtic. Having got to the final of the Texaco Cup in 1971, the hopes of the Tynecastle faithful of a dawn of a new era turned out to be false hopes once more.

By the time Celtic visited Tynecastle on league business at the end of April – in the days of an 18-team top league, clubs played each other just twice in a season – they had already wrapped up their seventh successive league championship. Jock Stein's men were ten points clear of their nearest challengers who, this season, were not Rangers but Aberdeen.

Rangers had other thoughts on their mind such as the final of the European Cup Winners' Cup against Moscow Dynamo in Barcelona's Nou Camp and by the time their league campaign had finished, they even had to share third place in the league with a team from Edinburgh who were not called Heart of Midlothian.

For the final league game of 1971/72, Hearts manager Bobby Seith gave some players on the fringes of the first team a chance against the league champions. Twenty-year-old striker Derek Renton had made an impact earlier in the season and Andy Lynch and the more experienced Donald Ford joined him in attack. Yes, younger readers, Hearts played with three strikers in the 1970s. Seith was even so bold as to name the one substitute permitted in the early 1970s as Eric Carruthers – another centre-forward who was still in his teenage years.

Celtic may have celebrated winning yet another league championship but there were a couple of clouds hanging over their end of season trip to Tynecastle. Firstly, ten days earlier they had experienced heartache against their old foes Inter Milan in the semi-final of the European Cup. Five years after Jock Stein's side had memorably defeated the Italians to become the first British club to win Europe's premier competition, Celtic were this time on the receiving end. After a goalless draw in the first leg in Italy, the Hoops strongly fancied their chances of finishing off the job at Celtic Park and therefore making it to a third European Cup final in five years. However, the Italians, as was customary, defended resolutely in Glasgow's east end and even after extra time, the tie remained goalless.

Uefa had recently introduced a penalty shoot-out to decide such deadlocked ties, so Celtic and Inter required the taking of penalties to determine the winner. Inter scored their regulation five kicks, Celtic four, with the home side's Dixie Deans stepping forward to take Celtic's fifth. Much to the bold Dixie's consternation and the horror of 75,000 Celtic fans, the former Motherwell striker blazed his penalty over the crossbar meaning Celtic were out of the European Cup.

Secondly, there was unhappiness among the Celtic support about their trip to Tynecastle. In the previous chapter, I wrote about Celtic defeating Hearts in Gorgie in a midweek Scottish Cup quarter-final replay. It was the occasion of the last 40,000 crowd at Tynecastle and there were those among the Celtic support who felt the congestion at the ground was unacceptable. Therefore, with the league title already sewn up and the league fixture at Tynecastle meaningless, many Celtic fans boycotted the trip to the capital city with the result that barely 10,000 fans headed to Gorgie for the game.

If the Celtic fans' boycott had caused controversy off the field, Hearts players showed their class on it – even before the game kicked off. In recognition of Celtic's latest league championship success, the Hearts players lined up on the Tynecastle pitch and applauded their Celtic counterparts on to the field of play. A Corinthian spirit sadly all too lacking today.

It was the visitors who were the first to threaten and striker Hood fired in an early effort that Hearts goalkeeper Kenny Garland did well to stop at full stretch. Hay then had another chance for the champions and his effort was again well saved by Garland who, if the opening stage of the game was anything to go by, was going to have a busy afternoon.

However, Hearts weren't letting the champions have things all their own way and clever play from Renton set Ford free but the striker's cross into the Celtic penalty box was uncontested and easily gathered by Celtic keeper Williams. It had been a bright start by both teams and in the tenth minute Celtic took the lead in controversial fashion. Kenny Dalglish's run took him into the Hearts penalty box where Jim Brown and Ian Sneddon challenged him. There seemed minimal contact but the Celtic player fell to the ground. A penalty said referee Mr Paterson, which Murdoch duly converted to give Celtic the lead. The decision didn't go down well among the home support.

Hearts sensed an injustice and fought back into the game. Shortly after, Ford had a fine chance to equalise but his effort from the edge of the penalty box flew over the bar. However, Hearts did equalise in the 22nd minute with a gem of a goal. A superb pass from Andy Lynch found Tommy Murray who effortlessly sauntered past Celtic skipper Billy McNeill.

As Hoops keeper Williams raced out to meet the onrushing Murray, the Hearts man deftly lobbed the ball over him and into the net to level the score at 1-1. Cue a disturbance in the enclosure in the main stand and police had to move quickly to quell the trouble, although it was later reported several arrests were made. The bad feeling between the home support and those Celtic fans that did go to Tynecastle was clearly boiling over.

The game itself became tousy. Hearts' Alan Anderson had to receive treatment for an eye injury, while Celtic's Brogan was lucky not to be cautioned for a bad challenge on Derek Renton. Six minutes before half-time, Hearts took the lead. Tommy Murray delivered a fine corner which was met superbly by Ford who powered a header past Williams. The Hearts fans were jubilant and they were almost celebrating again just two minutes later.

I say almost – that's because when McNeill tripped Donald Ford in the penalty box, referee Paterson had no hesitation in awarding the second penalty of the afternoon – this time to Hearts. However, Murray, in trying to place his spot kick, only succeeded in pushing the ball past the post. Seconds later, Anderson headed wide when he really should have scored and when half-time arrived, it was hard to believe the home side were only leading 2-1.

The second half began in the same manner the first half had ended – with Hearts in the ascendancy. Lynch was causing the Celtic rearguard more than a few problems and the second half was minutes old when he ran at the trailing Celtic defenders before passing to Ford. The Hearts striker delivered another fine ball into the Celtic area that clipped the crossbar and the Maroons were left to curse their luck again.

After Lynch himself had a chance shortly afterwards, Hearts scored the third goal their play richly deserved in the 53rd minute. Ford and Lynch exchanged passes before Lynch delivered a brilliant cross to Derek Renton who blasted the ball into the roof of the net. This was developing into a fine Hearts performance against the reigning league champions with Lynch, Ford and Renton threatening to cause havoc.

Despite Hearts' dominance, the Maroons scored only once more that afternoon – although this seems a bizarre thing to say considering who the opposition were. Jim Brown added a fourth goal with 13 minutes left when he fired the ball past Williams after yet more good work from Lynch. This was the cue for those Celtic fans that made the effort to take their leave and when referee Paterson blew his whistle for the final time that afternoon, the Hearts players left the field to tumultuous applause. A season that had promised much but delivered little had at least ended with a comprehensive gubbing of Jock Stein's league champions.

Celtic accepted defeat graciously – well, the club did, if not their supporters – and manager Stein was sufficiently impressed by the performance of Hearts' Lynch to offer the Tynecastle board of directors the princely sum of £30,000 to take him to Celtic Park ten months later. You may well have already guessed that Hearts accepted the offer.

Much was expected of young centre-forward Derek Renton after his goal against Celtic but, like so many other young players, the 20-year-old didn't fulfil the promise shown that afternoon. The following season he made only ten league appearances for Hearts and in one of those, he was sent off against St Johnstone. In the summer of 1973, he was released by manager Bobby Seith and signed for Berwick Rangers.

In truth, the following season, 1972/73, was one to forget not only for Renton but also for anyone associated with Heart of Midlothian. They began the season in a League Cup section containing Dumbarton, Airdrieonians and Berwick Rangers

– and failed to qualify from the group stages for the ninth year in succession. In the league campaign, Hearts were infuriatingly inconsistent. Losses to East Fife, St Johnstone and Dundee were offset by victories over Rangers at Ibrox and a fine Aberdeen team at Tynecastle. I won't dwell too much on Hearts' nadir in the league campaign – the Edinburgh derby of New Year's Day 1973 when Hibs scored seven fortuitous goals without reply at Tynecastle.

The devastating effect of this result was that Hearts won just two of their remaining 15 league games and ended the season in tenth place in Division One, behind the likes of Ayr United and East Fife.

As well as suffering in the League Cup, Hearts had Airdrieonians to thank for elimination from the Scottish Cup at the first hurdle. After a goalless draw at Tynecastle, Hearts lost the replay 3-1 at Broomfield – the scorer of the home side's first goal was a certain Drew Busby, who would later attain cult status wearing the maroon shirt. Hearts' other cup exploits came in the Texaco Cup and there was brief respite in a dismal season when they defeated English side Crystal Palace both at Tynecastle and at Selhurst Park by a 1-0 scoreline. However, it was Scottish opposition – Motherwell – who put paid to Hearts' hopes of progression when, after another goalless game in the first leg in Gorgie, they defeated the Maroons 4-2 at Fir Park.

The promise of Hearts' 4-1 thumping of Celtic in April 1972 never materialised and there was little doubt among the disillusioned Hearts support that changes had to be made. Credit to the Hearts board of directors though who, in the summer of 1973, also recognised the need for change. Manager Bobby Seith was given the go-ahead to bring players such as Drew Busby, Kenny Aird, Bobby Prentice, Willie Gibson and Ralph Callachan to Tynecastle as Hearts looked for an infusion of new blood.

The 1973/74 season would conclude with Hearts celebrating their centenary and what better way to celebrate than delivering the first piece of silverware to Edinburgh's west end since the League Cup in 1962?

That was the theory in any case. Reality, as supporters of this great club know only too well, can be something else entirely...

v Hibernian 4-1
Scottish League Division One
8th September 1973. Tynecastle

Hearts:	Hibernian:
Garland	McKenzie
Sneddon	Bremner
Clunie	Schaedler
Cant	Stanton
Anderson	Black
Jefferies	Blackley
Aird	Edwards
Ford	Smith
Busby	Gordon
Stevenson	Cropley
Prentice	Duncan

Referee: JRP Gordon (Newport-on-Tay)

THE 1973/74 season promised to be a big one for Hearts. The club's centenary year was 1974 and Scottish football celebrated 100 years of a football institution. Special presentations were made from clubs from all over the country, as well as the SFA and Scottish League. Hearts also held a centenary dinner at Tynecastle in February, to which many ex-players were invited and some famous names from the great sides of the 1950s attended an emotional reunion.

The planning of celebrations for the centenary year seemed to instil a new sense of purpose at Tynecastle, as if the club's 100th birthday would mark the re-launch of Hearts as a major force in Scottish football. As the 1973/74 season approached, Hearts, at last, made some major moves into the transfer market as the importance of the season ahead was recognised. Following the arrival of Kenny Aird from St Johnstone and John Stevenson from Coventry, manager Bobby Seith signed Drew Busby from Airdrieonians for £35,000. Another new arrival at Tynecastle was winger Bobby Prentice from Celtic and it was a revamped Hearts side that began the 1973/74 season hoping to secure a long-awaited trophy.

The first league game saw Hearts begin with a 3-2 win at Cappielow over Morton. If the Maroons were hoping to create a bit of history in their centenary season they achieved this feat in that very first fixture. Donald Ford became the only player in Tynecastle history to hit a hat-trick of penalties in one game and the fans travelling back from Greenock were hoping this was an omen in Hearts' quest for glory. Next up was the return of Hibs to Tynecastle and their supporters headed for Edinburgh's west end on 8th September 1973 eager to taunt their adversaries in maroon about the events of eight months earlier.

An indication of the sweeping changes made at Tynecastle was illustrated by the fact that only four of the Hearts team that began the New Year mauling started the rematch in September. Ian Sneddon and Jimmy Cant, as well as newcomers Busby, Stevenson and Prentice, were all sampling their first taste of an Edinburgh derby. Hibs had ex-Airdrie goalkeeper Roddy McKenzie making his capital derby debut, but it was to prove an unhappy occasion for Drew Busby's former team-mate.

A crowd of almost 30,000 created a frantic atmosphere and the game kicked off with Hearts looking the more confident side. Busby and Ford were already looking to have forged a meaningful partnership and there was plenty of width with both Aird and Prentice foraging down the flanks. Hibs seemed to be struggling to contain this new-look Hearts side and keeper McKenzie looked less than comfortable in his new environment.

It was from a mistake from the Hibs number one that Hearts opened their account after 20 minutes. Youngster Jim Jefferies floated a cross into the Hibs penalty box, which didn't appear to pose any threat. McKenzie, however, decided to come out and collect but – to the horror of his fellow defenders – completely misjudged the flight of the ball. In the ensuing confusion in the penalty box, Hibs full-back Schaedler headed into his own net after a desperate attempt to clear the danger and instead made it 1-0 to Hearts, though the cautious Jambos told themselves that at least there would be no repeat of the 7-0 massacre of Ne'er Day.

The Maroons had looked confident enough from the start but this goal merely gave a surge to the adrenaline. Hibs were forced to back-pedal as Ford and Busby came close, with Jefferies proving to be an unlikely threat with his crosses. If it was manager Seith's plan to fool Hibs with his side's formation, then it certainly worked and Eddie Turnbull's men looked strangely out of sorts.

The only thing missing from a polished first-half performance from Hearts was further goals, but half-time arrived with the Maroons well on top – a fact underlined when Hibs boss Turnbull hauled off former Hearts star Alan Gordon and Alex Edwards and replaced them with Tony Higgins and Ian Munro for the start of the second half.

Further goals did arrive after the interval – three of which occurred within as many minutes. In the 54th minute, Kenny Aird set off down the right wing with the Hibs defence chasing. At the edge of the penalty box, the former St Johnstone man fired in a shot that slipped under the body of keeper McKenzie and into the net for 2-0 and the Hearts support went wild. Aird had promised much since his arrival at Tynecastle and scoring against the Hibees saw him crowned a hero by an ecstatic home support.

The celebrations were still in full swing when, seconds later, Hibs moved to the other end of the park and pulled a goal back. The ball was fired in to the Hearts goalmouth where keeper Kenny Garland and youngster Jimmy Cant decided to leave it for each other, allowing Cropley to flick the ball into net to make the score 2-1. Now it was the turn of the Hibs fans to celebrate – but not for long.

Incredibly, Hearts restarted and headed straight for McKenzie in the Hibs goal. This time it was the turn of youngster John Stevenson to run at the Hibs defence and his pace took him past a startled Hibs back four. Keeper McKenzie brought the ex-Coventry player to a halt, but merely succeeded in teeing up Ford. The striker thrashed the ball into the net to make it 3-1 and send the Hearts support delirious once more.

Hearts' Greatest Games

It had been 180 seconds of sheer bedlam and Hearts, with their two-goal advantage restored, sensed revenge for the New Year nightmare. Ford and Busby proceeded to wreak havoc and twice Hearts hit the crossbar as Hibs tried manfully to stem the maroon tidal wave. McKenzie redeemed himself for his earlier mistakes by producing some fine saves as Hearts fans demanded their side go for the kill.

With just ten minutes to go, Hearts did get the fourth goal their play so richly deserved. From 30 yards out, the man with one of the most fearsome shots in Scottish football – Drew Busby – let fly with a screamer. McKenzie's day of misery was complete when he allowed the ball to squirm under his body and into the net. 4-1 for Hearts and Busby had opened his league account at Tynecastle in the best possible manner.

Those Hibs fans who had taunted their rival supporters on their last visit to Gorgie were now heading for the exits praying that the memory of that occasion wouldn't be tarnished by a thumping win for Hearts. The scoring ended at 4-1 and the maroon half of Tynecastle loudly acclaimed their side at the final whistle.

A side which had barely managed an average of a goal a game the season before had opened the centenary season with seven in two games and had avenged the New Year debacle. Hearts supporters spilled out on to the streets of Gorgie after the game in high spirits. They had criticised the manager and board of directors for not spending enough money on bringing quality players to Tynecastle. Now, at last, money had been spent – and on this early evidence, spent wisely.

Aird and Stevenson looked talented players who could stretch any defence, while the fans at last had a new hero to acclaim up front. Not since the days of Willie Wallace had Hearts had anyone to take the pressure off Ford. However, Busby looked to be the answer to a long-standing problem and Jambos everywhere licked their lips at the prospect of Hearts challenging for the league title.

The Maroons were buoyed by this impressive start and embarked on an unbeaten run that lasted until the end of October – and took them to the top of the league. Although Bobby Seith's men dropped a point in each of their next two league games – Motherwell and Dundee both grabbed 2-2 draws – Hearts really made the country sit up and take notice on 29th September 1973 when they travelled to Ibrox and inflicted on Rangers their heaviest home defeat for ten years. A result of 3-0 didn't flatter the Maroons in the slightest and jubilant Jambos weren't slow in reminding everyone that the last time Rangers lost by three goals in Govan was to Tommy Walker's Hearts side in November 1963.

Hearts were equally impressive in defeating Dunfermline 3-0 at Tynecastle a week later and then followed that with a stylish 2-0 win at Muirton over St Johnstone. With Hearts now sitting proudly at the top of the league, the interest in the clash with Celtic at Tynecastle on 27th October was phenomenal. A crowd of over 35,000 packed into the Gorgie ground to see if this revitalised Hearts side could topple the long-time champions.

However, Celtic had seen off previous challenges from the likes of Rangers and Aberdeen and Jock Stein's men won 3-1 to remove the Maroons from their lofty position. Shortly afterwards, Hearts lost 5-0 to Burnley in a Texaco Cup-tie – having knocked out Everton in the previous round – and the noise of the players' confidence crashing to earth was deafening. After scraping a 3-2 win at Arbroath and a 1-1 draw with Dundee United, Hearts then lost 3-1 at Aberdeen and hopes of a centenary championship were beginning to fade.

Things turned sour in December, when the Maroons could only draw with East Fife and lost at home to Ayr United and Morton. When Hibs exacted revenge by winning the New Year derby 3-1 at Easter Road, the party was over and Hearts slid down the table once more. Rangers also took revenge by winning 4-2 at Tynecastle in January and the championship dream was over.

Hearts ended the season in joint sixth place, 15 points behind the champions Celtic, with the fans dreaming yet again of what might have been. Many cited the humiliating defeat by Burnley as a turning point but, if it was, then the team's inability to pick themselves up from the floor should have sent alarm bells ringing around Tynecastle.

With Hearts letting the championship slip from their grasp, supporters turned to the Scottish Cup for the last chance of centenary glory. After Clyde were beaten 3-1 at Tynecastle in round three, things looked bleak for Bobby Seith's side when Partick Thistle left Gorgie with a replay after a 1-1 draw. However, there were signs of the early season sparkle returning to Hearts' play when they romped home in the replay at Firhill by 4-1 and faced Ayr United in the quarter-final.

It was a repeat performance. Hearts struggled to a 1-1 draw at Tynecastle and an Ayr side that had scored 12 goals in their previous two cup ties were installed as favourites with the bookies for the Somerset Park replay. Nevertheless, Hearts again produced a tremendous display and won 2-1 to reach their first semi-final for six years. Moreover, they got the semi-final draw they wanted when they avoided Celtic and were paired with Dundee United and it seemed that Hearts' centenary season might end with a little bit of glory after all, with a cup final appearance. However, after a 1-1 draw at Hampden, the teams returned to Mount Florida three days later where United won the replay 4-2 in what was another night of huge disappointment for all Hearts supporters.

There was little joy, either, for the Maroons in the League Cup. Dundee, St Johnstone and Partick Thistle were awkward rather than dangerous opponents but the Maroons managed just two wins to finish third in the section and were eliminated at the sectional stage for the 11th year running.

Thus, yet another season which promised so much for Hearts ended in disappointment. Fans had dreamt – for a few short weeks at least – of championship glory and had Bobby Seith produced a title-winning side on the occasion of the club's 100th birthday he would have been given the freedom of Edinburgh. Sadly, it wasn't to be – but the supporters at least had the memory of the day their side exorcised the ghost of Ne'er Day, 1973.

v Lokomotive L 5-1

European Cup Winners' Cup First Round Second Leg

29th September 1976. Tynecastle

Hearts:	Lokomotive Leipzig:
Cruickshank	Friese
Brown	Sekora
Kay	Hammer
Callachan	Groebner
Gallacher	Fritsche
Clunie	Roth
Aird	Moldt
Busby	Frenzel
Gibson	Lisiewicz
Park	Loewe
Prentice	Kuehn

Referee: J Dubach (Switzerland)

HEARTS MAY have been struggling in the mid-1970s but they did reach the Scottish Cup final in 1976 – only to lose 3-1 to Rangers. However, reaching the final in itself was a back-door entry to European competition in the form of the now-defunct European Cup Winners' Cup for the 1976/77 season. Hearts were back in the big time – briefly at least.

In 1969, Hibs played two German clubs, Lokomotive Leipzig and SV Hamburg, in the Uefa Cup. By a remarkable coincidence, those two clubs would return to Scotland's capital city seven years later to face Edinburgh's big team. In 1976, it was Hearts' turn to face Leipzig and things looked ominous after a 2-0 first-leg defeat in the first round in East Germany. Manager John Hagart set out a defensive formation and the Maroons played reasonably well but were beaten, meaning it would be a huge task to overturn the deficit in the return at Tynecastle. However, on a balmy September evening in Gorgie, Hearts produced a performance that is still talked about in pubs and clubs by those of a maroon persuasion today.

More than 18,000 Hearts fans packed Tynecastle hoping for the early goal that would catapult Hagart's men back into the tie. With Hearts needing two goals, Hagart gambled by starting with Kenny Aird, who had been struggling with a heel injury, but in Drew Busby and Willie Gibson there was an obvious goalscoring threat.

With a raucous atmosphere that sent shivers down the back of the neck, Hearts threw players into attack from the off. Just 30 seconds had gone when Jim Brown and Willie Gibson worked the ball across the Leipzig goalmouth where Busby lurked. Busby took the ball on the turn and smacked a typically ferocious effort against the post as Hearts posted their early intentions.

Gibson also went close and it was clear the East Germans didn't appreciate Hearts' bustling up-and-at-'em style. Leipzig were in retreat and after just 13 minutes, the mercurial Rab Prentice lofted the ball towards the unlikely figure of Roy Kay. The full-back moved into the penalty box and beat Leipzig keeper Friese with a low right-foot shot to give Hearts a crucial early lead.

Inspired by a frenzied crowd, Hearts swarmed forward and Prentice, Gibson and Aird fired in shots that had the German defence in a panic.

Leipzig didn't know what hit them but were always dangerous on the counter attack. Jim Brown was forced to clear a Groebner effort off the line before Tynecastle erupted as Hearts scored a second goal just before the half hour. Aird made light of his injury and drove forward. His effort on goal looked menacing enough but when team-mate Gibson stuck out a foot to divert the ball past Friese to put Hearts two goals ahead on the night, the Hearts fans went crazy. They could scarcely believe that their team, who hadn't won a league game thus far, were taking one of East Germany's finest teams apart.

However, as so often happens in European ties, it took just one slip of concentration to prove costly. Leipzig hit Hearts on the break and a sweeping move saw Fritsche score with a low shot just minutes before the referee blew for the break. Not only were the East Germans now back in front on aggregate, but they had scored an away goal that would count as double if the aggregate score was level at the end of the night.

Tynecastle was stunned. Hearts had been so impressive in that first half but it looked as if their efforts would count for nothing. They would have to score another two goals in the second half to progress. Matters were not helped when John Gallacher limped off at the break to be replaced by Jim Jefferies. Moreover, when the game restarted, the East Germans, buoyed by that away goal, looked more purposeful as they swamped the midfield, giving Hearts little space to breathe. However, they reckoned without the Maroons' indomitable spirit.

Urged on by a passionate support unaccustomed to big nights of European football, Hearts swarmed forward in pursuit of the goal that would level the tie on aggregate. Captain Jim Brown led by example. His determination forced a through ball to Gibson whose effort on goal was superbly saved by Friese. There then followed a frenzied succession of corners, which resulted in substitute Graham Shaw almost single-handedly attempting to notch the vital third goal as he followed a header that just cleared the bar with two shots at goal that had Friese scrambling.

It seemed that Hearts had to score and a third goal duly arrived with just 15 minutes left – from an unusual source. Full-back Brown collected a pass from Shaw and lobbed the goalkeeper from the edge of the penalty area to put Hearts 3-1 ahead and level the aggregate scores. Leipzig still stood to go through on the away goals rule but, with Tynecastle in frenzy, it took only 60 seconds for the tie to be turned on its head.

A Prentice corner was nodded on by Gibson to the inimitable Drew Busby who headed past a startled Leipzig goalkeeper to make it 4-1 to Hearts. Tynecastle was now a cauldron of noise and, with just six minutes to go and the East Germans now realising they had to score to remain in the competition, Gibson capped a magnificent night by adding a fifth goal from a cross by Busby to make the final score Hearts 5 Lokomotive Leipzig 1.

The fans could scarcely believe it and a pitch invasion by delirious Jambos at the end of the game invoked a rather needless fine from tut-tutting Uefa. It was a result and a performance that made Europe sit up and take note. Leipzig were touted by many as one of the favourites for the competition and the fact they were taken apart by a team that couldn't score against Dumbarton five months previously, was nothing short of startling.

The more excitable among the Hearts support were thinking of the Jambos being among the favourites to go on and lift the trophy. OK, but remember this was the innocent 1970s – and before the word "relegation" had entered Hearts fans' vocabulary.

Live football on television was an extremely rare event in 1976 (Hearts' defeat in the Scottish Cup final wasn't even live) with only the BBC and Scottish Television showing highlights of games. The BBC showed edited highlights of the Hearts – Leipzig tie at Tynecastle. Commentator extraordinaire Archie Macpherson clearly didn't rate Hearts' chances against Leipzig, so Auntie Beeb sent that doyen of sports commentators – Alan Weeks – to do the commentary. Weeks was more accustomed to commenting on ice-skating but it's doubtful if he spent a more exciting night in his career than that tumultuous September evening at Tynecastle. The fact he held up scorecards with 5.9 on them at the end of the game was a bit of a giveaway.

Drew Busby was immense that night. Busby was a hero to the Hearts fans throughout his five-year career at Tynecastle. As a young lad, Busby had played for Coventry City and Third Lanark in the 1960s before a spell with Vale of Leven Juniors alerted Airdrieonians to bring Busby back into the senior game. At Broomfield Park, Busby's scoring prowess forged a profitable partnership with another Drew – Drew Jarvie.

With Hearts looking to build a team capable of challenging for honours in the club's centenary season, manager Bobby Seith tried to sign the Airdrie pair but succeeded in getting only one – Busby (Jarvie headed north to sign for Aberdeen). The £35,000 Seith paid for the Glasgow-born player was a bargain. Busby, with his bustling style and penchant for scoring spectacular goals, was an instant hero to the fans.

The sight of Super Drew terrorising the Lokomotive Leipzig defence as Hearts fired five goals past the East Germans remains etched on the memory of those who saw it. There is a memorable photograph of Busby scaring the living daylights out of a young Alan Hansen on a visit with Partick Thistle to Tynecastle in 1973. The look of fear in Hansen's face is priceless!

In 1976, Hearts' next opponents in the Cup Winners' Cup were more German opposition – this time from across the Berlin wall. SV Hamburg were a year away from the audacious signing of Kevin Keegan from Liverpool, but were clearly intent on becoming a force not only in German football but in European football too.

Some 2,000 Hearts fans in buoyant, even expectant mood headed to Hamburg for the first leg but a cold blast of realism brought them down to earth. The omens weren't good even before the game kicked off. Jim Cruickshank had been displaced from the Hearts goal by rookie Brian Wilson shortly after the Leipzig triumph (it wasn't clear if the legendary keeper was injured or if he had had one of his famous and numerous spats with the Hearts management team). Hamburg won the first leg 4-2 and, if truth were told, the final scoreline flattered Hearts.

A goal from Drew Busby and an injury-time effort from Donald Park put some gloss on a shaky performance. Still, it was two away goals, which was no mean feat and we all looked forward with eager anticipation to the return leg at Tynecastle and what we hoped would be a repeat of the Leipzig experience.

However, Hamburg showed real quality and when they scored an early goal it signalled the end of Hearts' European dream. The Germans won 4-1 for an impressive 8-3 aggregate victory. Even accounting for Hearts' collapse, it was no surprise that SV Hamburg went on to lift the trophy in May 1977.

By that time, Hearts were in serious trouble. The cracks in Hearts' confidence began to deepen following the Hamburg defeat. Form deserted the Maroons, and what had promised to be a memorable season turned into a nightmare as Hearts plunged down the Premier Division table. For the first time in their history, Hearts were relegated to the First Division at the end of a rollercoaster season. It would be another eight years before European football would return to Tynecastle as Hearts began the yo-yo process between the Premier and First Divisions.

Hearts' relegation cast a huge shadow over Tynecastle. The Maroons seemed to prefer the cup competitions to the cut-throat Premier Division and they qualified for the knockout stages of the League Cup with some impressive displays – the pick being a 4-1 win at Motherwell. But after defeating First Division side Falkirk in a two-legged quarter-final, Hearts lost the semi-final 2-1 to Celtic at Hampden.

In the Scottish Cup, there was almost a repeat performance of the marathon run of the 1975/76 season. After defeating Dumbarton and Clydebank, Hearts were held to a goalless draw by First Division side East Fife in the quarter-final at Tynecastle. Things looked ominous for Hearts when they lost an early goal in the replay at Methil, but they hit back and secured a 3-2 win with a late winner from John Gallacher. Hearts' luck ran out in the semi-final when they lost 2-0 to Rangers at Hampden at the end of March, leaving John Hagart's men with the ultimately unsuccessful task of trying to avoid relegation.

Such thoughts were light years away from Hearts supporters on that September night in 1976. A night when Hearts made the rest of Europe sit up and take notice. And there was only one Drew Busby!

20 v Hibernian 2-1

Scottish Premier Division
4th November 1978. Easter Road

Hearts:	Hibernian:
Dunlop	McDonald
Brown	Duncan
Jefferies	Smith
McNicoll	Bremner
Liddell	Stewart
Fraser	McNamara
Gibson	Rae
Bannon	MacLeod
O'Connor	Hutchinson
Busby	Callachan
McQuade	Higgins

Referee: W Anderson (East Kilbride)

I N A BOOK called *Hearts' 50 Greatest Games*, you will not be surprised to learn there aren't many references to the late-1970s. The reason for this is simple. This was the darkest period of Hearts' history and one that the generation of Hearts supporters who grew up during it – including yours truly – aren't keen to refer to greatly.

I mentioned in the previous chapter about the cut-throat nature of Scotland's new Premier Division with its ten clubs playing league opponents four times a season. While this meant two home games per season against Celtic and Rangers and the subsequent increased revenue this would bring, it also meant that a ninth-placed finish in the league now resulted in relegation.

In the first half of the 1970s, Hearts seemed capable of little more than finishing in the top half of the league. The reality was Hearts were no longer good enough to compete in the new Premier Division – the elite of Scottish football. Hearts were relegated at the end of 1976/77 and the next five years would become known as the "yo-yo" years – Hearts would go down, then come back up, then go down again until the very existence of the club was at threat. It would be the early-1980s before some kind of stability returned to Tynecastle.

Hearts' relegation in 1977 saw manager John Hagart leave the club. It should be said that Hearts' board of directors didn't want him to go and saw him as the man to lead the club back to the top flight of Scottish football at the first attempt. After all, Hearts had played some good football at the beginning of 1976/77. However, it was a measure of Hagart that he blamed himself for Hearts' demotion – although most Hearts fans considered the decision by the club's board of directors to sell Ralph Callachan to Newcastle United in February 1977 as the final nail in the relegation coffin. It was difficult to see what more Hagart could have done when his best player was sold at a crucial time of the season – a situation that would, astonishingly, be repeated two years later.

Hearts' choice for a replacement for Hagart was a sensational one. Not only was Willie Ormond the manager of Scotland, he was part of the "Famous Five" forward line of the 1950s – with Hearts' arch-rivals Hibs. Despite Ormond's success with Scotland – it's argued with some justification he was in charge of the best Scotland team ever, one that returned from the World Cup finals in West Germany in 1974 as the only country unbeaten, even though they went out in the first round on goal difference – there were some among the Hearts support who struggled to accept a Hibernian icon as their manager.

Hearts were struggling financially even before relegation and they faced the prospect of playing league football in season 1977/78 not against Celtic, Rangers, Aberdeen and Hibs but against the likes of Dumbarton, Stirling Albion and Arbroath. When the Maroons began the season away at Dumbarton and could only manage a 2-2 draw, the gloom deepened.

However, Ormond galvanised his troops and the players' full-time fitness was enough to help them overcome many hurdles. It was notable that the Hearts support, far from deserting the team, was remaining loyal and attendances were in fact up from the previous term. In the absence of a New Year's derby game with Hibs, there was a huge crowd of 19,399 for the visit of fellow First Division title contenders Dundee to Tynecastle on 7th January 1978.

Hearts had been on a decent run of form at that point, which included a 7-0 thrashing of Arbroath at Gayfield on Christmas Eve where Willie Gibson and Drew Busby both scored a hat-trick (the fact they each received a crate of whisky from sponsors for their efforts was, I'm sure, purely coincidental!).

Hearts did show their other side on occasions and dropped points to Montrose and Queen of the South. However, in the days when two teams were promoted to the Premier Division, Hearts secured second place behind First Division champions Morton. It had been an unconvincing season but Hearts had returned to the top flight of Scottish football at the first time of asking. The question on everyone's lips was whether they were good enough to stay in the Premier Division. Sadly, the answer seemed apparent just a few weeks into season 1978/79.

Ormond arranged for Hearts to play in a sponsored pre-season tournament at Ibrox with Rangers and English side West Bromwich Albion. His aim was to get his charges prepared for life with top quality opposition. Hearts lost the opening game 3-1 to Rangers but did defeat West Bromwich Albion 2-0 and there were optimistic noises in Gorgie. Such optimism, however, was seriously misplaced.

Hearts began their return to life in the Premier Division with a crushing 4-1 defeat at home to Aberdeen – this despite taking the lead after just four minutes through youngster Eammon Bannon. Seven days later, Hearts lost 4-0 at Celtic Park and were bottom of the league after just two games. Even allowing for the quality of Aberdeen – then managed by Alex Ferguson – and Celtic, Hearts looked woefully short of the standard required for the Premier Division.

Ormond knew this better than anyone did but with no money for new players, he had to wheel and deal in the transfer market. One of his moves, however, puzzled many. He brought two players to Tynecastle who struggled to get into Partick

Thistle's first team – Denis McQuade and John Craig – but in return for their arrival, he swapped one of Hearts' better players – Donald Park.

There were signs of recovery when Hearts held Rangers to a goalless draw at Tynecastle in October but in truth, it was an awful game and the Maroons remained in the league's relegation places. A week later Hearts headed to Pittodrie and the return fixture with an Aberdeen team who had hammered them on the first day of the season.

Ormond gave a debut to striker Derek O'Connor, who he had signed from St Johnstone. It took O'Connor less than 60 seconds to help repay the £25,000 transfer fee when he scooped home the opening goal. Although Aberdeen equalised, it was another of Ormond's new signings, McQuade, who hit an unlikely winner with a 25-yard screamer with ten minutes to go.

When Hearts defeated Celtic 2-0 at Tynecastle the following week thanks to two goals from Drew Busby, Hearts fans began to believe Ormond had at last produced a team that was going places. It would become apparent just a few weeks later where those places would be.

Hearts headed for Easter Road on 4th November 1978 in unusually expectant mood. Despite those highly impressive results against Rangers, Aberdeen and Celtic, Hearts were still in ninth place in the Premier Division, although they were now six points ahead of bottom club Motherwell and just five behind league leaders Dundee United. It was indicative of how tight things were in the Premier Division.

The Maroons' recent record at Easter Road wasn't a good one. It had been ten long years since they had won there and, despite their recent good form, not many Hearts fans would have bet their rent money on them breaking this hoodoo. It was Hibs who started the game the stronger and it pained those watching Hearts fans on the Easter Road slopes to see their former hero Ralph Callachan orchestrate the Hibs midfield. Callachan had spent just 18 months at Newcastle United after his £90,000 transfer from Hearts and he returned to Edinburgh to join 'the other team' across the capital city.

It was a tense first half, with Hearts' defence of Dave McNicoll, Jim Brown and Jim Jefferies thwarting the Hibs attack at every opportunity. Brown and Jefferies were now seasoned campaigners and they refused to panic under what was, at times, intense pressure from the home side. Hibs' Ally MacLeod came closest in the first half and while his fellow forward Tony Higgins was always a physical threat, Hearts looked comfortable with a goalless scoreline at half-time.

The deadlock was broken just two minutes into the second half – but not in the way the home support in the 20,000 crowd expected. Hearts galloped forward in the opening moments of the second period and McQuade found himself in the Hibs penalty box – albeit with his back to goal. The lanky winger controlled the ball beautifully before turning deftly and hitting a sweet shot past Hibs keeper McDonald and into the net to give Hearts the lead. Cue bedlam among the Hearts fans behind the goal at the Albion Road end – but there was more joy to come.

Ten minutes later Derek O'Connor finished off a fine Hearts move after good build-up play by Busby, Bannon and the hard-working Cammy Fraser. Remarkably, it was now 2-0 to Hearts and the Maroons' long wait for a win at Easter Road – and more importantly, two crucial points – was a step closer.

Bannon was now controlling midfield with his intelligent passing; Fraser seemed to be immune to any Hibs challenge; Busby created panic in the home rearguard whenever he got close to the Hibs penalty box. Busby was renowned for his ferocious shooting ability and he fired in a couple of efforts that went wide of goal.

Of course, this being Hearts things are never meant to run too smoothly. With three minutes left, Gordon Rae took advantage of a lapse of concentration in the Hearts defence to pull a goal back – and for those final three minutes, Hibs' attempts to salvage an equaliser resembled the assault on the Alamo. However, Hearts weren't to be denied and the players and supporters danced for joy at the final whistle. Hearts had won 2-1 and were now in an almost lofty position of eighth in the league – but now just three points behind leaders Dundee United.

Sadly, this would prove to be the only time Hearts were out of the bottom two places of the Premier Division that season. It was typical of Hearts that, having drawn with Rangers and defeated Aberdeen, Celtic and Hibs they would slip up the following week when Partick Thistle – inspired by Donald Park – won 1-0 at an expectant Tynecastle. The loud popping sound at the end of the game was the Hearts balloon bursting.

After Hearts defeated bottom side Motherwell at Tynecastle in November, the Maroons wouldn't win another league game again until the end of February – ironically, this was a 3-2 win over Rangers at Tynecastle, a reminder of what the team could achieve if they put their minds to it.

At the end of March 1979, Hearts remained in ninth position in the league – but were six points behind Partick Thistle at a time when there were just two points awarded for a win. There was brief hope when Willie Ormond's men defeated league leaders Dundee United and bottom side Motherwell at Tynecastle within four days, but Hearts' fate was all but sealed when Partick Thistle came to Gorgie four days later and won 2-0 – a certain Donald Park scoring the second goal three minutes from the end. The wee man's distinct lack of celebration when he scored spoke volumes.

Hearts' second relegation in two years was finally confirmed at Pittodrie on 2nd May when a woeful performance resulted in a 5-0 hammering from Aberdeen. It had been a dismal season and there was no respite in the cups with Morton knocking Hearts out of the League Cup on an embarrassing 7-2 aggregate score, and Hibs exacting revenge for that league defeat in November by beating Hearts 2-1 at Easter Road in the Scottish Cup – a tie that was marred by crowd trouble.

Trouble was a word never far away from the corridors of Tynecastle in the late 1970s. However, a white horse upon sat a man called Mercer would soon ride into the streets of Gorgie…

v Hibernian 3-2
Scottish Premier Division
3rd September 1983. Tynecastle

Hearts:	Hibernian:
Smith	Rough
Gauld	Sneddon
Cowie	Duncan
Jardine	Callachan
R MacDonald	Brazil
MacLaren	McNamara
Bowman	Conroy
Robertson	Rice
Bone	Irvine
Park	Thomson
Mackay	Murray

Referee: RB Valentine (Dundee)

THE KNIGHT on a white horse I referred to in the previous chapter was an Edinburgh businessman called Wallace Mercer. Mercer saved Hearts from oblivion in 1981 when he wrote a cheque for £350,000 to purchase shares in the club and became the majority shareholder. He was a successful property developer, and while he would often cut a controversial figure during his decade and a half as Hearts supremo, it's frightening to think even now what might have happened to Hearts without his financial intervention and business expertise. Hearts will always owe a huge debt to Wallace Mercer.

In the summer of 1983, Hearts fans were optimistic once more as their team challenged in the top tier of Scottish football for the first time in two years. After a desperate 1981/82 season, when they failed to get promotion and were knocked out of the Scottish Cup by Second Division side Forfar Athletic, Hearts stumbled over the promotion finishing line by securing second place in the First Division at the end of season 1982/83 – and were at last back in the top flight.

Scottish football in general was in good shape in 1983. Aberdeen had emerged, under Alex Ferguson, as one of the leading sides in the country and, indeed, one of the top sides in Europe after winning the European Cup Winners' Cup in Gothenburg in the summer. So the task of making an impact on the Premier Division was all the harder for Hearts for, as well as the Old Firm and Aberdeen, there was Dundee United who had won their first ever league championship at the end of the 1982/83 season. However, there was a vibrant air in the west end of Edinburgh and a genuine optimism that Hearts had finally laid their woes to rest.

Alex MacDonald, appointed as Hearts' player-manager in 1982, may have been relatively inexperienced in managerial terms – although as a player, he had enjoyed more than a decade of success at Rangers – but he knew he needed more experienced players if Hearts were to avoid yet another relegation. It wasn't fanciful to suggest that, despite chairman Mercer's financial backing, the club's future would be in doubt if they were to be demoted again. Hearts did have talented youngsters such as Gary Mackay, Davie Bowman and John Robertson but MacDonald knew he needed players who had experience of the Premier Division – but he also knew he had little money to acquire them.

However, MacDonald was an astute manager. He persuaded veteran striker Jimmy Bone, a hero of Partick Thistle's League Cup-winning team of 1971, to return from a spell in Hong Kong to sign up for the Tynecastle cause. Although now 34, Bone was the ideal man to nurture the talents of young strike partner Robertson.

MacDonald also secured the return to Tynecastle of the hugely popular Donald Park, who Hearts fans believed should never have been allowed to leave Gorgie in the first place. With former Scotland youth captain George Cowie recruited from West Ham United to fill in the full-back position and players already at Tynecastle who had experience in the Premier Division, Hearts at least looked better prepared for the challenges that lay ahead. MacDonald was as honest as ever when he stated that Hearts' aim was to avoid relegation – anything else would be considered a bonus. What would transpire as the season progressed would be a spectacular bonus.

Having ditched the sectional stage as a format for the League Cup in the past few seasons, Scottish League officials adopted a curious logic for the 1983/84 competition. They began with two knockout rounds played over two legs – but then, inexplicably, drew the remaining 16 teams into four groups of four – in other words, a return to the sections that had proved less than popular throughout the years.

Hearts required penalties to see off Second Division side Cowdenbeath (although, after the tie they signed the Fife club's promising young centre-half Craig Levein) and finished second to Rangers in a section that also had Clydebank and St Mirren. However, only the group winners went through so it was another despairing year in the League Cup for the Jambos.

The league season though, was to get off to a spectacular start for MacDonald's men. An awkward trip to Perth on the opening day to face promotion bedfellows St Johnstone was rewarded with a 1-0 win thanks to a goal from veteran Bone. As the Saints were to face Aberdeen, Dundee United and Rangers immediately after the Maroons, it seemed likely the Muirton Park team would be left at the stalls in the race for survival. Hearts' next game attracted their biggest home crowd for nearly seven years when just over 20,000 fans swarmed to Tynecastle – for the meeting with Hibs.

Inspired by a noisy support, Hearts began in positive fashion and youngsters Robertson and Bowman both forced Hibs and Scotland goalie Alan Rough into action. However, Hibs then took over. The ever-dangerous Irvine was unsettling the Maroons' defence and it was no real surprise when Hibs opened the scoring after just 11 minutes. After a Murray shot had cannoned off Hearts keeper Henry Smith, Ralph Callachan rubbed salt into the wounds of those in maroon who used to idolise him, by lashing home the rebound to put Pat Stanton's side one goal ahead.

Hibs then dictated the game for the remainder of the first half, with young midfielder Rice controlling the centre of the park. But for some inept finishing Hibs could – and should – have added to their lead. However, for all their dominance, half-time arrived with the Hibees just the one goal in front and their fans on the Gorgie

Road terracing must have wondered if one goal would be enough. They were to get their answer in dramatic fashion in the second half.

MacDonald tried to pep up his Hearts players during the break but, as the second half got underway, it was clear that Hibs still had a stranglehold in midfield. Ten minutes into the second period, MacDonald brought himself on in place of youngster Gary Mackay and the transformation was almost immediate. Two minutes later, Hearts equalised with one of the best goals ever scored in an Edinburgh derby – and it proved to be the first of a derby record for another Tynecastle youngster by the name of John Robertson.

Home goalkeeper Henry Smith launched the ball forward and with wind assistance, it landed at the feet of the 18-year-old striker. With a breathtaking piece of skill rarely seen by Hearts fans since the golden age of the 1950s, Robertson controlled the ball with his right foot. With his back to goal, and a deftness of touch reminiscent of Scotland legend Kenny Dalglish, Robertson turned Hibs veteran Arthur Duncan, spotted goalkeeper Rough off his line and curled a magnificent left-foot shot past the startled Hibs custodian to level the score at 1-1. It was one of those goals that remained etched on the memory, and the fans in Gorgie who saw it still talk about it to this day.

It set an already intriguing derby alight and the Hearts fans celebrated wildly. However, their joy didn't last long. Eight minutes later Hibs, stung by the turn of events, regained the lead. Home defender Roddy MacDonald failed to clear a Thomson header and Irvine was on hand to steer the ball past Smith for 2-1 to Hibs and it looked as if the points were heading for Easter Road. Stanton's men had seemingly weathered the storm after losing the equaliser but the never-say-die attitude which Tynecastle boss MacDonald had instilled in his troops came to the fore in dramatic fashion.

With 20 minutes left, Hibs full-back Brazil, attempting to take the sting out of the game, was short with a pass-back to Rough. Robertson was on hand again to pounce and sweep the ball home to level the scores at 2-2. Tynecastle was now in frenzy as the Hearts support acclaimed the birth of a star who had been banging in goals in the First Division the season before, but was now proving himself in a big way in the top league.

Play now swung from end to end and the match was turning into one of the best derbies seen in years. With just 13 minutes to go, Robertson showed that he could turn goal maker as well as goal taker when he delivered a glorious 25-yard crossfield pass, which carved open the Hibs defence and reached Donald Park. The wee man, who revelled in derby games, quickly despatched the ball into the penalty box where Bone headed past Rough to put Hearts in the lead for the first time at 3-2.

The home support erupted and while Hibs threw everything into attempting to get the equaliser, Hearts held on for a famous victory. The joyous scenes at the end of the game told their own story as the maroon-shirted players hugged each other and punched the air with delight. It was Hearts' first victory over their rivals for almost six years, their first derby win at Tynecastle for almost a decade and, remarkably, only their third league win at Tynecastle over Hibs in two decades. It had been one of the best games between the two sides since the halcyon days of the 1950s and was the clearest signal yet that Hearts were heading in the right direction.

It was two wins out of two for Hearts and, buoyed by this success, the Maroons, to the astonishment of the country who weren't used to such performances from a promoted side, went on to win their next three league games – one of which was a highly impressive victory over Rangers at Tynecastle. Incredibly, after five games, Hearts shared top spot in the Premier Division with champions Dundee United and Celtic, with a 100% record and Tynecastle fans pinched themselves to make sure it wasn't a dream.

Their run ended when Aberdeen won 2-0 in Gorgie, but MacDonald's men kept on producing highly creditable results that included wins over St Johnstone, St Mirren and a hard fought 1-1 draw at Celtic Park where Henry Smith saved a penalty. Hearts, unusually for a side that had gained promotion, were proving hard to beat and as 1984 began, delighted Jambos were beginning to think more about the prospect of a Uefa Cup place rather than the expected fight against relegation.

The Maroons did stutter heavily at Dens Park in January and in the return fixture at Celtic Park a few weeks later, but with youngsters Bowman, Mackay and Robertson maintaining form, Hearts clinched fifth place in the Premier Division at the end of a hugely satisfying season – and did indeed clinch a place in the following season's Uefa Cup, much to the delight of Jambos everywhere.

In the Scottish Cup, there was the potential for Hearts to slip up in their tie against First Division side Partick Thistle but the Maroons won 2-0 at a barely playable Tynecastle. The luck of the draw deserted MacDonald's men in the next round, however, when they were faced with the perilous trip to Tannadice to face league champions Dundee United. Hearts' famous battling spirit was to come to the fore once more with a pulsating performance, but the dismissal of Jimmy Bone turned the game in United's favour and the Taysiders squeezed through 2-1.

Hearts supporters eagerly awaited the following season with the added anticipation of a plum draw in the Uefa Cup – French cracks Paris St Germain. The 1983/84 season had been an unqualified success and had seen the birth of a new star at Tynecastle. A star who, at just 18 years, had already taken the first steps to acquire the name "John Robertson, Hammer of the Hibees"!

v Paris St Germain 2-2
Uefa Cup First Round Second Leg
3rd October 1984. Tynecastle

Hearts:	Paris St Germain:
Smith	Baratelli
Cowie	Lemoult
Whittaker	Jeannol
Levein	Janvion
Kidd	Bathenay
Black	Couriol
Bowman	Niederbacher
Bone	Bacconnier
Park	Rocheteau
Robertson	Susic
Johnston	Toko

Referee: U Ericsson (Sweden)

HEARTS' PERFORMANCE in finishing fifth in the Premier Division at the end of the 1983/84 season was astonishing for a promoted side – in fact it was astounding when you consider this was enough for entry, in the days before the break-up of the Soviet Union and the expansion of Europe, as we know it today, into the following season's Uefa Cup.

And when the draw for the first round was made in July, Hearts fans could scarcely believe the news. Hearts were paired with Paris St Germain. French football was on a high, with the national side having lifted the European Championship in the summer of 1984. Now, Hearts were heading for the same Parc des Princes venue. Hearts fans could hardly wait to head for Paris.

Manager Alex MacDonald continued his work in rebuilding this Hearts squad from what was a shambolic team three years earlier to one that would be an established Premier Division outfit. He added to the squad by bringing in two more players who had experience at the top end of Scottish football – defender Brian Whittaker from Celtic and utility player Kenny Black from Motherwell.

Black had been a full-back of some promise at Rangers but his temperament let him down on occasions and he joined Motherwell where he relished the combative midfield role. MacDonald was beginning to establish a trait of signing players discarded by the Old Firm but who would go on to blossom at Tynecastle.

Unexpectedly, Hearts began 1984/85 with two league defeats – and one of those was at home to newly promoted Morton, for whom former Jambo Willie Pettigrew made a substitute appearance. However, the Maroons steadied the ship by inevitably beating Hibs at Easter Road but a lacklustre win over newly promoted Dumbarton and another home defeat by St Mirren had anxious Hearts fans fearing another relegation battle.

Hearts' return to the real big time – European football – came on 19th September when the boys in maroon ran on to the Parc des Princes to face Paris St Germain. Despite a spirited performance, the gulf in class was obvious. PSG, with one of the best midfield players in the world in Dominique Rocheteau, were one of the leading sides in Europe whereas Hearts had failed to beat Alloa Athletic less than 18 months before.

Hearts defended resolutely in the opening 20 minutes, but once Susic opened the scoring with 22 minutes gone, there was no doubt which side would win. The Frenchmen ran out easy 4-0 winners of the first leg, although the chant of Bonjour, Bonjour, Nous Sommes les Gorgie Garcons from 3,000 Hearts supporters in the famous old Parisian stadium bemused the residents of the French capital.

The tie may have been over as a contest after that first leg but the return at Tynecastle a fortnight later still attracted a crowd of 10,023 keen for a look at the star-studded line-up of Hearts' glamorous opponents.

Alex MacDonald was honest enough not to raise fans' expectations by declaring his hope of an early Hearts goal to give the Jambos a chance. However, Hearts very nearly did open the scoring in the opening minutes when PSG's Baratelli fumbled an early cross from George Cowie and the ball was scrambled away from the on rushing John Robertson.

However, Hearts' early impetus only seemed to irritate the classy French side. The Yugoslav-born Susic tormented the Hearts defence and he turned Cowie inside out before delivering the perfect cross to the Austrian Niederbacher, who took a touch before gliding the ball past keeper Henry Smith after just ten minutes to put the French aces 5-0 up on aggregate.

Gorgie heaved a collective sigh but watched a remarkable contrast in styles – the flamboyant technique and flair of the French against the hard-working and totally committed Scots, even at five goals down. Robertson and Davie Bowman both tested Baratelli before Hearts gained reward for their efforts when Robertson scored the club's first goal in European competition since Willie Gibson's counter at Tynecastle in 1976.

Kenny Black sent over a cross that fell to the feet of veteran striker Jimmy Bone. Now 35 years of age, Bone laid the ball to Robertson who drove the ball home from ten yards. Level on the night, but still four goals down on aggregate, Hearts were at least salvaging some pride and Black was a constant threat with his powerful shots from outside the penalty box.

However, hopes of going in at half-time with at least the second leg scores level were dashed when the inspirational Susic crossed for Jeannol to net a second for PSG in the 44th minute. Nonetheless, Hearts received a well-deserved ovation from the fans at half-time, in recognition of their efforts.

In the second half, the French superstars were content to spray passes all over the Tynecastle pitch. When they did threaten, it was inevitably through Susic and early in the second half, he linked with Toko to set up Rocheteau but thankfully, for Hearts, the Frenchman's effort struck the crossbar. Hearts, for their part, wanted to gain some credibility by at least securing a draw against one of the best sides in Europe and George Cowie came close to equalising the tie on the night when his effort was punched away by Baratelli.

The French still looked the more likely to score, however, and Toko – who had given Hearts full-back Walter Kidd a torrid night to the extent that "Zico" as he was affectionately known by Hearts fans received a booking for his efforts – produced a brilliant piece of skill to chip Smith who managed to clutch the ball at the second attempt.

Player-manager MacDonald brought himself on along with Derek O'Connor as Hearts tried to secure a draw on home soil at least. Their wish was granted when Robertson – who else? – netted the equaliser by lobbing Baratelli with just four minutes to go to earn Hearts a fine 2-2 draw.

A 6-2 defeat on aggregate it may have been, but it had been a fantastic adventure for everyone and conclusive proof that Hearts were back among the big boys. It was a great experience for the youngsters in the Hearts line-up such as the ever-impressive Robertson (who wouldn't have looked out of place in the PSG line-up), Davie Bowman and centre-half Craig Levein.

The European adventure was over and now Hearts had to turn to more pressing domestic matters. After nine games, they were just a point off the bottom of the Premier Division and they faced an impressive Dundee United team. Thankfully, Hearts showed what they could do and won 2-0 but MacDonald wasn't the kind of manager to believe his team had turned the corner on the back of one good result.

Yet again, he turned to his former club Rangers and paid £30,000 for the services of striker Sandy Clark. MacDonald used his considerable skills of persuasion as former Airdrieonians and West Ham United striker Clark had initially stated his preferred option was to stay and fight for a first-team place at Ibrox. However, Clark eventually signed for the Maroons – a move he certainly never regretted as it would establish him once again as one of the top strikers in Scotland.

As if to prove the point, he scored on his debut in a 3-2 win against Morton to avenge the Greenock side's win at Tynecastle earlier in the season. Three weeks later, Hearts repeated this feat by winning 3-2 at St Mirren Park – Clark scoring twice – as Hearts began to move clear of the relegation zone. However, the following week Celtic cruised to a 5-1 win at Tynecastle and the Maroons' confidence was dented once more.

Defeats to Dundee and Aberdeen followed, before a 5-2 thrashing at Dundee United just before Christmas. The game at Tannadice was notable for Jimmy Bone scoring Hearts' 5,000th league goal and also the debut of defender Neil Berry who came on as a substitute – and scored an own goal! Berry, though, would become an established member of the Hearts team for more than a decade.

Despite these losses, Hearts went on to record three wins in a row – including defeating Hibs in the New Year Edinburgh derby at Easter Road – to allay fears of becoming embroiled in a relegation dogfight.

The league season petered out somewhat and Hearts ended the campaign in seventh position in the Premier Division – a somewhat disappointing finish given the previous season's heroics but indicative of the progress the team had made under the tutelage of Alex MacDonald.

The final game of the league season seemed to sum things up. Hearts lost 5-2 at St Mirren but were not helped when goalkeeper Smith had to leave the field because of injury after an hour – and with Hearts having no substitute custodian, he had to be replaced by veteran defender Sandy Jardine. It wouldn't be the last time Hearts would have cause to curse the Paisley Saints on the last game of a season.

At least Hearts had a decent showing in the League Cup. The sectional stage had now been discarded and Hearts defeated East Stirlingshire, Ayr United and Dundee in a knockout format. This set up a two-legged semi-final with Dundee United.

The Maroons lost the first leg 2-1 at Tynecastle but this didn't stop 5,000 Hearts fans heading to Tannadice for the return leg. Despite a brave effort, United's class was just too much for the Maroons on the night and they won 3-1 to head for the final on a 5-2 aggregate.

However, Hearts' cup performances whetted the appetite for the Scottish Cup and they disposed of Inverness Caledonian – as they were known in their Highland League days before they joined the Scottish League – 6-0 at Tynecastle, helped by four goals from Gary Mackay. Next up for Hearts was an awkward trip to Brechin City and it took a late John Robertson goal to snatch a 1-1 draw and avoid an embarrassment. Hearts duly won the replay 1-0 at Tynecastle.

The quarter-final draw gave Hearts the team no one wanted – reigning league champions Aberdeen. However, the game was at Tynecastle, which at least gave MacDonald's side a fighting chance of knocking out Alex Ferguson's men. And for a while, it seemed this would happen. In front of over 23,000 fans, Sandy Clark gave Hearts the lead early in the second half and the home support roared their encouragement. However, slack defensive play allowed the Dons' Eric Black to head home a late equaliser and force a replay at Pittodrie.

Some 5,000 Hearts fans headed to the Granite City four days later – although thanks to a lack of organisation by the home club, many didn't get in to Pittodrie as Aberdeen permitted some home fans into the Beach End, where the away support was congregated. To compound a night of misery, Hearts' Roddy MacDonald was sent off in the first half after clashing with Eric Black – and with him went Hearts' chances of Scottish Cup glory. The home team won 1-0 on a hugely controversial night.

At least the 1984/85 season had seen Hearts return to European competition after an eight-year break. The Paris St Germain tie was to prove to be the first of many "Jambos on Tour" occasions which would see Hearts fans take in the delights of Dublin, Vienna, Munich, Bologna, Bordeaux and Basel in the years which followed. PSG were a superb team and simply outclassed Hearts in 1984. It was a valuable lesson for youngsters John Robertson and Craig Levein who, two decades later, would both manage Hearts on similar European occasions.

v Rangers 2-0
Fine-Fare Premier Division
28th December 1985. Ibrox

Hearts:	Rangers:
Smith	Walker
Kidd	Dawson
Black	Munro
S Jardine	McPherson
Berry	Paterson
Levein	Durrant
Colquhoun	McCoist
I Jardine	Russell
Clark	Nisbet
Mackay	Ferguson
Robertson	Cooper

Referee: W Knowles (Inverurie)

AS THE 1985/86 season began, it was evident that some of Hearts' elder statesmen were finding the relentless pace of Scottish football quite difficult, something manager Alex MacDonald was very well aware of. His task was to rebuild the Hearts team with a limited budget – something the former Rangers player excelled at.

Veteran Willie Johnston knew it was time for him to depart Tynecastle in 1985. MacDonald saw Celtic's young winger John Colquhoun as the ideal replacement. He paid £50,000 for Colquhoun's services in the summer and it was another sign that Hearts were looking ahead rather than at the past. MacDonald and his assistant Sandy Jardine were beginning to forge a Hearts team that was becoming difficult to beat. Although this wasn't quite the case at the beginning of season 1985/86.

Hearts began the season with the visit of Celtic. It was a hot August afternoon with a huge crowd and all the anticipation that the first game of the new campaign brings. There was an inevitability about Colquhoun – making his competitive debut for Hearts – scoring the first goal of the season against the club who had sold him just a few weeks earlier.

Hearts played well that day and our collective optimism seemed justified with Hearts hanging on to their deserved lead until the dying moments of the game, when Paul McStay equalised to rob them of a point. It may have been the first game of a long season, but that McStay strike would prove highly significant on the last day of the league season nine months later.

However, as any Hearts fan of a certain age will tell you, it doesn't pay to get overly optimistic. The next few weeks would see the Maroons slump. Defeats to Rangers, Aberdeen, Motherwell and Clydebank meant that, come the end of September, it was looking like another relegation battle was on the cards. Hearts also crashed out

Hearts, Tottenham and Scotland legend Dave Mackay

Hearts, Scottish League Cup winners, 1958

*Hearts gifted striker
Donald Ford*

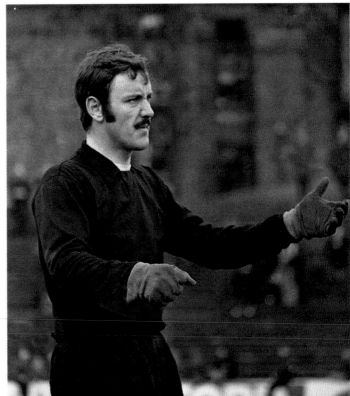

*Hearts legendary
goalkeeper Jim
Cruickshank*

Drew Busby - Hearts cult hero from the 1970s

The Hammer of the Hibs - legendary striker John Robertson

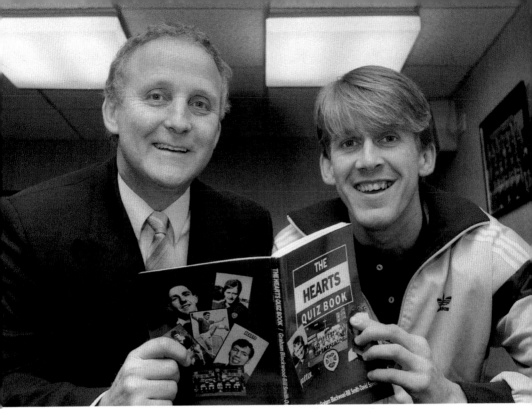

Two Hearts legends from different eras - Alex Young and Gary Mackay

'Big Slim'- Hearts' Dave McPherson

Wayne Foster scores a late winner to knock Hibs out of the Scottish Cup 1994

'Fozzie' celebrates his winner against Hibs 1994

Injured captain Gary Locke celebrates Hearts' Scottish Cup win, 1998

Hearts goalkeeper Gilles Rousset with the Scottish Cup, 1998

Colin Cameron scores Hearts' opening goal from the penalty spot, Scottish Cup final 1998

*John Robertson and Colin Cameron, Scottish
Cup winners 1998*

*Gary Locke and match winner Stephane Adam
with the Scottish Cup 1998*

Mark De Vries scores against Bordeaux, UEFA Cup 2003

Hearts celebrate a famous UEFA Cup win in Basel 2004

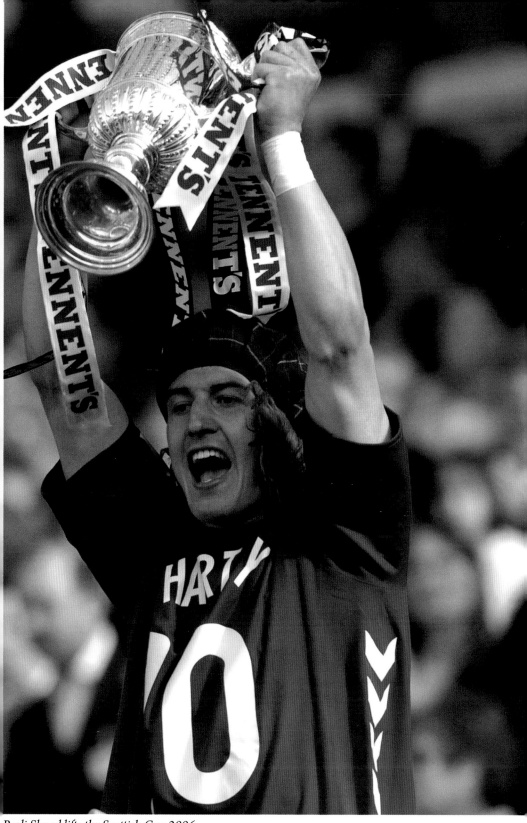

Rudi Skacel lifts the Scottish Cup 2006

The drama of the penalty shoot-out - Scottish Cup final 2006

It's all over as Hearts win the penalty shoot-out, Scottish Cup final 2006

*Robbie Neilson and **that** tackle, Scottish Cup final 2006*

Hearts win the Scottish Cup 2006

Hearts' rising star, David Templeton

Darren Barr scores the first of Hearts' five goals against Hibs, Scottish Cup final 2012

Ryan McGowan celebrates with his team-mates, Scottish Cup final 2012

Rudi Skacel torments Hibs, Scottish Cup final 2012

Suso is fouled and Hearts are awarded a penalty kick - Scottish Cup final 2012

The Hearts are having a party! Scottish Cup final 2012

Former Hearts manager Paulo Sergio with the Scottish Cup 2012

Hearts owner Vladimir Romanov points out Hearts have beaten Hibs yet again

of the League Cup at Aberdeen. Injuries to key players didn't help, but Hearts were struggling – although an Edinburgh derby victory over Hibernian was most welcome. Some things never change.

When new signing Iain Jardine equalised against Dundee to secure a 1-1 draw on 5th October, no one thought much about it. Though we didn't realise it at the time, this result was the prelude to one of the most astonishing runs of results in Scottish football history.

A week later, Hearts travelled to Celtic Park and thanks to a John Robertson goal in the first half, secured their first league win in the east end of Glasgow in 16 years. It was Celtic's first defeat of the season and was a result no one expected – not even those dyed-in-the-wool Jambos. Robertson suffered a neck injury in that game that initially looked serious but, thankfully, didn't keep him out of any matches.

That victory was the catalyst for this Hearts team to believe they were capable of beating anyone on their day. A week later Hearts beat St Mirren 3-0, before champions Aberdeen headed for Tynecastle on a rain-lashed Wednesday evening. By now, Hearts' self-belief was soaring and Craig Levein scored the only goal of a memorable night as Hearts inflicted on the Dons only their second defeat of the season.

The late autumn of 1985 saw Scotland involved in a play-off against Australia for a place in the World Cup finals in Mexico the following summer. The country was in mourning following the death of manager Jock Stein in Cardiff, where the Scots secured the draw they required against Wales to make the play-offs. Now, a two-legged affair was required with the Scots, now under the temporary tutelage of Aberdeen boss Alex Ferguson, having to go to Australia for the second leg.

Scotland won 2-0 on aggregate – thanks to a two-goal victory in the first leg at Hampden – but the knock-on effect on the domestic game was substantial. Some clubs had games postponed while their top players were heading to the other side of the world in the middle of the league campaign.

Hearts' awful start to the season meant no one was looking in the direction of Gorgie Road when selecting which players would take Scotland to the world stage a few months hence. Hearts, therefore, weren't affected by postponements and they produced some impressive performances – and, more importantly, were racking up the points.

Rangers came to Tynecastle in mid-November and were comprehensively outplayed by the Maroons 3-0. Motherwell and Clydebank were then despatched with relative ease. By the time the festive period came along, Hearts had accumulated an impressive tally of points to the extent that when Alex MacDonald's side defeated St Mirren four days before Christmas, Hearts were top of the league – for the first time since 1973.

True, most of the other teams who had league championship aspirations had several games in hand, but Hearts had the points in the bag. MacDonald and Sandy Jardine were eager to play down talk of Hearts being championship contenders, but when the Maroons headed to Ibrox three days after Christmas to face Rangers, one couldn't help but think this was a significant fixture.

There was some doubt about whether the game would be played as, on the morning of Saturday 28th December 1985, Rangers' undersoil heating system had developed a fault – meaning large parts of the Ibrox playing surface resembled an ice rink. The players had to adapt accordingly and after the inevitable whirlwind start by Rangers, it was Hearts who looked the more assured team.

MacDonald was beginning to prove to be a master tactician. While not changing the starting 11, he placed striker John Robertson in a slightly deeper role than he was used to – leaving John Colquhoun and Sandy Clark as the two main forwards.

After weathering the early Rangers storm, Hearts began to move forward with more menace than their hosts. The slippery surface seemed to be causing havoc with home defenders McPherson and Paterson and this proved costly after 16 minutes. A long pass was played forward from the Hearts defence towards the diminutive figure of Colquhoun. McPherson appeared to have it covered but "Big Slim" – who would join Hearts later in his career – slipped on the treacherous surface.

Colquhoun latched on to the ball, fended off a half-hearted challenge from Paterson and drove the ball beyond the static home keeper Walker. The 5,000 Hearts fans in the Broomloan Stand leapt for joy, as did I in the main stand, actions that attracted suspicious glares from those around me – and a shake of the head from my accompanying father.

Hearts sensed Rangers' unease and this feeling intensified when they doubled their lead ten minutes later. It wasn't dissimilar to the first goal. This time Iain Jardine delivered a superb long pass to the ever-alert Colquhoun, who eluded Dawson's challenge before striking a superb effort that beat keeper Walker and rasped into the net to give Hearts a two-goal lead.

Hearts fans celebrated again; my celebrations were somewhat muted, given I was concerned for my personal safety as the mood of the Rangers fans turned from frustration to anger. However, inside I was dancing for joy. I had never seen Hearts win at Ibrox but they looked like they could score every time they went up the park.

It was 2-0 to the visitors at half-time and there was the expected Rangers onslaught as the second half began. McPherson tried to atone for his earlier error by setting up McCoist minutes after the re-start and the striker should have done better than to blaze his shot wide. With the enigmatic Cooper looking menacing on the wing, Rangers looked dangerous, but for all their possession, they never seriously troubled Hearts keeper Henry Smith who was revelling in the occasion.

Indeed, if anyone looked like scoring it was Hearts. Sandy Clark rose majestically to direct a powerful header that for all the world looked like goal number three until home defender Munro headed off the line. As the game drew to its conclusion and Rangers looked to be running out of ideas, Colquhoun danced his way into the penalty box once more before being the victim of a crude foul by keeper Walker.

It had to be a penalty but referee Knowles astonished the visiting support by awarding a free kick on the edge of the penalty box – for an earlier foul by a Rangers player. Had Mr Knowles allowed advantage to be played, Colquhoun would have had a penalty. The final score was Rangers 0 Hearts 2 and if few were prepared to take Hearts seriously as championship contenders before, they were now revising their thoughts.

Hearts remained top of the Premier Division and, significantly in the eyes of many, were now five points clear of a struggling Rangers side – in an era when there were just two points for a win. The victory was just one in what would be a long unbeaten run for Hearts that began in October and would stretch all the way until May – heartbreakingly until the final game of the season.

Buoyed by their achievements, Hearts began 1986 in equally impressive form. In January, they defeated defending champions Aberdeen 1-0 at Pittodrie – Colquhoun was again the scorer that day – and began to stretch their lead at the top of the league. Hearts' triumph at Pittodrie drew Alex Ferguson to the conclusion that the Dons would no longer be champions at the end of the season.

Rangers' woes continued and they didn't seriously challenge again for the title that season. Hearts' nearest challengers appeared to be Dundee United, and when the boys in maroon headed to Tannadice in April – accompanied by 7,000 buoyant fans – and recorded an astonishing 3-0 win over Jim McLean's team, it seemed the way was clear for Hearts to clinch their first league championship in more than a quarter of a century. However, one team was beginning to claw back the points deficit by winning their games in hand – Celtic.

When the final day of the league season arrived on 3rd May 1986, Hearts were two points clear at the top of the table. The only team who could catch them were Celtic – but even then, Hearts were four goals to the good on goal difference. Hearts needed just a draw, a single point from their final game at Dundee. Celtic needed a goals avalanche at St Mirren – and hope Hearts would lose their first competitive game in eight months.

I won't dwell on what happened – more than a quarter of a century on, it's still painful to write about. Suffice to say Hearts lost 2-0 at Dens Park – Dundee substitute Albert Kidd writing his name into Scottish football folklore by scoring his first and second goals of the season in the final eight minutes. At the same time, Celtic were cruising to a 5-0 win at St Mirren Park – and thereby snatched the league title from under the noses of the despairing Hearts players. Hearts' unbeaten run of 31 league and cup games was at an end. Their title dreams were shattered.

This run had also seen the team reach their first Scottish Cup final in ten years. Coming as it did just seven days after the trauma of Dens Park, victory over Aberdeen was never likely. The Dons won the final 3-0 – Hearts' traumatic end to the season was complete when skipper Walter Kidd was sent off.

Hearts ended the season with nothing but runners-up places. Nonetheless, they had given thousand of fans huge enjoyment for most of the season.

Hearts' memorable victory at Ibrox just after Christmas 1985 established the Maroons once again as one of Scotland's leading sides. Even if the club's anthem – which includes the words "Follow the Hearts and You Can't Go Wrong" – is something of a misnomer, the pride in being a Hearts supporter had returned. Denied of silverware, no one could deny the fans that.

v Celtic 1-0

Scottish Cup Fourth Round
21st February 1987. Tynecastle

Hearts:	Celtic:
Smith	Bonner
Kidd	McGrain
Whittaker	Rogan
S Jardine	Aitken
Berry	Whyte
R MacDonald	Grant
Colquhoun	McClair
Black	McStay
Clark	Johnston
Foster	MacLeod
Robertson	McInally

Referee: G Cumming (Carluke)

THE TRAUMA of that day at Dens Park on 3rd May 1986 would never leave the Hearts fans who were there. Subsequent Scottish Cup triumphs would help ease the pain but it's not fanciful to suggest some form of counselling should have been offered to the thousands of heart broken Jambos in Dundee that day.

I took considerable consolation from the fact I at least had the birth of my first child, Laura, to keep me occupied during the summer of 1986. The question on most fans' lips – certainly those of Hearts supporters – was how would the boys in maroon recover from such devastation?

The answer was a rather worrying one, if the beginning of the 1986/87 season was anything to go by. Manager Alex MacDonald had added just one player to the squad which came so close to glory – former England youth striker Wayne Foster – and he arrived on a free transfer having been released by Preston North End.

Hearts began the league season with a goalless draw at St Mirren – starting the campaign at Love Street was seen by many Jambos as mischief-making by the Scottish League's fixture computer – before narrow wins over Hamilton Academical and Falkirk.

The Maroons were struggling but had the chance to recover some form against First Division side Montrose in the League Cup at Tynecastle. However, despite dominating the game from start to finish, Hearts could not find the net and the Gable Endies scored with just about their only attempts at goal in the 90 minutes to secure a 2-0 win – a result that startled Scottish football. My mood wasn't helped any when a former school friend of mine from Aberdeen – Innes MacDonald – set up one of the Montrose goals.

When Hearts lost their next game in the league at Dundee United, alarm bells began to ring. However, who better to turn to in times of crisis than your near neighbours? Hearts travelled to Easter Road at the end of August and recorded a handsome 3-1 win over Hibs and all seemed right with the world once more.

Three days later, Hearts entertained Manchester United in a friendly and recorded a creditable 2-2 draw against a side who were shortly to dispense with the services of manager Ron Atkinson and replace him with Aberdeen boss Alex Ferguson. The draw against United seemed to breathe new life into the Maroons and they then defeated Clydebank, Aberdeen and Motherwell to move into second place in the Premier Division, a point behind league leaders Dundee United.

However, points were then dropped to Dundee, St Mirren and the Old Firm. Hearts defeated league champions Celtic at Tynecastle at the beginning of December but, by now, the Glasgow side had opened up a gap at the top of the league and it seemed unlikely Hearts would run them as close for the league flag this term – although a 7-0 thrashing of Hamilton Academical at Tynecastle proved what Alex MacDonald's side were capable of.

As is so often the case, Hearts' best hopes of success lay in the Scottish Cup and their opponents in the third round – the one where the top-flight teams entered the competition – were First Division side Kilmarnock, who visited Gorgie on the last day of January. Memories of the League Cup nightmare against Montrose flashed back when the Ayrshire side came close to creating another shock result but they were delighted enough to take Hearts back to Rugby Park after a goalless draw.

In the replay, it looked like more disappointment for the maroon hordes when Killie scored just on half-time, but Wayne Foster equalised midway through the second half. In the 1980s, teams tied in Scottish Cup ties simply replayed until someone won a game outright. A 1-1 draw at Rugby Park meant a second replay. Hearts lost the toss of the coin for the venue so had to head back to Ayrshire on a cold Monday evening in February. This time the Maroons made no mistake and won 3-1 to set up a mouth-watering tie with Celtic at Tynecastle.

The media wasted little time in declaring this a match between the nearly men of last season and the side who snatched their glory away from them. Worryingly, Hearts seemed to be hit by a bug prior to the game and it seemed some of the team would be less than 100% fit. Certainly, the early stages of the match indicated all was not well – literally – in the Hearts team as Celtic camped themselves inside the Hearts half.

With centre-half Craig Levein injured, Hearts' defensive partnership was Brian Whittaker and the evergreen – if you'll pardon the phrase – Sandy Jardine. Celtic's front two of Johnston and McInally were proving a handful but another former Old Firm defender, Hearts' Roddy MacDonald, was proving their equal.

After 18 minutes, it seemed the visitors had opened the scoring but McInally's effort crashed off the crossbar with Hearts keeper Henry Smith well beaten. However, a weary looking Hearts team weathered the storm and began to make forward moves themselves. After half an hour, Sandy Jardine's deftly struck free kick found the head of MacDonald who had ventured into the Celtic penalty box and his effort smacked off the post. After a cagey start, Hearts were now well in a game that swung from end to end and the pace of Wayne Foster was clearly troubling the not-so-young Celtic full-back Danny McGrain. Half-time arrived with the game still goalless and at that stage, it was anyone's guess who would progress to the quarter-final.

Hearts had the first chance of the second half when, five minutes in, John Robertson fired in an effort that was just inches over the crossbar. Minutes later, Celtic full-back Rogan headed a cross from Kenny Black against his own crossbar as Hearts sensed blood, with a huge home support in the crowd of nearly 29,000 roaring them on. Celtic, though, weren't out of the picture and Johnston looked dangerous every time he attacked the Hearts goal.

It was quite remarkable how the game was still goalless and with just ten minutes left, a replay at Celtic Park was looking on the cards. Given Hearts' less than impressive record in the east end of Glasgow, this was not exactly an enticing prospect. It was then, however, that Hearts were awarded a free kick when Walter Kidd, of all people, was fouled by Aitken 20 yards from the Celtic goal.

Robertson stepped up and it looked like the wee man was going to deliver a cross towards the head of strike partner Sandy Clark. However, Robertson stepped forward and suddenly burst into a sprint – which, with all due respect, wasn't typical of him! He hit a ferocious effort towards goal that took the slightest of deflections. The ball spun beyond the despairing Celtic goalkeeper Pat Bonner and into the net and it seemed like the noise that erupted from the home support might just blow the roof off the old enclosure that covered part of the Tynecastle terracing.

It was a magnificent strike, a magnificent goal and the little striker temporarily disappeared under his jubilant team-mates. Given the events in the closing stages of *that* game at Dens Park, we all nervously checked our watches about 100 times in the closing nine minutes. Celtic swarmed forward and it's fair to say Hearts were hanging on somewhat. However, hang on they did for a 1-0 win, a famous victory. Hearts don't often knock either of the Old Firm out of the Scottish Cup and this epic victory helped ease the pain of losing the league title to Celtic nine months earlier.

Hearts' next Scottish Cup opponents were Motherwell and, as against Kilmarnock, they made it difficult by being held to a 1-1 draw at Tynecastle before winning the replay at Fir Park thanks to a late goal from John Colquhoun. The 1986/87 season was when Hamilton Academical eliminated Rangers from the Scottish Cup, meaning the semi-finals were free of the Old Firm.

Uefa Cup finalists Dundee United were favourites for the trophy and Hearts avoided them in the semi-final, having been paired with St Mirren. A second successive Scottish Cup final appearance was on the cards and nearly 20,000 Jambos headed for Hampden Park for what many thought would be the formality of victory.

However, St Mirren had already held the Maroons to three goalless draws that season and Hearts – admittedly without the injured John Robertson – reserved their worst performance of the season for arguably the most important game. They lost 2-1 to the Paisley Buddies who went on to defeat Dundee United in the final. As a last twist to a bitter end to the season, St Mirren's victory deprived Hearts of a place in the Uefa Cup the following campaign.

Hearts' season petered out after the semi-final loss to the Saints. After being held to a draw with Aberdeen at Tynecastle, they then lost to Rangers and, almost a year to the day since the awfulness of Dens Park, lost once again to Dundee, this time 3-1 at Tynecastle. Hearts finished in fifth place in the Premier Division but this wasn't enough to secure a place in the following season's Uefa Cup.

The European campaign of 1986 was sadly short-lived. Hearts were drawn against Dukla Prague but had the misfortune to be at home for the first leg. They got off to a dream start when Wayne Foster scored in the first minute but the Czechs hit back and it took a late goal from John Robertson – who had been surprisingly left on the substitutes' bench until early in the second half – to secure a 3-2 win.

Aficionados of European football knew very well that losing an away goal, let alone two, was a recipe for disaster. And so it proved as Hearts, despite a brave performance, lost 1-0 in the Czech capital a fortnight later to go out on the away goals rule after the tie had been squared at 3-3 on aggregate.

After the drama of the previous season, 1986/87 proved to be something of a let-down. It's fair to say some Hearts fans were asking if the club was ready to take the next stage from being a now established Premier Division team to one that would actually win silverware. They had golden opportunities in 1986 and 1987 but failed to take them.

It's also fair to suggest chairman Wallace Mercer was thinking something similar. In the weeks following the Hampden defeat to St Mirren, Mercer thought long and hard about what to do next. The semi-final defeat hurt badly and for the first time in his tenure, he felt he had let the fans down.

Nagging doubts about the team's mentality would begin to surface as the decade wore on. Hearts had proved they could match the Old Firm on occasions, as was evident when they knocked Celtic out of the Scottish Cup. Nonetheless, one couldn't help but doubt if the players had the mental toughness required to win silverware. Sure, there had been remarkable progress in a short period.

Sure, there had been remarkable progress in a short period in the space of five years, Hearts had gone from First Division also-rans to a team challenging for honours. They had come so close but yet so far to winning a league and cup double in 1986. However, Hearts fans now wanted more than merely to challenge for honours. There had been a trophy drought at Tynecastle that had now lasted a quarter of a century. Hearts fans longed for a silver cloud or two.

v Dundee 4-2
Fine-Fare Premier Division
31st October 1987. Tynecastle

Hearts:	Dundee:
Smith	Geddes
Burns	Forsyth
Whittaker	Glennie
Levein	Shannon
Berry	Smith
McPherson	Chisholm
Foster	Mennie
Black	Brown
Colquhoun	Wright
Mackay	Coyne
Robertson	Angus

Referee: G Evans (Bishopbriggs)

ENTRE-HALF Dave McPherson was a defender who was thought very highly of at Ibrox but when Hearts boss Alex MacDonald enquired about bringing the defender to Tynecastle, Rangers were not difficult to deal with. Nevertheless, Hearts had to splash out a club record fee of £325,000. Although part of this fee was for fellow Rangers defender Hugh Burns, it was widely believed £275,000 was for the signature of "Big Slim".

As the 1987/88 season progressed, Hearts also spent £60,000 on utility player Mike Galloway and obtained forward Mark Gavin on a free transfer. The acquisition of Burns and McPherson in particular, excited the Hearts support who saw these signings as an ambitious declaration of intent from their club. As season 1987/88 began, such optimism did not seem misplaced.

Hearts lost just one of their opening 12 league games – thanks to a goal four minutes from the end from Celtic's Mark McGhee in Glasgow. It wouldn't be the last time McGhee would cause heartache for the Jambos with a late goal that season.

Ten days after that unfortunate loss, Hearts dismantled Dundee United 4-1 at Tynecastle. Come October, Hearts counted themselves unfortunate to have to settle for a draw against champions Rangers; Aberdeen were defeated at Tynecastle before the Hearts goal machine destroyed Falkirk 5-1 at Brockville.

With a strike force of John Robertson, John Colquhoun and Wayne Foster, Hearts' pace up front was tormenting defences throughout the land. It was a satisfying October – with the exception of one blip that I won't detail too much, other than to say Hibernian won their first Edinburgh derby in nearly a decade at Easter Road.

Two 3-0 wins over Morton and Motherwell saw Hearts go clear at the top of the Premier Division and set them up nicely for a Halloween clash with old adversaries

Dundee at Tynecastle. A crowd of nearly 14,000 headed for Tynecastle to see if the league leaders could maintain their impressive form. They got their answer after just 45 scintillating minutes.

Hearts swarmed around Dundee from the first whistle. Foster and Colquhoun ran the Dees' defence ragged and shots rained in on keeper Bobby Geddes. Kenny Black orchestrated the midfield with precision passing that carved open the Dundee defence almost at will. Chance after chance was set up for Robertson but, uncharacteristically, the wee striker missed those chances and, being the eternal pessimists that we are, Hearts fans began to wonder if this was going to be one of those days.

Dundee could barely get out their own half and Hearts keeper Henry Smith could have sat alongside me in the bench seats under the old enclosure as he hardly touched the ball, and after 15 minutes, the Dundee defence eventually caved in. McPherson ambled forward into the penalty box where his obvious aerial ability – standing at six feet three inches helped – saw him nod the ball towards Robertson. The wee man was not noted for his heading ability but he stooped to nod the ball past Geddes to put Hearts a goal ahead.

Having secured the breakthrough, Hearts wasted little time in doubling their advantage. Colquhoun split the visiting defence with a pass to Robertson who finished with aplomb after 17 minutes. Just three minutes later, Dundee must have thought about finding a white flag from somewhere when another Hearts defender, Brian Whittaker, was brought down in the box and Hearts were awarded a penalty. Robertson stepped up to complete what we all believed would be a five-minute hat-trick. However, Geddes saved well from the wee man's kick and, astonishingly, Dundee were still in the game, albeit 2-0 down.

Hearts were playing with verve and style not seen at Tynecastle for years. Dundee just couldn't cope with the mazy runs of Colquhoun, the direct runs of Foster, the passing of Black and the ever-dangerous Robertson. Hearts continued to create chance after chance and Robertson came agonisingly close to his hat-trick while Colquhoun could and should have scored.

It wasn't until ten minutes before the break that Hearts scored the third goal their play richly deserved. This time it was Foster who delivered a sublime pass to Colquhoun and the former Celtic man duly lashed the ball past Geddes to give Hearts a surely unassailable three-goal lead.

Indeed, Hearts continued to make chances up to the break but there was no more scoring, something a shell-shocked Dundee team were grateful for. Hearts left the field at half-time to a standing ovation. OK, most Hearts fans at Tynecastle in 1987 were standing anyway, but you get the picture. It had been a truly magnificent first-half performance from the boys in maroon and it's not an exaggeration to say that Hearts could have been six or seven goals ahead at half-time such was their brilliance, a fact even the Dundee manager Jocky Scott acknowledged at the time.

It was one of those games where you didn't want half-time to come as you didn't want Hearts' free-flowing football to end – and I wondered if they would be able to pick up such a frenetic pace again after the interval. They did, although perhaps understandably, they didn't dominate the game in quite the same manner in the second period. Scott had reorganised his troops for the second half and while Hearts continued to create chances, the Dees seemed more resolute.

On the hour mark there was another goal – but this time it was scored by Dundee's Tommy Coyne who took advantage of hesitancy in the Hearts defence. However, any hopes those from Dundee had of an unlikely fightback were soon dispelled as Hearts upped the pace again. Black's reward for a sublime performance was to score Hearts' fourth goal as he flicked home a cross from the tireless Foster. Game over – in truth it had been over after 20 minutes when Hearts were in cruise control.

Keith Wright did pull a goal back for the visitors near the end – he would soon face Hearts on a regular basis, wearing a green and white shirt in the Edinburgh derby – but Hearts' victory was never in doubt and the game ended Hearts 4 Dundee 2. Hearts remained three points clear of Celtic at the top of the league, six clear of Aberdeen, who lost that day to Celtic, and an astonishing seven clear of Graeme Souness's Rangers.

Their performance that day was the best I had seen from a Hearts side in nearly 20 years. The fact Hearts won in the end by just two goals was scarcely believable to those of us who were present. Had Hearts taken all of their chances they would have reached double figures. The skill on display was sublime, the pace at times frightening (for the opposition!) and the goalscoring threat was present every time the maroon shirts swarmed forward – which at times in that first half was incessant.

I was living in Aberdeen at that time and headed back to the Granite City raving about Hearts' performance. Of course, being Aberdeen, few people there were interested in my views about Edinburgh's leading team. Their own team was in decline with Alex Ferguson having left for Manchester United a year earlier and the dominance that Aberdeen held over Scottish football for the first half of the 1980s had gone with the manager.

Hearts continued to play stylish football and score goals almost at will for the rest of the season. After the Dundee game, they lost just one league fixture – a 3-2 defeat at Ibrox – until the end of February, when an inexplicable dip in form came at Brockville when Hearts, having won 5-1 there earlier in the season, lost 2-0.

However, the 1987/88 season was one of those campaigns with a 12-club Premier Division – meaning 44 league games had to be played in addition to League Cup and Scottish Cup ties. Hearts were playing some wonderful football and although the depth of their squad couldn't match that of Rangers, for whom money was no object, the Maroons were serious contenders for the league title.

In an attempt to retain their championship, the Ibrox club splashed out millions of pounds to bring established England internationals north of the border. However, money doesn't always talk and it was Celtic who were leading the way in the league title race. They were seven points ahead of Rangers when Hearts returned to Ibrox in early April 1988. Hearts knew if they could record a rare win in Govan, they would leapfrog Rangers into second place.

When Jan Bartram gave the home side a first-half lead, things didn't look good, but a storming second-half comeback for Hearts turned the tables. There was particular joy for Dave McPherson who headed home Hearts' equaliser before a rare incident in Glasgow towards the end of the game – a penalty for the visitors – was converted by John Robertson and clinched the points for the Maroons.

Hearts ended the season as they had done two years earlier – as runners-up to Celtic in the league. There was huge satisfaction from league performances this season. Not since the days of Bauld, Wardhaugh and Conn had Hearts played such free-flowing, attacking football scoring goals for fun. There was an ironic end to the season when Hearts failed to score in their final three league games, but they secured runners-up spot and had split the Old Firm again.

Much as it was a joy to watch Hearts in 1987/88, there was the inevitable crushing disappointment. Hearts reserved their worst performance of the season for a League Cup quarter-final tie with Rangers, which they lost 4-1.

For the third season running, Hearts reached the semi-finals of the Scottish Cup. In 1988, they faced Celtic at Hampden Park – a Celtic team chasing a league and cup double in their centenary year.

In front of a full house of 65,000, the game was a typical semi-final. Tense, nervous – and quite awful. However, with half an hour to go, Hearts took the lead when Brian Whittaker, playing against his old team, floated in a cross towards the towering Dave McPherson.

Slim missed the ball, but so did Celtic goalkeeper Pat Bonner and the ball sailed into the net. Cue bedlam in the Hearts end. It was a lead Hearts held until three minutes from time, when goalkeeper Henry Smith dropped a seemingly harmless cross, allowing Mark McGhee to prod home the equaliser.

I remember saying to my mate on the slopes of Hampden that there was little chance of me returning to Hampden for a midweek replay when Celtic, sensing blood, stormed forward again. Frank McAvennie launched another cross into the Hearts penalty box, Smith dropped the ball again and Andy Walker slammed home an unlikely winner.

As was the case 12 months earlier, Hearts had blown the cup semi-final at Hampden and the devastated maroon-clad fans leaving Mount Florida couldn't believe they had been kicked in the teeth again.

Their mood wasn't helped a few days later, when Hearts accepted a bid of £750,000 from Newcastle United for hero John Robertson. Depression turned to anger among the fans. Hearts had played some wonderful football that season but yet again when it really mattered, their mentality was being questioned. Now a player who had been afforded hero worship from the fans was on his way out.

It was an unfortunate end to the season, but the fact Hearts finished ahead of money-laden Rangers was something that tended to be overlooked in the aftermath of the Hampden loss. Looking back to that sparkling 4-2 victory over Dundee in October 1987 reminded me of when Hearts were at their very best.

26 v Bayern Munich 1-0

Uefa Cup Quarter-Final First Leg
28th February 1989. Tynecastle

Hearts:	Bayern Munich:
Smith	Aumann
McLaren	Grahammer
McKinlay	Pflugler
McPherson	Johnsen
Berry	Augenthaler
Levein	Flick
Galloway	Koegl
Ferguson	Reuter
Colquhoun	Wohlfarth
Black	Thon
Bannon	Ekstrom

Referee: H Kohl (Austria)

T WAS an unusual Hearts team that kicked off the 1988/89 season – for there was no John Robertson to lead the line, the legendary striker having been transferred to Newcastle United for £750,000 towards the end of 1987/88.

His replacement was man of many clubs Iain Ferguson, after Hearts paid Dundee United £350,000 for his services. Following in the footsteps of a player who was idolised by the Hearts support was never going to be easy, but Ferguson wasted little time in making an impact, scoring a hat-trick in a 5-0 League Cup win over St Johnstone at Tynecastle in August 1988.

Hearts were scoring plenty of goals in the League Cup – they put another four past Dunfermline Athletic in the quarter-final – until they reached the semi-final where they lost 3-0 to Rangers at Hampden.

Hearts' set-up this season looked different, although the return to Tynecastle of 1970s favourite Eammon Bannon was a welcome sight. Both Bannon and Ferguson were an intrinsic part of the Dundee United team that had reached the final of the Uefa Cup in 1987 and their experience was considered vital for Hearts' European campaign.

I use the term "campaign" loosely as, until this point, Hearts' sojourns to the continent were all too brief. However, Hearts were given an unusually kind draw in the first round of the Uefa Cup in the late summer of 1988.

Irish side St Patrick's Athletic were not expected to provide Alex MacDonald's men with a stern test and so it proved as Hearts won the first leg in Dublin 2-0, thanks to a penalty from Wayne Foster and the first of a record haul of European goals from the previously unheralded Mike Galloway. Galloway scored again in the return leg at Tynecastle along with Kenny Black as Hearts cruised to a 4-0 aggregate victory.

The ante was increased when Hearts' second round opponents were announced as Austria Vienna, a big name in European football at that time. The first leg was at Tynecastle, meaning Hearts would seek a lead to take to one of the most beautiful cities in the world. Over 14,000 fans turned out on a chilly October evening and, despite enormous Hearts pressure, the game ended goalless. Few people outside Gorgie fancied the Maroons' chances of scoring in the famous Prater Stadium.

Even fewer fancied Walter Kidd and Mike Galloway to combine for the latter to score the only goal of the game to send the 2,000 travelling Hearts fans into ecstasy – and serve notice that Hearts weren't in this competition just for the fun of it.

However, the third round of the Uefa Cup was not for the faint-hearted. A quick look at the potential opponents would be enough to send shivers down the spine of your average Hearts fan, although no doubt chairman Wallace Mercer was rubbing his hands with gleeful anticipation. However, Hearts avoided the likes of Bayern Munich, Juventus, Roma, Napoli, Bordeaux, Inter Milan and Stuttgart when the draw was made. Instead, the Maroons were paired with unknown Yugoslav outfit Velez Mostar. Relief at avoiding the big guns was tempered with the news that Hearts had to play the first leg in Gorgie – never a favoured option in European competition.

On a memorable November night, in front of a passionate crowd of over 17,000, Hearts attacked the Velez goal incessantly. They were rewarded with a first-half goal from Bannon and Galloway's fourth of the Uefa Cup campaign before John Colquhoun drove home a glorious third in injury time to send the Hearts fans wild with delight.

Hearts survived an ordeal both on and off the park in the return leg in Mostar – in between dodging missiles being thrown on the pitch and being showered with broken bottles – losing 2-1, but secured a place in the quarter finals on a 4-2 aggregate. Galloway – inevitably – scored Hearts' away goal and fans celebrated a happy Christmas in the knowledge that European football was still on the menu for 1989.

They were even happier with the news that John Robertson was on his way back from his ill-fated spell on Tyneside – Hearts paid Newcastle United £750,000 to bring the prodigal son home – and along with the capture of highly rated Dundee full-back Tosh McKinlay, 1989 appeared to hold much promise.

The old cliche that there are no easy teams left in the quarter-final of a cup competition was trotted out on more than once occasion. And so it proved, when Hearts were paired with Bayern Munich when the draw was made for the last eight of the Uefa Cup. The first leg was played at Tynecastle and more than 26,000 fans – including a smattering of expectant Germans – headed for Gorgie on a cold February night.

Bayern were confident and the talk in the Munich camp before the game was of how much of a lead they were going to take back to Germany for the return leg. Moreover, as the game began in a tumultuous atmosphere, it appeared Hearts had been listening a tad too closely to their more illustrious opponents.

The Maroons began cagily with the three Macs at the back – McLaren, McKinlay and McPherson – preferring to cautiously play the ball back to safety rather than incur the wrath of a Bayern team not unaccustomed to such occasions. Further forward,

John Colquhoun appeared to be sucked into a midfield role leaving Iain Ferguson as the lone striker, but with Galloway and Bannon providing support.

After 13 minutes, a misplaced pass from Ferguson went to Thon who delivered a superb pass to the Swedish striker Ekstrom, whose flick just went past the post. Shortly after, Ekstrom fell down in the penalty box after a challenge form Craig Levein but the Austrian referee ignored German pleas for a penalty.

Hearts, if truth were told, were struggling to make an impact. A highlight of their European campaign had been the strength of Galloway up front, but Bayern had clearly done their homework and Galloway was struggling to even touch the ball, far less maintain his impressive scoring record. However, after half an hour, Hearts finally threatened when Bannon delivered a tantalising cross which keeper Aumann could only punch out. Tosh McKinlay swept the ball into the net, but Hearts celebrations were soon muted when the referee blew for a foul on the German goalkeeper.

Bayern were clearly rattled by the physical nature of the game. Kenny Black, never averse to a challenge or two, lunged in on Reuter and the German reaction was not unexpected. Thon responded with a brutal tackle on Colquhoun and as tempers frayed, the game threatened to get out of hand. If the referee was loath to show anyone a yellow card, he had little choice when Alan McLaren kept his foot high when he went for a 50-50 ball and the teenager was booked.

Bayern had threatened on a couple of occasions in the first half but there was precious little incident around either penalty area. Alex MacDonald had stressed before the game the importance of not conceding the dreaded away goal and when half-time arrived, we hoped Hearts would at least look like scoring a goal in the second period.

Hearts did indeed throw off their shackles after the re-start. Just three minutes had gone of the second period, when Levein sprayed a long pass to Galloway. The former Halifax Town player turned the ball across goal, out of the reach of Ferguson but towards Bannon whose effort cannoned off a Bayern defender to safety. The 26,000-plus crowd roared their approval as hopes rose that the Jambos would make the breakthrough.

After 54 minutes, Ferguson rifled in a free kick that brought a fine save from Aumann and the huge Jambo contingent sensed the breakthrough was imminent. It came two minutes later. Black was brought down on the edge of the penalty box, just in front of the Tynecastle shed. The unlikely figure of Tosh McKinlay stood alongside Ferguson as the Germans tried to figure out the threat. McKinlay discreetly rolled the ball to Ferguson who let rip with a rasping shot that flew high into the net. Delirium at Tynecastle – Hearts were ahead against Bayern Munich! Standing in the shed, I was hurtled several rows down the terracing as Hearts fans celebrated wildly.

Spurred on by a cacophony of noise from the home support, Hearts continued to drive forward with Ferguson and Colquhoun going close to extending the lead. However, Bayern were dangerous on the counter-attack and the ever-dangerous Thon seemed set to score a vital away goal only to be denied by a last-gasp tackle from McKinlay. Thon's frustration soon showed when he was booked for another crude challenge on Colquhoun who took an arm in the face from Pflugler shortly afterwards – but the referee missed the incident.

It was patently obvious that Bayern were rattled and their discomfort should have increased eight minutes from the end, when Dave McPherson found himself all alone in the Bayern penalty box – only to scoop the ball over the bar from ten yards out.

The Germans didn't know what hit them and they clearly took the option for damage limitation as the game drew to its close. When the referee blew his whistle for full time, Hearts had secured their most memorable victory in European football. They had beaten the mighty Bayern Munich 1-0 and they headed for the Olympic Stadium a fortnight later in high spirits.

Of course, this wouldn't be Hearts without a hard luck story. Wearing their away candy-striped shirts, Hearts survived an edgy start in Munich to look the likelier team to score until Klaus Augenthaler smacked in a shot from 35 yards which left keeper Henry Smith helpless. Alex MacDonald had warned his players beforehand about the threat of Augenthaler and was clearly annoyed that his players didn't heed his words.

The scores were now level on aggregate, but still Hearts had opportunities to notch a priceless away goal. John Colquhoun, in particular, had two glorious chances – one of which clipped the post. Inevitably, the second goal was scored by the home side's Johnsen, towards the end of the game. Bayern won 2-0 on the night and 2-1 on aggregate.

While the Germans had criticised Hearts for their physical approach in the first game in Edinburgh, they were quick to praise MacDonald's side after the return game, saying Hearts were one of the best teams to play at the Olympic Stadium for some time.

Three days after Munich, Hearts' Scottish Cup run ended in anger as McLaren and McKinlay were sent off in a 2-1 defeat by Celtic at Parkhead. With Hearts' league form continuing to stutter – they finished sixth in the Premier Division after a distinctly average domestic campaign – there was precious little left to play for as season 1988/89 drew to a close.

There was one further highlight, however. John Robertson had not enjoyed the best of luck since his return to Tynecastle in December. He had scored just twice – both goals coming in the same game against Celtic – but injury had hampered his progress in a maroon shirt. When Hibernian came to Gorgie in April 1989 and took the lead, it seemed Hearts' dismal league season would end the way it began.

However, the Jambos equalised through Bannon and with minutes remaining it was left to the Hammer of the Hibs to score the winner. Robertson could not contain his glee as he hit Hearts' second goal and danced off to celebrate with the Hearts hordes at Tynecastle's School End.

It was one of the few league highlights from a season in which Europe dominated. And the memory of the night Bayern Munich were humbled at Tynecastle still burns bright more than two decades on!

v Hibernian 3-0
B&Q Premier Division
15th September 1990. Easter Road

Hearts:
Smith
McLaren
McKinlay
Levein
Berry
Wright
Robertson
Mackay
Foster
Sandison
Colquhoun

Hibernian:
Goram
Miller
Sneddon
Mitchell
Cooper
Hunter
Hamilton
Wright
Findlay
Houchen
McGinlay

Referee: J McCluskey (Stewarton)

EARLIER IN this book, I portrayed chairman Wallace Mercer as riding into Gorgie on a white horse in 1981 when he signed a cheque for an amount in the region of £350,000 to save Heart of Midlothian FC from the likelihood of liquidation. It was the beginning of the rebirth of Hearts and they moved from First Division also-rans to Premier Division title contenders within five years.

When the 1980s ended, Hearts were signing players for £750,000 – John Robertson's return from Newcastle United and Derek Ferguson's transfer from Rangers both costing this amount – and Mercer had ambitious plans for Hearts. One of those plans, however, was fatally flawed. His proposal in the summer of 1990 to buy a majority shareholding in Hearts' Edinburgh rivals Hibernian – and close them down.

More than two decades on, such a move still seems incredible, but at the end of the 1989/90 season Mercer set the wheels in motion by agreeing a deal which would see him purchase more than 60% of the shares in the Easter Road club's parent company, Edinburgh Hibernian plc. There were those who initially thought Mercer was playing a late elaborate April Fools Day prank, but it soon transpired he was deadly serious.

The superiority complex some Hearts fans felt at the breaking news soon disappeared when it became clear Mercer's vision was of creating an "Edinburgh United" in an effort to challenge the Old Firm's dominance of Scottish football and moving to a custom built stadium on the outskirts of Scotland's capital city – for this would also mean the end of Heart of Midlothian FC as we knew it.

There was outrage not only in Edinburgh, but also throughout Scottish football. Hibs fans immediately launched a campaign to save their club called "Hands off Hibs" that was supported by the likes of The Proclaimers, one of Scotland's leading musical names. Prominent former Hibs players such as Pat Stanton and Tony

Higgins joined the campaign as did thousands of Hibs fans across the country – and Hearts fans too.

Hearts striker John Robertson irked his club chairman by joining the campaign and the Mercer family home was the subject of attacks from some of those angrily opposed to the proposal. Mercer famously described such attacks as typical of the tribalisation that affected the Edinburgh clubs, a stance that did nothing to calm already turbulent waters.

Mercer claimed there was strong support among football fans within the Edinburgh business community for the plan and he had the full support of the Hearts board. It was an assertion many people found difficult to believe. Mercer said "there were sound football and economic reasons" behind the proposal. Economic reasons I can perhaps understand. Football reasons? To use the uniqueness of the Scots language where two positives can form a negative – aye, right.

It took six weeks of vociferous campaigning before the move collapsed when Hibs chairman David Duff blocked the move by refusing to sell his percentage of Hibs shares. Finally, on 13th July, Mercer announced he was dropping his £6.2m bid but couldn't resist walking away without firing a parting shot. He insisted he had won the business argument hands down and claimed he had support from 66% of Hibs shareholders, which in normal circumstances would be a convincing majority.

However, he admitted he had underestimated the strength of feeling from not only Hibs supporters but also supporters from his own club. The takeover was off and Hibs – and Hearts – lived to fight another day. Nevertheless, Mercer's relationship with many Hearts fans soured from that point on. Yes, he had saved Hearts from oblivion in 1981 and under his leadership, the club were vibrant and competing for honours once again. His innovation in transforming a club dying on its knees to one that was commanding respect not only in Scotland but also in Europe, was admirable. Yes, we were all grateful for that. However, some of Mercer's recent decisions had irked many Hearts fans.

The decision to sell John Robertson to Newcastle United in 1988 was the first to cause resentment. Robertson was the Hearts fans' favourite by the length of Gorgie Road and even though he was sold for a club record fee, his departure left a gaping hole in the team. Re-signing Robertson eight months later for the same fee was seen by many as a tacit admission by Mercer that he had got it wrong.

Then there was Hearts' Uefa Cup tie against Bayern Munich in 1989, described in the previous chapter. Mercer and the Hearts board had arranged a deal with a German television company to show the game live in Germany. However, the deal had not been authorised by Uefa and Hearts were given a huge fine of £93,000.

There was also the not insignificant matter of the sacking of Sandy Jardine. After Hearts' agonising near-miss of a league and cup double in 1986, Mercer elevated Jardine to the position of joint manager with Alex MacDonald. It was a role he held for two years until Mercer decreed that "two hands on the tiller weren't working" and he dismissed Jardine in 1988 – but kept MacDonald, a move that stunned and mystified the majority of the Hearts support.

Mercer's aborted takeover of Hibs meant therefore, that the 1990/91 season would see Hearts under intense scrutiny. Perhaps it was the unease this created that contributed to a dismal start to the season. The visit to Tynecastle of English star Paul

Gascoigne with Tottenham Hotspur for a pre-season friendly attracted a crowd of over 18,000 and an admirable 1-1 draw didn't hint of the trouble to come.

Hearts began the league campaign with a 1-1 draw at home to St Mirren before losing 2-0 at Dunfermline Athletic. Hearts then headed to Pittodrie for a midweek League Cup tie with Aberdeen – one of the first games to be shown live on the new satellite television channel BSB. Hearts produced an awful performance. Those fans who had made the effort to make the long journey north on a Wednesday evening were less than pleased to see new £750,000 signing Derek Ferguson sitting on the substitutes' bench.

Their displeasure turned to anger when MacDonald made a substitution at half-time with his team 2-0 down – he chose not to bring on Ferguson and opted instead for veteran defender Walter Kidd. The fans weren't slow to make their feelings known. Hearts lost 3-0.

A few days later, Rangers cruised to a 3-1 win at Tynecastle and the fans directed their anger towards Mercer and MacDonald. Two days later, Mercer took action – he sacked MacDonald in a move that rocked Scottish football. Hearts were in turmoil.

Mercer appointed coach Sandy Clark as interim manager until a successor to MacDonald was appointed. Clark had something of a baptism of fire – Hearts' next game was a trip to Easter Road and a game with the team Wallace Mercer had attempted to run out of business a few weeks earlier.

The atmosphere at an Edinburgh derby is usually electric but given the circumstances of a few weeks before, this one was charged to the point of exploding. Wisely, Mercer heeded police advice and stayed away from the game. Tension was high enough, particularly among the home support.

Hearts had injury concerns before the game, as well as a lack of form. Caretaker boss Clark picked fringe players George Wright and Jimmy Sandison – the latter in for the injured Dave McPherson – and while they weren't first-team regulars, they were thrown into the white heat of probably one of the most contentious Edinburgh derbies ever.

Hibs, as you might expect, started on the offensive, buoyed by their support, desperate to prove a point. However, Hearts' defensive rocks Alan McLaren and Craig Levein were coolness personified and coped ably with anything the home side could throw at them. Up front, there was the Hammer of the Hibs – John Robertson, now at the peak of his powers.

After a frenetic start to the game, there were 13 minutes played when Hearts took the lead. Robertson, on the left, beautifully controlled the ball with a touch that left home defender Miller in a tangle. The wee man then went round centre-half Hunter as if he wasn't there, before chipping a delightful cross into the Hibs penalty box. The ball was meant for Wayne Foster but Hibs' McGinlay, in attempting to stop it reaching the Hearts player, merely succeeded in deflecting the ball past goalkeeper Goram to give Hearts the lead.

Hibs supporters' agony was a mirror image of the ecstatic jibes from the Maroon Army on the slopes of the Albion Road end. It was all too much for some of the home support, one of whom ran on to the pitch. Another fan followed from the Hearts enclosure in the main stand and police and stewards raced on to the field of play. Both men were arrested and players and officials from both clubs appealed for calm as more fans threatened to invade the pitch. The mood had turned ugly and it was clear the police were struggling to restore order.

The decision was taken for the players to leave the park for eight minutes, as an announcement warned the 16,500 spectators the game would not restart until the crowd had settled down. Eventually, the players returned to the field but there was an uneasy calm which many thought wouldn't last.

After 23 minutes, Hearts doubled their lead. John Colquhoun's corner from the left was met ever so sweetly by the head of Levein whose effort flew past Goram, thanks in no small part to Robertson's deft shimmy to allow the ball to sail in. This was the cue for yet more trouble on the terraces although, thankfully, the game wasn't held up this time.

It was, in truth, a scrappy match but Hearts were well in control. Gary Mackay was dominant in midfield with Robertson a thorn in the Hibs defence – as he always was. Wayne Foster's pace also troubled the Hibs rearguard and it was no surprise when Hearts scored a third goal on the stroke of half-time.

The hard-working John Colquhoun released Foster on the right wing with a peach of a pass. Foster delivered a brilliant cross into the Hibs penalty box where Robertson headed home with much glee – and much to the home supporters' disgust. Half-time arrived with Hearts three goals ahead and there were more ugly scenes as fans spilled on to the pitch once more.

There endeth the scoring – and most of the action. Hearts had secured a much-needed and richly deserved two points. There wasn't a great deal of football played, and one might argue that this game should not be included in *Hearts' 50 Greatest Games*. However, I have included it, not for the quality of the football on display, but for the circumstances behind such an emphatic win. Rarely has an Edinburgh derby been played in such a torrid atmosphere. Hearts showed they feared no one, certainly not the louts who ran on to the pitch with the intent of causing trouble. Sandy Clark's men ignored the frenzied pre-match hype and got on with at least trying to play football.

During a troubled afternoon off the pitch, Lothian & Borders Police, who said they were "extremely disappointed and concerned" about the fans' behaviour, arrested 36 people. After the game, the Scottish League promised an enquiry. As usual, the enquiry didn't do very much.

The first Edinburgh derby after Wallace Mercer's aborted takeover of Hearts' city rivals was always going to be a fraught one, but it was one that maintained Hearts' dominance over Hibs that had lasted nearly a decade. When the dust had settled, Hearts were on their way back up the league.

28 v Dnieper 3-1
Uefa Cup First Round Second Leg
3rd October 1990. Tynecastle

Hearts:	Dnieper:
Smith	Horodov
McLaren	Yudin
McKinlay	Gueraschenko
Levein	Sidelnikov
Kirkwood	Bezhenar
McPherson	Kudritsky
Colquhoun	Bagmut
Wright	Mamchur
Robertson	Son
I Ferguson	Hudymenko
Bannon	Shakhov

Referee: E Halle (Norway)

ORMER SCOTLAND international Joe Jordan was the surprise choice as the man to replace Alex MacDonald as Hearts manager. One of the best strikers ever to play for Scotland, Jordan had been manager at Bristol City where his impressive style of management had not gone unnoticed by bigger clubs. Indeed, Jordan had turned down the opportunity to manage Aston Villa just months earlier, so his appointment at Tynecastle was seen as a real coup.

Although Jordan had no previous link with Hearts – unusually for a Gorgie boss – it was clear that chairman Wallace Mercer had looked at Ibrox, where Graeme Souness had transformed Rangers, and thought Jordan could emulate his international team-mate. The difference was that Souness was given a blank chequebook – Jordan would have very little money as Hearts' finances worsened.

On paper, Hearts looked a strong team. With the much heralded defensive pairing of Craig Levein and Dave McPherson at last playing alongside each other for a decent run of games, the influential Derek Ferguson in midfield and the goalscoring prowess of John Robertson up front, Hearts looked good enough to give any team a run for their money.

However, the full-back positions were a worry, with neither George Wright nor Jimmy Sandison having the consistency to make those positions their own. In midfield, it seemed too much was expected of Ferguson, who found it difficult to gel with Gary Mackay and Davie Kirkwood, while up front, far too much was expected of Robertson.

Two years after their memorable run that took them to the quarter-final, Hearts were also looking forward to another run in the Uefa Cup. I quite fancied making a journey to the continent to see Hearts play in Europe – at this point, I hadn't done so before. However, my heart sank when the draw was made, when I saw Hearts paired with Dnieper Dnepropetrovsk. It was the era of glasnost and the Soviet Union was about to come to an end but I still didn't fancy a trip to a club who played just a few miles from the site of the Chernobyl nuclear disaster in 1986.

On 19th September, in the first leg 'behind the iron curtain', Hearts produced a marvellous display and secured a 1-1 draw with, inevitably, Robertson scoring the crucial away goal. Nearly 19,000 Jambos packed Tynecastle a fortnight later to see Hearts try to finish the job. They weren't to be disappointed.

The return of McPherson to the side – Big Slim had missed the first leg through suspension – was welcome, while European veteran Eammon Bannon was encouraged to make as many forward runs as possible and to deliver telling passes to Robertson and Iain Ferguson. There was a feeling that the pair were too similar in style to play effectively together but they fairly rumbled the visitors on a memorable October evening.

The game kicked off with the big crowd urging Hearts to glory and within seconds of the start, a brilliant piece of skill by Robertson seemed to light the blue touch paper. He dummied a through ball from Tosh McKinlay that let Iain Ferguson through. The former Dundee United striker lashed the ball beyond keeper Horodov to seemingly give Hearts a dream start. However, the linesman on the stand side dampened celebrations by signalling for offside and Dnieper were let off the hook. It was a close call, as Ferguson seemed onside to most onlookers.

Thereafter, Hearts began to look a bit unsure of themselves. The 1-1 draw in Ukraine meant a goalless game in Gorgie would be enough to secure Hearts' place in the second round and the Maroons seemed to be in two minds as to whether to go on the offensive or play it tight. Dnieper sensed Hearts' unease and looked menacing on the counter-attack. Sidelnikov forced Henry Smith into making a couple of saves and it was clear Hearts still had work to do to ensure their progression in the competition.

George Wright was being encouraged to get forward as often as possible and he had a chance after 15 minutes, when he found himself with time and space on the edge of the Dnieper penalty box. However, Wright's effort sailed high into the packed Tynecastle terracings. Jordan signalled to McPherson that he wanted to use the defender's height in attack to unsettle Dnieper's defence and the visitors found the former Rangers man a handful.

After 20 minutes, Hearts were awarded a free kick on the edge of the penalty box. McKinlay, an astute crosser of the ball, delivered a fine ball into the danger area where confusion reigned among the Dnieper defenders. Keeper Horodov completely missed the cross but McPherson didn't and produced a superb diving header to put Hearts in front both on the night and on aggregate.

Two minutes later, Hearts came forward again. John Colquhoun crossed from the right towards Iain Ferguson who managed to flick the ball on to Robertson. As Robertson was about to pull the trigger he was pushed off the ball by Gueraschenko and the Norwegian referee had no hesitation in pointing to the penalty spot. Robertson picked himself up and fired his penalty past Horodov to put Hearts 2-0 ahead and a step closer to the second round.

Dnieper seemed to lose the plot for a brief spell after this and Hearts did their best to capitalise on their indiscipline. There was almost a third goal when Horodov fumbled the ball but Davie Kirkwood's eagerness to punish this error saw him lunge in and he was booked for fouling the Dnieper custodian.

The Maroons' game-plan then suffered a setback after 35 minutes, when Wright hobbled off injured. However, his replacement was a Tynecastle legend – Gary Mackay. The midfield player, a Hearts fanatic as well as long serving player – would ensure the Maroons kept their focus. Henry Smith was thankfully keeping his, when he produced a stunning save from Shakhov to keep the score at 2-0.

However, with just four minutes until the break Dnieper got the breakthrough few could grudge them. McKinlay fouled Bagmut and now it was Dnieper's turn for a penalty kick. Shakhov beat Smith from the spot – the first goal Smith had conceded at Tynecastle in European competition in over 400 minutes – and the tie was back in the melting pot again. But not for long!

Hearts immediately raced to the other end of the park and forced a corner. Colquhoun's cross was headed towards goal by Alan McLaren for Robertson to nod past Horodov. As the half-time whistle blew, Hearts were, remarkably, 3-1 ahead on the night, 4-2 on aggregate.

It was all or nothing for Dnieper in the second half and there were some anxious moments, particularly when Kudritsky's effort flew just inches over the crossbar and Hudymenko was denied by the alertness of Smith, who dived at the forward's feet. Hearts, though, weren't averse to trying to secure the fourth goal that would put the tie beyond the Soviets and Horodov, who seemed to go down in instalments, eventually saved a shot from Iain Ferguson.

Colquhoun's effort towards the end of the game was also close to settling things but it seemed Dnieper, sensing the tie ebbing away from them, had resorted to some tough tackling. Colquhoun and Ferguson were the victims of some crude challenges, but despite this, Hearts saw the game out and there were no further goals. Hearts won 3-1 to go through 4-2 on aggregate and it was one of the more impressive European results for the Gorgie Boys.

Along with 19,000 other Jambos, I celebrated and waited for the Uefa Cup second round draw to be made. I quite fancied a trip to Milan, Roma, Lisbon or Monaco but knowing Hearts' luck, I crossed my fingers in the hope we weren't faced with a trip to Katowice or Moscow. In the event, Hearts did receive a decent draw – Serie A side Bologna. The Italians were not perhaps in the same class as the Milan clubs or Juventus, but the fact they had finished high enough up the Italian league the previous season to qualify for the Uefa Cup told its own story. As luck would have it, I had just started a new job in the autumn of 1990, so my plans to follow Hearts in Europe were put on hold. With the first leg against the Italians being in Gorgie, the importance of Hearts getting a win to take over to Italy was crucial. What happened was one of the most bizarre games in Hearts' European history.

John Robertson missed the game through injury, which meant Hearts relied on a forward trio of Wayne Foster, Iain Ferguson and John Colquhoun. The surprise for me was seeing record signing Derek Ferguson on the substitutes' bench with Davie Kirkwood retaining his midfield role. I thought Ferguson, a sublime talent who was never given a chance by Graeme Souness at Rangers, would be ideal to play against the Italians but manager Joe Jordan saw it differently. And, after a stunning first-half performance, it was clear the Hearts boss was correct.

Hearts produced one of their finest performances in European competition and hit three magnificent first-half goals to leave the stunned Italians 3-0 down at the interval. Foster scored twice and Iain Ferguson added his customary European goal and the Tynecastle crowd of 11,000 stood transfixed at half-time after a breathless performance from the Maroons.

The fact the size of the attendance was a good bit down on the previous round was due to the club's insistence on hiking admission prices. Bologna may have been in the top half of Serie A, but they weren't box office and many fans decided against shelling out £10 for a ticket, feeling they were being shafted just once too often.

Scotland boss Andy Roxburgh was in the Tynecastle stand (although whether he forked out a tenner is unclear) and he was mightily impressed – as we all were – with Hearts' first-half performance. Another goal or two and they could surely assume they would be in the draw for the third round. After all, they could easily have been five goals ahead at half-time. However, this is Hearts we're talking about. A club that snatches defeat from the jaws of victory on an alarmingly regular basis.

Bologna's forays into the Hearts half were few and far between, even as the second half began. As keeper Smith prepared to launch another ball downfield towards Ferguson and co. the time it took him to do so was deemed too long by the referee, who thought our Henry was time wasting and so promptly awarded a free kick to Bologna on the edge of the Hearts penalty box.

You know what happened next. Bologna scored, secured a crucial away goal and a game that Hearts should have had wrapped up by half-time was now back in the balance. The Maroons looked stunned by this unexpected turn of events and the final score of Hearts 3 Bologna 1 was scarcely believable. Inevitably, Hearts' trip to Italy a fortnight later ended in despair. Bologna turned the tables and won even more easily than the 3-0 scoreline suggested – Hearts were out of the Uefa Cup on a 4-3 aggregate.

It was a bad season for Hearts in the cups. As well as losing 3-0 to Aberdeen in the League Cup, they went out of the Scottish Cup at the first hurdle to First Division side Airdrieonians – now managed by former Heart Jimmy Bone. A fifth-placed finish in the Premier Division was quite respectable for the Maroons given all they had gone through in season 1990/91 – a rollercoaster ride if ever there was one!

v Celtic 3-1

B&Q Premier Division
16th November 1991. Tynecastle

Hearts:	Celtic:
Smith	Bonner
McLaren	McNally
McKinlay	Galloway
Levein	Creaney
Mackay	Mowbray
McPherson	Gillespie
Crabbe	O'Neil
D Ferguson	McStay
Baird	Coyne
Millar	Nicholas
Robertson	Collins

Referee: A Roy (Aberdeen)

THE 1991/92 season would be Joe Jordan's first full one in charge of Hearts and the one he would be best judged on. It was clear the former Manchester United star wanted to exert his own influence on a team that had been managed by Alex MacDonald for ten years and whose loyalty to some players perhaps meant there was complacency among some players about their place in the first team.

With chairman Wallace Mercer's backing, Jordan brought several new players to Tynecastle in the summer of 1991. Using his considerable contacts in England, Jordan paid £350,000 to Middlesbrough for the services of striker Ian Baird, a former Leeds United player, and £200,000 to Portsmouth for former Manchester United defender Graeme Hogg. He also brought in winger Steve Penney on a free transfer from Brighton & Hove Albion and midfielder Glyn Snodin, also on a free transfer, from Leeds United.

In October 1991, an era when there wasn't a window period restricting transfers, Jordan paid £100,000 to Raith Rovers for another striker – another Ian Ferguson. While the Hearts team was changing, the nucleus of the 1980s side – Henry Smith, Craig Levein, Gary Mackay and John Robertson – was still there. A decade after three of them made their Hearts debuts, they were no longer the promising youngsters upon so much rested. They were now experienced campaigners – with all four of them now full Scotland internationals.

There was the usual optimism as the 1991/92 season kicked off – but this time it was justified as Jordan's men made a highly impressive start. Hearts' league campaign began, rather unusually, with two away fixtures – a 2-1 win at Dunfermline Athletic followed up by a 3-2 win over Airdrieonians, who were now managed by Alex MacDonald and whose side contained former Jambos Walter Kidd, Jimmy Sandison, Sandy Stewart and Davie Kirkwood.

When Hearts defeated league champions Rangers the following week at Tynecastle – Scott Crabbe's first-minute goal deceiving Gers keeper Andy Goram – the Maroons sat joint top of the Premier Division alongside Celtic and Aberdeen. By the end of September, Hearts were still unbeaten and out on their own at the top of the league, with Jambos everywhere beginning to believe the new era under Jordan would finally see success arrive at Tynecastle.

Hearts' first league defeat came at Celtic Park with a 3-1 defeat on 5th October, but they were still at the top when the Hoops made the return trip to Scotland's capital city five weeks before Christmas. Of course, it was far too early to be called a title decider – particularly as Celtic weren't even in second place, they were third behind Rangers – but the game was seen as a true test of Hearts' league championship credentials. A crowd of over 22,500 swarmed to Tynecastle on a November afternoon to see one of the games of the season.

Hearts began the game strongly, with former Rangers midfield maestro Derek Ferguson orchestrating the midfield alongside seasoned campaigner Gary Mackay and the ball-tackling skills of John Millar. However, despite a couple of early chances for striker Baird – affectionately nicknamed "Yogi" by the home support – and Robertson, it was Celtic who took the lead after just 15 minutes with a somewhat fortuitous goal.

McStay's somewhat wayward pass towards the Hearts penalty box took a deflection off striker Coyne and the ball spun away from home keeper Henry Smith to give the visitors an early lead. It was tough on Hearts but urged on by the huge home support, they tried to force their way back into the game.

Striker Baird's big, bustling physical presence was clearly rattling the visiting defence, in particular, his former Middlesbrough team-mate Tony Mowbray. Fellow strikers Robertson and Scott Crabbe applied the more delicate touches and Hearts would switch from the direct long ball style to a more intricate passing move that had Celtic at full stretch.

However, it wasn't all one-way traffic. Celtic, with striker Charlie Nicholas back in their ranks following his sojourn with Arsenal and brief spell at Aberdeen, threatened to score on more than one occasion. Former Hearts player Mike Galloway, now wearing the green and white hoops, was also a thorn in the Hearts side. At half-time, Hearts remained a goal behind but they headed for the dressing room with the loud cheers of their fans in their ears – it had been a pulsating first half. However, it was nothing compared to the second 45 minutes!

Just minutes after the restart came the defining moment of the game. After neat build-up play, Celtic's Nicholas set up Coyne whose superb header was about to fly into the net to put the Celts two goals ahead until Smith produced a quite magnificent one-handed save from near point blank range to tip the ball past the post for a corner. The Hearts fans were in raptures and Tynecastle rocked with applause from the home support. The Celtic fans on the Gorgie Road terracing behind the goal where the save took place could only howl in anguish. Coyne held his head in his hands and looked towards the black November sky.

It was a stupendous save, one of the best ever seen at Tynecastle and one likened by many to the one a certain England goalkeeper made in the 1970 World Cup finals against Brazil. Alex Cameron of the *Daily Record* wrote: "It was a save which qualified

Smith for the Olympic gymnastics team." It turned the game – for moments later, far from being 2-0 down, Hearts were level.

Ten minutes into the second half, Tosh McKinlay delivered a Hearts free kick into the Celtic penalty box. Home defender Dave McPherson used his height to knock the ball down where the on rushing George Wright drilled it into the net past Bonner. The Celtic defenders claimed Wright was offside but referee Sandy Roy was having none of it.

Buoyed by such a start to the second half, Hearts continued to surge forward and six minutes later, astonishingly, were 2-1 ahead. Again, McKinlay was the instigator with a corner that fell kindly to Craig Levein. The big defender fired the ball past Bonner, who complained vociferously that he was fouled – but no one, least of all referee Roy, was listening. Tynecastle erupted. While the atmosphere had been electric since kick-off – it usually is when the Old Firm come calling to Gorgie – there was now a deafening blast of noise.

With 12 minutes left, Celtic were swarming around the Hearts goal in desperate search of an equaliser. Then McPherson broke away and linked up with Robertson. After some fine work by Robertson, the ball broke in the Celtic penalty area for Scott Crabbe, who gleefully tucked away Hearts' third goal – and the one that clinched the points for a delirious home side.

When the full-time whistle blew, it was 3-1 to Hearts and the joyous scenes among the Hearts support was a sign they truly believed this side was ready to mount a serious challenge for the league championship for the first time since the heart-breaking season of 1985/86.

It was a hugely entertaining game. Afterwards, Joe Jordan said his players had learnt their lessons of the corresponding fixture at Celtic Park, when it finished 3-1 to Celtic, by cutting out the mistakes they had made that afternoon. Even Celtic's manager, the former Arsenal and Republic of Ireland player Liam Brady, said the better team won.

Hearts followed up this impressive victory with two more impressive results, by winning 2-0 at Aberdeen and 1-0 at Dundee United in the week that followed. Thus, in the space of seven days, Hearts had defeated the three teams who dominated Scottish football in the 1980s. Was it Hearts' turn to rule the roost? It might have been had Rangers not had a blank chequebook with which to rectify such matters.

Hearts continued in impressive form, although they were held to a 1-1 draw by Falkirk – managed by former Hearts stalwart Jim Jefferies – at Tynecastle at the beginning of December. Three days after Christmas, Hearts cruised to a 5-0 win at St Johnstone to continue their highly impressive form away from home. That result maintained Hearts' two-point lead over Rangers at the top of the Premier Division – and both Hearts and Rangers had pulled well clear of the others, with Joe Jordan's side an astonishing ten points clear of third-placed Celtic, at a time when there were still just two points given for a league win.

On the first Saturday of January 1992, Hearts headed for Celtic Park and recorded a 2-1 win thanks to goals from Scott Crabbe and John Millar. This killed Celtic's faint hopes of winning the title and the battle for the league championship was now confirmed as a two-horse race between Hearts and Rangers.

Hearts fans could scarcely believe it. Could their team go one better than the one that went so close to glory under Alex MacDonald and keep their nerve? The question was answered the following week when Aberdeen came to Tynecastle. Inspired by youngster Eoin Jess who hit a double, the Dons cantered to a 4-0 win that didn't just stop Hearts' title challenge express in its tracks, it derailed the bid completely. It was reported that some Hearts players suffered from a stomach bug before the game, which may have explained their lethargic performance, but the effect of such a devastating loss – Hearts' first defeat in the league for four months – was cataclysmic.

The following week, Hearts lost 2-1 at Airdrieonians, much to the delight of the Diamonds boss. This meant Rangers' visit to Tynecastle on 1st February 1992 was vitally important. Just two points separated the teams at the top of the league and more than 24,000 packed into Tynecastle for a game that would have a huge bearing on the destiny of the league flag. A second-half strike from Rangers' Ally McCoist was the only goal of the game and meant Hearts fell four points behind the money-laden Glasgow giants – a gap that would not be closed.

Ironically, it was Celtic who snuffed out the dying embers of Hearts' championship hopes when they exacted revenge by winning 2-1 at Tynecastle on 29th February. The Maroons did end the season as runners-up in the league but they finished nine points behind champions Rangers and only one ahead of Celtic.

Sadly, Hearts' impressive league form did not transfer to the cup competitions. After defeating Clydebank and Hamilton Academical in the League Cup, Hearts lost a Tynecastle quarter-final 1-0 to Rangers. In the Scottish Cup, Hearts needed a Tynecastle replay to defeat St Mirren 3-0 – John Robertson scoring a hat-trick – before defeating Dunfermline Athletic and Falkirk.

When Hearts avoided Celtic in the semi-final draw and were paired with Airdrieonians, the fans were jubilant – just the draw they wanted, conveniently forgetting the Diamonds had already beaten Hearts in the league. The two teams fought out a quite awful goalless draw at Hampden so reconvened at the national stadium ten days later for the replay. This was another awful game and one that had an awful ending for Hearts as Airdrieonians won a penalty shoot-out after the teams were tied at 1-1 after extra time.

A crushingly disappointing end to a season that had promised so much – and as that 3-1 triumph over Celtic in November proved, it was yet another case of what might have been for Hearts.

v Slavia Prague 4-2

Uefa Cup First Round Second Leg
30th September 1992. Tynecastle

Hearts:	Slavia Prague:
Smith	Janos
Hogg	Petrous
McKinlay	Suchoparek
Mackay	Silhavy
Levein	Jurasko
Van de Ven	Tatarcuk
Robertson	Binic
McLaren	Penicka
Baird	Kuka
Snodin	Necas
Bannon	Lerch

Referee: R Larsson (Sweden)

THE JOE JORDAN era at Tynecastle faced its sternest test yet as the 1992/93 season got underway. The honeymoon period was well and truly over. At the end of Jordan's first full season in charge – 1991/92 – Hearts had finished as runners-up to Rangers in the Premier League. However, some fans of the maroon persuasion weren't entirely happy, despite Hearts' league standing looking better than it had done for five years.

Jordan had adopted a more cautious approach than his predecessor had and the fans didn't take an immediate shine to some of the players he brought in during the summer of 1992. Midfielder Ally Mauchlen played in the same Motherwell team as Gary McAllister some ten years before and was small in stature – but some of his "tackles" made you wince. Full-back Tommy Wilson arrived on a free transfer from Dunfermline Athletic and Dutchman Peter Van de Ven cost £90,000 from Aberdeen.

Hearts' second-placed finish in the Premier League in 1992 meant another tilt at the Uefa Cup. The Maroons' first round opponents were Slavia Prague. The Czechs weren't the biggest name in European football – but then again, neither were Hearts. However, Jordan was doubtless happy to avoid Real Madrid, Juventus, Manchester United, Roma and Benfica – can you imagine those teams in today's Europa League?

The Hearts manager was also happy that the first leg was played in Prague and Hearts defended resiliently on a balmy September evening, conceding the only goal of the game five minutes from the end, in front of a paltry crowd of less than 5,000. They couldn't secure the away goal that would make life so much easier for the return leg but, a fortnight later, a crowd of over 16,000 headed for Gorgie – and another memorable European night for the JTs.

The big crowd received a boost as the teams warmed up. For, doing strenuous exercises was Alan McLaren, a defender who had blossomed into one of the most talented in Scotland. McLaren had made his Scotland debut that summer against the USA and Canada and, with added responsibility following the departure of Dave McPherson back to Rangers, it was clear the youngster had a big future in the game. McLaren had missed the previous seven games – including the first leg in Prague – due to injury and his return to the Hearts team was a welcome sight.

Interestingly, McLaren was deployed in a ball-winning role in midfield with Hogg and Van de Ven the central defensive partnership. Slavia Prague fancied their chances after winning the first leg, and listed among their substitutes was 18-year-old Patrick Berger, of whom great things were expected.

The game kicked off with typical fervour from a noisy Hearts support but the Czechs showed they weren't going to be intimidated, with barely legal tackles going in on John Robertson and Hogg in the opening few minutes. Silhavy, in particular, could well have caused Robertson serious injury but he escaped punishment, a decision he would take advantage of soon after.

Hearts seized the initiative though, and while Jordan had appealed to the fans to be patient, reasoning that even a goal in the last minute would be enough to force extra time, the Maroons opened the scoring after just ten minutes. It was a night that Gary Mackay, given a free role in midfield thanks to McLaren's ball-winning responsibilities, revelled in. He delivered a fine pass to Iain Baird who fed Glyn Snodin. The Englishman fed a through ball for Robertson to set up Mackay, who had maintained his run.

The Scotland midfield man appeared to stumble as he was about to pull the trigger but he maintained enough composure to fire in a shot from just inside the penalty box past keeper Janos and into the net to put Hearts a goal ahead on the night and level the aggregate scores.

The Czechs were rattled, their game-plan of frustrating Hearts scuppered just minutes into the game. Midfielder Tatarcuk appeared to have been shot by a sniper in the tenements on Gorgie Road – as no one else was near him when he fell to the ground, it seemed to be the only explanation – and, remarkably, the Swedish referee stopped play while the Prague player received treatment. What for exactly, was far from clear and the Hearts fans made their irritation known in no uncertain terms. Irritation that turned close to hostility when the player was allowed treatment on the pitch, thereby holding the game up for several minutes.

If Slavia's ploy was to distract Hearts after their excellent start, then it worked. After 15 minutes, they forced their first corner of the game. Necas swung the ball over and found the aforementioned Silhavy, who flicked it past a startled Henry Smith to level the score on the night. Hearts fans' worst fears were realised – the away goal meant their heroes now had to score two more goals to avoid going out in the first round.

Nevertheless, roared on by the crowd, Hearts refused to throw in the towel. Six minutes later, Eammon Bannon belied his advancing footballing years with a powerful run, which took him from defence towards his forwards. Robertson took a pass from his balding team-mate, returning it down the right wing for Bannon to swing in a superb cross into the Slavia penalty box. Rising, as if a phoenix, was Baird who bulleted a header past Janos to put Hearts back in front. Hearts still required another goal but there was time aplenty to get the crucial third strike.

As half-time approached, tension rose in both camps with Penicka, having committed foul after foul all evening, at last getting his name entered in the referee's notebook. Almost as if to redress the balance, however, Tosh McKinlay then found himself booked for the heinous crime of stealing a yard at a throw-in.

However, with two minutes until the break, Tynecastle roared again, when Craig Levein superbly headed Bannon's corner kick home. Hearts went in at half-time 3-1 ahead on the night, 3-2 up on aggregate, but knowing the Czechs just needed to score again to tilt the tie back in their favour.

The brutal nature of Slavia's game was starkly illustrated when the second half got underway. Silhavy, the Czechs' self-proclaimed hard-man, lunged in, not once, but twice on Robertson. Both were 'challenges' off the ball and both were missed by a Swedish referee who was in danger of losing the plot. A belief underlined when Tatarcuk launched a scything tackle on Baird – only for referee Larsson to send Penicka packing from the field. Mistaken identity it may have been, but there was little doubt Slavia deserved to be down to ten men as the Hearts players were in danger of receiving serious injury. Hearts were on top, but the inevitable sucker punch duly arrived with 25 minutes left. A tiring Alan McLaren left the field to be replaced by Tommy Wilson and as the Hearts defence reorganised, Slavia moved forward. Necas delivered the perfect through ball to Kuka who lobbed keeper Henry Smith to make the score 3-3 on aggregate – but with the Czechs having two vital away goals.

However, the most dramatic moment of the night was still to come. With little over ten minutes left, and Hearts facing yet another European knockout on the away goals rule, the Maroons were awarded a free kick 30 yards from goal. With Baird and Robertson jostling in the penalty box, the Slavia defenders had their hands full to keep the strikers at bay. They didn't reckon on the diminutive figure of Glyn Snodin, who ran like an express train to the dead ball and smacked it as hard as he could. From 30 yards out, the ball soared past the despairing Slavia defensive wall and into the roof of the net.

Tynecastle erupted! It was a goal worthy of winning the Uefa Cup itself and Snodin was engulfed by delirious team-mates as Hearts moved ahead decisively on aggregate. The gamed ended Hearts 4 Slavia Prague 2 and another famous European night at Tynecastle entered Gorgie folklore.

The game was one of the few highlights of what was a curious season for Hearts. Joe Jordan continued to add to his squad but some of the fans questioned some of his signings. They were happy enough with Jordan's signing of Peter Van de Ven from Aberdeen, but wondered why the man who was an integral part of the Dons team was being played in central defence. Van de Ven was, like many Dutch players, adept at playing in more than one position, but his impressive displays for Aberdeen had been in midfield.

In October, there was a more audible reaction from Hearts supporters. Local hero Scott Crabbe was a dyed-in-the-wool Jambo as well as a goalscorer of some note. Dundee United had expressed an interest in taking him to Tayside and while Jordan accepted their offer, Crabbe told the manager he didn't want to go. His allegiance to Hearts was greater than his need for regular first-team football but it was clear to Crabbe that Jordan didn't have him in his plans. Reluctantly, he agreed to move to

Tannadice in a move that saw Hearts receive £215,000 and winger Allan Preston, a player who rarely featured in Dundee United's first team.

It was a deal that alienated some of the Hearts support and Preston made his debut in a lacklustre 1-1 draw with St Johnstone at Tynecastle – before being replaced by Eammon Bannon. The attendance of less than 8,000 was another worrying sign that all was not well in Gorgie.

Preston did make an impact in his next game by scoring in a 1-1 draw at Celtic Park but the Maroons were struggling to score goals. Hearts' next opponents in the Uefa Cup were Standard Liege and Hearts' performances and results against the Belgians – 1-0 defeats at Tynecastle and in Liege – seemed to sum up the season. One couldn't escape the feeling Hearts were regressing rather than progressing.

At the end of November, Hearts headed to Pittodrie and produced their worst performance of the season so far, as Aberdeen handed out a 6-2 thrashing. Defeats by Falkirk and Airdrieonians then followed and the unrest on the terracing increased. Hearts remained in the top half of the Premier Division but performances were far from convincing. By April, they were 20 points behind league leaders Celtic and the season was fizzling out.

After successive defeats from Rangers, Aberdeen and Motherwell, Hearts made the short trip to Brockville Park on 1st May 1993 to face Jim Jefferies' soon to be relegated Falkirk. Hearts lost 6-0. It was the end of the line for Joe Jordan, who was sacked two days later amid rumours some of the Hearts players didn't want to play for him.

Hearts ended the season in fifth place in the Premier Division. The Old Firm put paid to any hopes in the domestic cups, with Celtic defeating Hearts at Tynecastle in the League Cup and Rangers inflicting yet more Scottish Cup semi-final heartache on the Maroons by winning 2-1 at Celtic Park.

At the end of the season, Hearts were looking for another manager. The gamble on Joe Jordan had not worked – increasing the pressure on Wallace Mercer to get his next appointment right.

v Hibernian 2-1

Tennents Scottish Cup Fourth Round
20th February 1994. Easter Road

Hearts:

Smith
McLaren
McKinlay
Levein
Berry
Millar
Colquhoun
Mackay
Robertson
M Johnston
Leitch

Hibernian:

Leighton
Miller
Beaumont
Farrell
Tweed
Lennon
McAllister
Hamilton
Wright
Jackson
O'Neill

Referee: L Mottram (Forth)

JUST AS he did when Alex MacDonald left in 1990 and Hearts sought a replacement manager, coach Sandy Clark stepped into the breach following the departure of Joe Jordan from Tynecastle at the end of the 1992/93 season.

As a player, Clark was one of Tynecastle's favourite sons and while he didn't have extensive experience as a manager – he had a less than productive year in charge of Partick Thistle – his permanent appointment as Hearts manager in the summer of 1993 was well received by the majority of supporters.

Clark knew what was required to play for Hearts and knew what the club meant to the fans. However, he also knew there would be no money to spend on new players. Following the Hillsborough disaster in 1989 and the tragic loss of life, the Taylor Report came into effect, which meant top-flight clubs in the United Kingdom had to have all-seated stadia. Tynecastle would not be exempt – meaning the old terraces would have to be replaced by shiny new stands – naturally, at a considerable cost.

The days of Hearts shelling out £750k for a player – however brief – were now at an end, and Clark had to resort to the format used by MacDonald of wheeling and dealing for bargains.

Clark had been coaching the youth players at Tynecastle – with considerable success. Hearts had lifted the BP Youth Cup, a prestigious national competition and the Tynecastle youth system was widely seen as one of the best in Scotland. Clark's intention was to blood some of these youngsters such as striker Kevin Thomas, winger Allan Johnston and defender Gary Locke. Jordan had given Thomas his debut in February, while Johnston and Locke were given their first-team debuts by Clark at the end of the 1992/93 season after Jordan had left Tynecastle.

With Hearts having to fund the redevelopment of Tynecastle, Clark had little choice but to turn to his successful youth team. However, no one had to tell him those youngsters would require experienced heads to help them progress – just as Clark himself had done with John Robertson in 1984. Even so, the arrival of striker Justin Fashanu at Tynecastle in July 1993 raised more than a few eyebrows.

Fashanu was a controversial character off the field, with a lifestyle that seemed to be meat and drink to the tabloid press, with tales of exploits with television soap stars and the like. At the beginning of his career, Fashanu was a rising star with Norwich City and he scored a memorable goal for the Canaries against Liverpool in 1980 that resulted in him getting the goal of the season award from the BBC's *Match of the Day* viewers.

Nottingham Forest manager Brian Clough was sufficiently impressed to part with a million pounds to take Fashanu to the City Ground, but this proved to be one of Clough's less successful transfers. Things didn't work out for Fashanu and whether it was down to his lifestyle or just bad luck, the striker drifted from club to club, drifting down the lower leagues before ending up at Torquay United.

It was then that the call came from Scotland – ironically, from Alex MacDonald at Airdrieonians, who took the big man to Broomfield. After the Diamonds got relegated, Fashanu had a brief spell in Swedish football before signing for Hearts in July 1993. Sandy Clark saw "Fash the Bash", as some fans called him, as the ideal man to pass on his experience to the young strikers at Tynecastle.

What little money Clark did have, he spent on one player – centre-half Jim Weir, who was bought from Hamilton Academical for £300,000. Weir was likened to former Scotland centre-half Gordon McQueen but more likely as a result of his physical similarity rather than style of football. However, as Weir had been courted by Celtic and teams from England, his signing was seen as something of a coup for Hearts.

After losing their opening Premier Division game 2-1 to Rangers at Ibrox, Hearts began the season in decent enough form, although there was concern at the lack of firepower. Fashanu was popular with the fans but he didn't score until early September in a 2-1 win over Partick Thistle – and then proceeded to get himself sent off for elbowing a Thistle player. It was clear he wasn't going to be a prolific scorer. Hearts then failed to score in a home League Cup tie with Jim Jefferies' Falkirk, who won 1-0.

Hearts were involved in the Uefa Cup once more, but they were given a tough draw against Spanish aces Atletico Madrid. Hearts had struggled to score goals, but when they went 2-0 up against the Spaniards in the first leg at Tynecastle, there was hope the corner had been turned. However, they conceded a crucial away goal and lost the return in Madrid 3-0 a fortnight later, to crash out 4-2 on aggregate.

Hearts' lack of goals continued to be a concern, as was the fact they were in the bottom half of the league. However, as he had done with the signing of Fashanu, manager Sandy Clark pulled a rabbit out the hat with another remarkable signing in October. Striker Maurice Johnston hit the headlines in 1989 when he was paraded as Celtic's new signing – before joining arch-rivals Rangers a few weeks later. After his spell at Ibrox, Johnston signed for Everton for £1m in 1991. Now, incredibly, he was available on a free transfer and despite numerous offers, opted to accept Clark's approach to come to Tynecastle. Astonishingly, Hearts now had two strikers who each cost £1m at some stage in their careers. However, like Fashanu, Johnston wasn't as prolific as some Hearts fans had hoped for.

Results continued to be patchy. However, two days after Christmas, a John Robertson penalty in the 93rd minute secured a 2-2 draw against Rangers at Ibrox. When the Scottish Cup began in January 1994, Hearts were given a tricky away tie at Partick Thistle. Johnston scored the only goal of the game against the team with which he had started his career and, on the way back to Edinburgh, we listened on the radio for the fourth round draw. When it came, we punched the air with delight – Hearts had been drawn against Hibs at Easter Road.

Now you may have noticed, dear reader, there's a theme in this book that indicates that Hearts, no matter how poorly they are playing, usually do quite well against their city rivals. Therefore, we headed for Easter Road on a cold Sunday afternoon in February – the game had been chosen for live television coverage – in our usual expectant mood whenever Hearts play Hibs.

Just under 21,000 fans created the usual frenetic Edinburgh derby atmosphere but as this was a Scottish Cup tie, there was more of an edge than usual. Hibs were enjoying a better season than their bigger city rivals were – but against this, was the fact that Hearts had gone a remarkable 20 games against Hibs without tasting defeat. Fashanu wasn't available for selection – but the Hammer of the Hibs, John Robertson, was. Robertson took his place alongside Johnston.

Given the importance of the occasion and Hearts' less than impressive scoring record that season, there was an astonishing start to the game. Just two minutes had been played when John Colquhoun played a ball out wide to Tosh McKinlay. The former Dundee man skipped past Miller before cutting the ball back in the Hibs penalty box. Inevitably the player who was first to react was Robertson and the wee man fired the ball into the net beyond keeper Leighton to give Hearts a sensational early lead.

Thereafter, Hibs threatened with winger McAllister causing problems for the Hearts defence with his trickery. However, it was doubtful if there was a better defensive partnership in Scotland than Alan McLaren and Craig Levein and with Neil Berry playing just behind in the sweeper role, the Hearts defence coped well with what Hibs could throw at them.

Hearts weren't averse to attacking either, with the experienced Johns – Colquhoun and Robertson – causing danger for the home team whenever they got the ball. While Johnston was well policed by the home defence, the Hibs players knew the danger of paying too much attention to "Super Mo" was to give Robertson that wee bit more freedom.

It was a tough first half, as one might expect from an Edinburgh derby Scottish Cup tie and some of the bone-crunching tackles would have made lesser mortals wince.

Just as Hearts looked like they would be heading in at the interval a goal to the good, Hibs equalised three minutes before the break. O'Neill delivered a cross into the Hearts penalty box. Inexplicably, Hibs striker Wright was left unchallenged to head home the equaliser, and now it was the turn of the home fans to celebrate.

Moments later, Alan McLaren was booked for a nasty foul on Jackson and as the Hearts defender gestured vehemently at the Hibs player as he lay on the ground, the fear among the more cautious Hearts supporters – that's most of us incidentally – was that McLaren would be sent off. He was clearly angered by the loss of the goal but thankfully, he managed to keep his cool – though the tempo of the game, already high, had risen to dangerous levels. When McAllister hit the post when it seemed easier to score, there was little doubt Hearts were relieved to hear the half-time whistle with the game still level.

The second half continued in the same, almost brutal, fashion with chances becoming few and far between. Given Hearts' lack of punch in front of goal this season, Sandy Clark's decision to replace Robertson with Wayne Foster with 25 minutes left baffled most of us on the terracing. Was Clark settling for a replay at Tynecastle? We hoped not. As the game raged on, there were just three minutes left when it seemed both sides had indeed settled for that.

Then Hearts legend Gary Mackay delivered a long pass from defence for which he was famous. His target was Foster whose pace was enough for him to elude the attention of home defender Beaumont. As Foster raced towards the Hibs penalty box, home keeper Leighton rushed out to meet him. Foster was coolness personified as he drilled the ball through the legs of Leighton and into the net. Those of us who knew Foster wasn't the most prolific of scorers – he hadn't scored a goal for nearly two years after all – looked to the Albion Road terracing to see where he had put his wayward effort.

I could swear there was a split second of silent disbelief as we heard the net swish with the impact of the ball. Foster rushed to the fencing on the terracing to celebrate with the ecstatic Hearts fans and promptly became the sixth player to be booked that fraught afternoon. Seconds later, the game ended – Hearts had secured a famous victory.

Hearts' quarter-final opponents were Rangers at Ibrox – you won't be surprised to learn the Maroons lost 2-0 and so crashed out of the Scottish Cup.

Hearts were left to fight a relegation battle and didn't secure their Premier Division place until they defeated Dundee United 2-0 at Tynecastle in the penultimate game of the season. It had been a disappointing campaign – but one that spawned a song that is still heard today whenever Hearts play Hibs: "Wayne, Wayne, super Wayne!"

v Rangers 4-2

Tennents Scottish Cup Fourth Round
20th February 1995. Tynecastle

EXACTLY A year to the day after Hearts' memorable Scottish Cup victory at Easter Road, they were involved in another epic Scottish Cup tie, this time at Tynecastle. However, much had changed in the intervening 12 months.

After 13 years, chairman Wallace Mercer decided it was time to hand the reins of principal shareholder at Tynecastle to someone else. His legacy was that he transformed Hearts from a shambling First Division club on the brink of part-time football to an established Premier Division club that regularly competed for silverware. Tynecastle Park was in the throes of being developed into Tynecastle Stadium and while the club's financial debt may have risen, Hearts were still able to compete with the best.

The debt Hearts owed to Mercer was immeasurable – in fact, it's fair to say the club owed its very existence to the man someone once called "the Great Waldo". Mercer sold his shares to another successful businessman, catering supremo Chris Robinson, in 1994. It was the end of an era – and the start of another one, a new era that would finally bring the much yearned for silverware, but would ultimately end in acrimony.

Robinson's first action as the new chairman of Hearts was to install a new manager. Sandy Clark left Tynecastle after the team struggled for much of his sole season in charge. Robinson turned to someone with no Hearts connections whatsoever – although Tommy McLean did play for Kilmarnock in that infamous last game of the season at Tynecastle in 1965.

McLean had led Motherwell to Scottish Cup success in 1991 and, like his brother Jim at Dundee United, was widely respected in the game. Robinson believed McLean would bring much needed discipline to Tynecastle. In truth, 1994/95 turned out to be similar to the previous season, although controversy was never far away.

Like his predecessor, McLean had little money for new players and set about organising the Hearts team so they would at least be difficult to beat. If pre-season friendlies are meant to be an indication of how the campaign ahead will transpire, then the omens were not good. Hearts played a friendly against Raith Rovers at Starks Park on 9th August. What should have been a nondescript match four days before the start of the Premier Division season made national headlines.

Hearts defenders Craig Levein and Graeme Hogg became embroiled in an on-field argument that resulted in Levein delivering a punch to Hogg that nearly knocked him out. Referee Bill Crombie had no alternative but to send both players from the field. Unsurprisingly, Hearts lost 2-0 and Tommy McLean was apoplectic.

Subsequently, both players were suspended from Hearts' opening game of the league season, a 3-1 loss at Aberdeen. Hearts then drew with Motherwell before entertaining Hibs at Tynecastle. Having gone 22 games in a row unbeaten against Hibs, Hearts' run had to end sometime, but it was the manner of the visitors' 1-0 win that irritated the home support. Hearts looked a disjointed lot and, it has to be said, Hibs didn't have to do a lot to earn their first win over Hearts in more than five years.

After the opening league game at Pittodrie, McLean had dropped goalkeeper Henry Smith and replaced him with Nicky Walker. It was a move that didn't go down well with the Hearts support, to whom Smith was a cult hero, despite his propensity for the odd gaffe or two. Against Hibs, the Hearts defence looked unsure and the home team's cause wasn't helped when midfielder Gary Mackay was sent off. The discipline McLean had sought to bring to the team was nowhere to be seen.

Four days after the defeat to Hibs, Hearts entertained First Division side St Johnstone in the League Cup. The Maroons eased into a 2-0 lead after half an hour, before full-back Stephen Frail was sent off for deliberate handball. In the second half, ten-man Hearts collapsed as the Perth Saints scored four goals to win 4-2. Hearts were a shambles and McLean himself appeared perplexed as he brought on Tommy Harrison only to substitute the substitute by taking the youngster off about 20 minutes later. It might well have been during this game that the supporters' chant of "you don't know what you're doing" was born.

After a 3-0 league defeat at Ibrox, Hearts did steady the ship somewhat with home wins over Dundee United and Kilmarnock and there were further Tynecastle successes over Celtic and Aberdeen. Nonetheless, things just didn't seem quite right and, as they were the previous season, Hearts were in the bottom half of the league table.

Fans hoped the Scottish Cup would bring a bit of respite. Hearts were drawn away to First Division side Clydebank and were relieved to escape with a 1-1 draw. Hearts huffed and puffed in the Tynecastle replay but won 2-1. My abiding memory from that game was not another struggling performance but of some Hearts fans giving light-hearted jibes to the Bankies' veteran winger Davie Cooper, the former Rangers, Motherwell and Scotland star who was still playing just a couple of weeks short of his 39th birthday.

Shouts of "where's yer zimmer frame, Cooper?" were acknowledged by a grin by the great man who must have heard such chants every week. A few weeks later, Cooper was dead. He collapsed with a brain haemorrhage when he was coaching youngsters for a training video. A nation was stunned.

After defeating the Bankies, Hearts were given a home draw in the next round – against Rangers. Given Hearts' poor league form and the fact a rampant Rangers team were 14 points clear at the top of the Premier Division, not even the most optimistic Hearts fan believed their team would win. Perhaps the Sky Sports people did, though, as they switched the game to a Monday night for live television coverage.

By now, Tommy McLean had brought in another goalkeeper – 23-year-old Craig Nelson from Partick Thistle, with Nicky Walker heading to Firhill as part of the deal. McLean had been making subtle changes to the Hearts team as the season progressed and had also secured the services of Rangers' reserve striker David Hagen, defender Colin Miller and former Hibee Willie Jamieson.

Perhaps McLean's most important player, however, was the former Rangers, Aberdeen and Scotland midfield player Jim Bett, ironically signed by McLean's predecessor Sandy Clark in May 1994, but on the proviso Bett completed his season with Icelandic club Reykjavik that ended in October. Bett was a calming influence in midfield – in a season when Hearts desperately needed a calming influence!

Hearts did get a pre-match boost for the cup-tie when it emerged Rangers' hugely influential striker Mark Hateley had failed a fitness test. Their French international defender Basile Boli was also missing and some Hearts fans felt there might just be a chance for their team.

On a cold, wet Monday evening, it was the visitors – with former Heart Alan McLaren now wearing blue following his transfer to Rangers – who began the match in the ascendancy with Danish winger Brian Laudrup causing the home defence problems. However, Hearts' central defensive duo of Craig Levein and Dave McPherson were immense, as was full-back Miller. Hearts were coping admirably with anything Rangers could muster. Then, after 22 minutes, the deadlock was broken. Hearts were awarded a free kick some 25 yards from goal. There seemed little threat, particularly as Miller stepped up to the breach. The Canadian – not noted for his goalscoring prowess – sprinted forward and unleashed a powerful shot that barely lifted the ball from the rain-sodden Tynecastle pitch but fairly whizzed past keeper Maxwell, hit the inside of the post and nestled into the net to give Hearts an unlikely lead. The Hearts fans danced for joy – although with the new Wheatfield Stand now in operation, were quickly told to sit in their seats again.

Rangers immediately tried to hit back but Hearts stood firm against the onslaught and indeed might have scored again through John Robertson. With half-time imminent, Hearts fans looked at their watches hoping their side would go in at the interval a goal ahead to impress the watching millions on Sky.

The score didn't remain at 1-0 as another goal was registered right on the half-time whistle. However, it came from a corner to the home team. Jim Bett's inswinging cross was met by the head of Rangers defender Craig Moore. Inexplicably, the Australian headed the ball across his own six-yard box where Hearts' Dave McPherson launched his big mop of hair to nod the ball into the net for 2-0, and there was bedlam at Tynecastle as the half-time whistle blew!

Those of us who have followed Hearts for more than a few years were steadfastly avoiding any chickens that weren't yet hatched. We had witnessed this scenario so many times before. And we weren't proved wrong, as Rangers inevitably came roaring back in the second half.

Just two minutes after the restart, Gough crossed for Durie, the former Hibs player, to head past Craig Nelson although Laudrup ensured there was no dubiety about the goal by thrashing the ball into the net and at 2-1 to Hearts, nerves were jangling once more.

They were in shreds ten minutes later, when Rangers came forward again and full-back Cleland's cross was headed powerfully home by Durie to level the tie at 2-2. Rangers' management team of Walter Smith and Archie Knox leapt from the dugout and punched the air with delight. Hearts were on the rack now and downtrodden fans like me would have gladly accepted a replay at that stage. However, the game was to take another dramatic twist just two minutes after Rangers' equaliser.

Hearts came forward in a bid to restore their lead. Jim Bett fired in an effort from the edge of the penalty box, which, while on target, was straight at Maxwell. However, the Rangers keeper let the ball squirm from his grasp and the ball spun loose in the penalty box – a dangerous thing to happen when John Robertson is around. Robertson pounced like the goalscoring predator he was and scooped the ball into the net to put Hearts back in front at 3-2. There was still half an hour to go – but the home support was delirious once more.

Play then raged from end to end with Maxwell making up for his error by saving brilliantly from Stephen Frail, while Gough sent a header inches wide for the visitors. With just a minute left and Hearts desperately hanging on, McPherson broke from defence and set off on a galloping run for which he was famous. He simply kept on running until he reached the edge of the Rangers penalty box, before dragging the ball back for substitute Kevin Thomas, who rifled the ball past Maxwell to end the game at Hearts 4 Rangers 2.

The quarter-final draw saw Hearts at home again, this time against Dundee United. John Millar was the hero this time, scoring twice in a 2-1 win to set up a semi-final clash with Hearts' old adversaries Airdrieonians. Would the Maroons learn from their mistakes from the past? You can guess the rest – suffice to say the Diamonds won 1-0 to inflict more cup heartache on Edinburgh's finest.

Hearts ended a dismal league campaign needing to beat Motherwell in the final game of the season at Tynecastle to avoid a dreaded relegation play-off. Thanks to second-half goals from Brian Hamilton and a last-minute strike from Robertson, they did.

The Scottish Cup triumph over Rangers was easily the highlight of a season to forget for Hearts. However, changes were afoot. Tommy McLean left Tynecastle at the end of the season – and his replacement would be a man steeped in the tradition of this footballing establishment, one who would finally put the glory into Glorious Hearts.

v Rangers 3-0

Bells Premier Division
20th January 1996. Ibrox

Hearts:	Rangers:
Rousset	Goram
Locke	Ferguson
Ritchie	Robertson
McPherson	Gough
McManus	McLaren
Bruno	Petric
Johnston	Miller
Colquhoun	Cleland
Lawrence	Durrant
Fulton	Durie
Pointon	Laudrup

Referee: B Orr (Kilbarchan)

AFTER TOMMY MCLEAN left Tynecastle, Hearts chairman Chris Robinson knew he could ill-afford to make another managerial appointment mistake. He knew the ideal man would be someone who had a proven track record of producing good, entertaining football teams without having any money to do it with. Someone who could wheel and deal in the transfer market, who had a reputation in developing promising young players – and someone who shared the same passion for Hearts as its loyal support. There was only one man for the job – step forward Jim Jefferies.

Jefferies had played for Hearts in the 1970s and 1980s and had been captain of the club during the dark days of relegation. After leaving Tynecastle, he made an early managerial impression at Berwick Rangers, before producing minor miracles at Falkirk. He led the Bairns to the Premier League and established them as a top-flight side. When the cash-strapped club sold their best players, Jefferies simply went out and recruited others.

He was in the process of doing this in the 1992/93 season but couldn't prevent Falkirk's relegation from the top flight; however he was in charge of the aforementioned 6-0 rout of Hearts, with signs the rebuilt Bairns were ready to bounce straight back up again.

It has to be said that Jefferies had to be persuaded to come to the Tynecastle hot seat. He rejected Robinson's initial offer, out of a sense of loyalty to Falkirk. However, Robinson sensed Jefferies' lack of conviction in stating he wanted to remain at Brockville and he returned to re-offer the post a few days later. Jefferies may have had initial misgivings about turning down the job he yearned for, but when he was given a second chance, he grabbed it with both hands. He duly became Hearts manager on 4th August 1995.

After the initial euphoria – by both the man himself and the fans who saw him as the prodigal son – Jefferies was faced with rebuilding Hearts in the 1995/96 season. He relished the task, but not even he realised just how much rebuilding was required.

Hearts began the Premier Division campaign with a 1-1 draw with Motherwell and followed this up with a 4-1 win over the team Jefferies had just left. It won't surprise you to learn there was a large Falkirk support at Tynecastle that day and not all of them were keen to show their appreciation for their former manager.

However, Hearts then suffered heavy defeats to Celtic and Rangers and losses to Aberdeen and Kilmarnock. After an early League Cup defeat at Dens Park via a penalty shoot-out, it occurred to the manager that five of that Hearts team had played at the same venue where they infamously lost the league nine years earlier. It was a remarkable statistic and clear evidence that things had to change.

As Hearts slumped to the bottom of the league after a less than auspicious start – ironically following a 2-0 defeat at his old club Falkirk – Jefferies brought in new players. Goalkeeper Gilles Rousset played at Brockville that afternoon and the Frenchman was soon joined by Italian defender Pasquale Bruno and Swedish striker Hans Eskillson, who all arrived within weeks of each other. Jefferies also gave youth its chance and added the likes of Paul Ritchie to the already established youngsters such as Gary Locke and Allan Johnston.

Sandy Clark had given the last two named their chance and Johnston, in particular, was a considerable talent. An old-fashioned winger, Johnston, on his day, brought the Hearts fans to the edge of their new plastic seats in the new, impressive Wheatfield Stand, which had replaced the old enclosure.

Inspired by the new recruits and youngsters, Hearts began to haul themselves up the Premier League with stirring wins over Partick Thistle, Kilmarnock and Hibernian. Come January 1996, Hearts were playing with style, albeit they were still inconsistent. They destroyed Motherwell 4-0 at Tynecastle, with Johnston in particularly impressive form.

Ten days later, Hearts headed for Ibrox and the somewhat daunting task of facing up to champions Rangers. Walter Smith's side had not conceded a goal in eight games and had lost just one league game all season. They were without their talisman Paul Gascoigne, but they still had the arguably even more gifted Brian Laudrup in their ranks. How would Hearts' youthful defence cope?

It was a sign of Hearts' evolvement under Jefferies that two stalwarts – Gary Mackay and John Robertson – could only find places on the substitutes' bench. Rangers began the game, as they always do on their home turf, in confident mood but it didn't take long for Hearts' diminutive front two of John Colquhoun and Alan Lawrence to make their presence felt.

With just six minutes played, Colquhoun stole the ball from defender Petric and sped down the left wing. After playing a one-two with Lawrence, he cut the ball back for Johnston to drill a shot past Goram and give Hearts an unexpected but extremely welcome early lead.

This set the tone for the afternoon. Hearts now had their noses in front and would invite the home side to come charging at them – leaving plenty of opportunities to hit on the break, something Hearts did with remarkable frequency and with menace. With the experienced former Rangers player Dave McPherson marshalling young

Paul Ritchie in central defence, the Maroons coped ably with all the home side could throw at them.

Ferguson had a tame shot easily saved by Rousset and, despite having plenty of possession, the home side were struggling. For all Rangers' huffing and puffing, Hearts looked the likelier side to score. The pace of Colquhoun, coupled with the menace of Allan Lawrence, troubled Rangers' defence all afternoon. Hearts could and should have had a penalty when Fulton and Colquhoun linked up with fine passing movement to feed Lawrence who was bundled over in the penalty box by home defender Gough. Inevitably, the referee said no penalty.

Just before half-time, Lawrence again had a chance when he raced in on goal from a pass from Johnston but fired his shot just over. Rangers upped the pressure as half-time approached but youngsters Locke and Ritchie handled everything that came their way. Indeed Lawrence came closest to scoring but his well-struck effort was well saved by Goram.

It took half an hour for Rangers to carve out a half-decent chance and even then, the legs of Rousset in the Hearts goal blocked Laudrup's effort. At the interval, Hearts were well worth their 1-0 lead; in fact, there was an element of disappointment among the almost disbelieving visiting support that their team were only one goal ahead.

Rangers brought on Dutch striker Van Vossen at the start of the second half but it was Hearts who made the first chance when Stevie Fulton's cross into the penalty box was cleared by a desperate Rangers defence. Shortly after, a quite ridiculous decision by referee Bobby Orr, when he deemed Rousset had picked up a pass back and awarded a free kick to the home side, resulted in nothing – thankfully.

On the hour, Gough gave the ball away and a superb slick passing move from Hearts presented Lawrence with yet another chance to double the visitors' lead. Goram blocked Lawrence's effort and Colquhoun really should have buried the rebound instead of driving the ball wide.

However, Hearts did double their lead soon after. A sublime pass from Neil Pointon played through Johnston, who raced through before deftly chipping Goram to put his side two goals ahead. Rangers threw on Mikhailichenko but Hearts remained untroubled, apart from a magnificent save from Rousset when he tipped over a header from Gough. Towards the end, there was a case of déjà vu.

The tenacious Pointon hooked another delicious pass forward to Johnston, and "Magic" raced through on goal before rounding Goram to slot the ball home for 3-0. Incredibly, Johnston should have had a fourth goal soon after, when another through ball saw him race in on goal but Miller made a timely intervention just as Johnston was about to pull the trigger.

By this time, all the noise at Ibrox was emanating from the ecstatic travelling Hearts support – most of the Rangers fans had headed for the exits, giving rise to the gag "why is Allan Johnston nicknamed Magic? It's because he made 45,000 Rangers fans disappear".

The game ended with the astonishing scoreline of Rangers 0 Hearts 3 – astonishing in that it was only three for Hearts, something manager Jim Jefferies alluded to after the game. It could easily have been 5-0 to the visitors.

The result was Hearts' best in a remarkable season, which at one point saw the Maroons slip to the bottom of the league but ended with a comfortable mid-table finish. As always, the key to success was finding consistency. Three weeks after their Ibrox triumph, Hearts slipped to a 3-1 defeat to Aberdeen at Tynecastle. However, they would soon avenge this result with a place in the Scottish Cup final.

Hearts had reached the Scottish Cup final in 1906, 1956, 1976 and 1986 so perhaps it was no surprise they reached the final again in 1996. Their run was far from easy – they defeated Partick Thistle at Tynecastle, then achieved hard-fought victories over Kilmarnock at Rugby Park and St Johnstone at McDiarmid Park before Aberdeen were beaten 2-1 in a tense Hampden semi-final.

There have been frequent arguments in recent years between supporters of Hearts and Aberdeen as to their respective claims to be the biggest club in Scotland after the Old Firm. Both can present decent cases but, to my mind, the argument was settled at that semi-final. Just under 30,000 fans were present – two thirds of them from Scotland's capital city.

The Hearts support that day was magnificent and vociferous from the start – and particularly at the end, when Allan Johnston scored a late winner. Quite what the Aberdeen players must have thought when they ran on to the Hampden pitch for the kick-off to see large sections of empty seats in their end can only be guessed at. It could hardly have filled them with inspiration. As the result proved, Aberdeen were not so much the third force as a spent force.

Hearts' opponents in the final were Rangers – who exacted full revenge for their Ibrox hammering by thrashing Jim Jefferies' men 5-1. The final is remembered for a superb performance from Brian Laudrup, who scored a hat-trick – and a not so superb performance from Hearts keeper Gilles Rousset, who let an effort from Laudrup slip through his fingers early in the second half. With that error went Hearts' hopes of lifting silverware for the first time since 1962. Rousset, however, would more than make amends two years later.

Despite the Hampden disappointment, hope had sprung again among the Hearts support in 1996. The Magic Show in January that resulted in a 3-0 thrashing of the champions in their own back yard was testament to that!

v Aberdeen 4-1

Bells Premier Division
1st November 1997. Pittodrie

Hearts:	Aberdeen:
Rousset	Leighton
Locke	Anderson
Pointon	Smith
Weir	Rowson
Salvatori	Kombouare
Ritchie	O'Neil
McCann	Miller
Fulton	Jess
Robertson	Windass
Cameron	Dodds
Flogel	Glass

Referee: J McCluskey (Stewarton)

B Y THE beginning of the 1997/98 season, Jim Jefferies' rebuilding of Hearts was mostly complete. Having already plundered his former club Falkirk to make midfielder Stevie Fulton one of his first signings for Hearts, Jefferies returned to Brockville for central defender Davie Weir. Other notable captures were winger Neil McCann, midfielder Colin Cameron and striker Jim Hamilton.

Jefferies continued to bring in players during the summer of 1997 and two notable additions were French forward Stephane Adam and Austrian utility player Thomas Flogel. Now, the term utility player can mean several things, including he is rubbish in any position. That was certainly not true in Flogel's case – he was someone who was dependable in midfield, defence or attack – as he proved in some style throughout season 1997/98.

The critics wondered whom, if anyone, would challenge the Old Firm in the summer of 1997. What would transpire in season 1997/98 was one of the most remarkable seasons in Scottish football and one that would make history.

There was an unusual start to Hearts' 1997/98 campaign. Their opening fixture, against champions Rangers at Ibrox, was played not on a Saturday, but a Monday night to suit the needs of live television. Despite the home side not having Paul Gascoigne and Ally McCoist available, they had their new Italian striker Marco Negri and he scored twice as Rangers won 3-1, Colin Cameron grabbing a late consolation for the Maroons.

However, Hearts soon began to find their feet and a fortnight later they faced Aberdeen at Tynecastle. Before the game, Aberdeen striker Dean Windass had scoffed at Hearts' stated intention of going for third place in the league, the Yorkshireman saying that Aberdeen were aiming higher and going for the championship itself.

Jefferies duly posted Windass's comments on the walls of the home dressing room. He required no team talk as Hearts went out and played the Dons off the park in a 4-1 win, with McCann producing a Johan Cruyff moment when he turned the visiting defence inside out. Windass? He didn't score but did receive a booking, which was warmly applauded by a goading home support.

Hearts produced some great football that autumn and were emerging as genuine title contenders. By the time the return fixture with Aberdeen was due to take place on 1st November 1997, Hearts were joint top of the league with Celtic with Rangers a point behind.

Hearts headed to the Granite City in confident mood, while Windass was keeping himself to himself this time as well he might – his team, far from going for the championship, were languishing in second bottom place in the Premier League.

Hearts were without the influential Stephane Adam, who was suspended, so manager Jefferies opted for the popular Flogel to partner John Robertson – making his 500th appearance for Hearts – in attack. Aberdeen were without their £1m signing Paul Bernard due to an ankle injury.

A huge Hearts support made its way to Pittodrie but weren't rewarded with anything in a curious first half. A feature of Hearts' performances that season was the whirlwind start they made to many games – but the only whirlwind in this game was the customary gale blowing from the North Sea. Hearts looked strangely lethargic early on and the home side looked the more likely to score, which they thought they had done after ten minutes, when Dodds swept home a cross from Windass – only for the linesman to flag for offside. Minutes later, Windass himself thought he had opened the scoring, only for Paul Ritchie to block his effort.

Although Hearts had chances, it was the Dons who were applying the pressure and they were rewarded after 22 minutes when Rowson fired in an effort that Hearts keeper Gilles Rousset could only parry and Windass duly slotted home the rebound. However, the goal seemed to waken Hearts from their slumber. McCann began to show why he had just been named in the Scotland squad and produced a piece of magic when he jinked past a couple of defenders before chipping the ball just past the post. On the half-hour mark, a deflected effort from Flogel bounced off the crossbar and the travelling Hearts fans began to believe their team was revving up. Hearts went in at the interval 1-0 down but Jefferies was about to weave his magic.

The visitors began the second half like a team transformed. They swarmed around the Aberdeen goal from kick-off and it took just eight minutes for them to level the score. Full-back Gary Locke crossed from the right towards Robertson whose delicate touch put McCann clear for the former Dundee player to slot home. It was just reward for a vibrant opening to the second half for Hearts and the game turned on this fine goal.

The home side began to wilt under the visitors' pressure and, 12 minutes later, Hearts deservedly went in front. This time McCann was the provider as he found Flogel with a neat pass. The Austrian showed tremendous strength to hold off the challenge of an Aberdeen defender to drive the ball past veteran home keeper Leighton – and Hearts never looked back.

Jefferies' side continued to sweep forward with McCann majestic on the wing, Colin Cameron dominant in midfield and Flogel a forceful presence up front.

McCann should have scored Hearts' third goal with 20 minutes left, only to be denied by a last-gasp tackle by Aberdeen's Kombouare.

However, the third was merely delayed. With 13 minutes left, Robertson skipped past a floundering Smith in the Aberdeen defence to fire in an effort that took a deflection off the defender on the way to nestling in the back of the net and with the score 3-1 to Hearts this was the cue for the home support to exit en masse.

To rub salt into already considerable wounds, Hearts added a fourth goal when the industrious Stefano Salvatori delivered a cross to which Flogel delivered a sublime finish with eight minutes left. Jubilant Hearts supporters chanted "easy, easy" to those Aberdeen fans still left and there could and, perhaps should, have been more goals for the visitors as substitute Jim Hamilton had a chance to net against his hometown team but failed to finish the chance off. In the end, it finished Aberdeen 1 Hearts 4 and the game was a watershed in what would turn out to be a momentous season for Hearts.

Jefferies' side showed they were serious about challenging Celtic and Rangers for the league title by winning their next four games. A week after hammering Aberdeen, Hearts entertained Hibernian in the Edinburgh derby. Inevitably, Robertson opened the scoring and substitute Jose Quitongo entered Tynecastle folklore by securing a 2-0 win with the second goal two minutes before the end.

After St Johnstone were beaten by a last-minute Colin Cameron penalty in a 2-1 win, Hearts took on Kilmarnock at Tynecastle and produced a feast of attacking football. Veteran Pat Nevin inspired Killie that afternoon and his opening goal after just five minutes set the tone for a classic game. A Stephane Adam hat-trick, added to goals from McCann and Quitongo – who was fast becoming a cult figure among the Hearts fans – helped the home side to an astonishing 5-3 win, a result that took Hearts a remarkable four points clear at the top of the Premier League.

The fortnight before Christmas however, saw Hearts' title fervour doused somewhat. Firstly, Hearts went to Celtic Park and defended resolutely, until ten minutes from the end when Craig Burley scored the only goal of the game. It was Hearts' first defeat in the league since they last played Celtic at Tynecastle in October. Those who opined that the real test of this Hearts team would be when they played the Old Firm were wearing smug grins the following week when the other half of the Glasgow duo visited Tynecastle – and thrashed the Maroons 5-2.

Two of Rangers' five goals came when they were down to ten men after the sending off of Gattuso and a crestfallen Hearts support shuffled silently out of Tynecastle with their dreams of seeing the first league flag flying in Gorgie for nearly 40 years almost – but not quite – in tatters.

It wasn't the best of festive periods for Hearts. The New Year Edinburgh derby was played at Tynecastle and when Stevie Fulton scored twice in the opening ten minutes to put Hearts two goals ahead against a struggling Hibernian side, some of us licked our lips at the prospect of the Gorgie Boys exacting revenge for a certain result on New Year's Day 1973. However, inexplicably, Hearts took their collective feet off the gas (to use an Americanism) and the visitors came back from the dead with two second-half goals to snatch an unlikely draw.

Hearts, though, refused to be written off and they embarked on an unbeaten run of 13 games. In February, they drew with Celtic at Tynecastle thanks to a last-gasp scrambled equaliser from that man Quitongo, whose ecstatic celebrations added to the bedlam at Tynecastle that afternoon. Three weeks later, Hearts thought they had avenged that thrashing from Rangers when they led the champions 2-1 in the snow at Ibrox – only for Jorg Albertz to score a last-minute equaliser. It was a sign, however, that Hearts now believed they could match Celtic and Rangers and after the draw in Govan, they now sat second in the league, just two points behind Celtic as the Old Firm began to show unfamiliar signs of faltering.

It was then, however, that the wheels of Hearts' title chase, while not falling off, began to skid somewhat. Kilmarnock and Motherwell held Jefferies' side to draws – the game against the Fir Park team, in particular, was a tension-laden midweek fixture and Motherwell's late equaliser seemed to deflate Hearts' championship challenge. Hearts' next fixture was at Easter Road against a Hibernian side staring relegation in the face. Hearts looked like a team drained of energy on an April afternoon that was frequented by snow showers and lost 2-1.

The bitter defeat at Easter Road signalled the end of Hearts' brave and creditworthy challenge for the league title. This was confirmed a fortnight later, when Rangers visited Tynecastle and repeated their performance of Christmas, coasting to a 3-0 win although Hearts, missing the hugely influential Colin Cameron, more than matched the outgoing champions in a pulsating first half.

In the end, Hearts finished in third place in the Premier League, seven points behind new champions Celtic. It had been a fantastic effort by Jefferies' team who had played magnificent football at times throughout the course of a memorable campaign. The strength in depth of Hearts' squad was always going to be a factor. Hearts had a decent sized squad but it was obvious what the best starting 11 was.

The feeling persisted that Hearts should have added to the squad early in 1998, as the push for the title gained momentum. True, finances at Tynecastle were tight but it would have perhaps sent a message to the Old Firm that Hearts were serious in their challenge to be the best in Scotland.

The league campaign may have ended in disappointment. Nonetheless, a third-placed finish guaranteed a place in the following season's Uefa Cup. Moreover, there was still the not inconsiderable matter of the Scottish Cup to come. As at Pittodrie Stadium on that cold November afternoon when they saw their side win 4-1, Hearts supporters would have cause for celebration – only this time it would be the mother of all parties!

v Rangers 2-1
Tennents Scottish Cup Final
16th May 1998. Celtic Park

Hearts:	Rangers:
Rousset	Goram
McPherson	Porrini
Naysmith	Stensaas
Weir	Gough
Salvatori	Amoruso
Ritchie	Bjorklund
McCann	Gattuso
Fulton	Ferguson
Adam	Durie
Cameron	McCall
Flogel	Laudrup

Referee: W Young (Clarkston)

WHEN THE top-flight sides entered the Scottish Cup at the beginning of 1998, some commentators had been so impressed with Hearts' league displays they thought the Tynecastle side were a good bet to take the trophy – even though it had been 36 years since silverware last graced the west end of the capital city. The Old Firm, they reckoned, would be too involved with the championship but Jambos boss Jim Jefferies wasn't worried about that being an apparent backhanded compliment.

Hearts were given a home draw against Second Division side Clydebank in round three and were somewhat fortunate to win 2-0 given that the Bankies created the better chances in the game. It was Third Division opposition in round four when Albion Rovers visited Edinburgh and Angolan winger Jose Quitongo inspired Hearts to a 3-0 victory before their penchant for home ties was illustrated again in the quarter-final with a 4-1 win over Ayr United.

Hearts' eighth semi-final appearance in the Scottish Cup in 12 years had many people believing their name was on the trophy when they avoided both the Old Firm and were paired with First Division side Falkirk. Hearts' luck in the cup held firm. Despite their poorest display of the season, during which the Bairns outplayed them, Hearts emerged 3-1 victors (two goals in the last two minutes sinking their lower league opponents) and their second Scottish Cup final appearance in two years beckoned.

Their opponents were the side that had thrashed them 5-1 in the Scottish Cup final of 1996 – Rangers. Ibrox boss Walter Smith conceded that Hearts were a much-improved team from the one that capitulated two years earlier, but the Govan men were still firm favourites for the trophy. Nearly 49,000 supporters headed for Celtic Park – Hampden Park was being refurbished – on a warm May afternoon to witness one of the most emotional cup finals in recent years.

It was a sign of the cosmopolitan times that, of the Rangers side, only Gordon Durie and Ian Ferguson were born in Scotland (Richard Gough was born in Stockholm while Andy Goram and Stuart McCall were born in England of Scottish parentage). Even the Hearts side contained two Frenchmen, an Italian and an Austrian.

Pre-match blows affected both sides. Rangers' influential German, Jorg Albertz, was sent off for violent conduct the previous week at Tannadice and was therefore suspended, while injury ruled out Swede Jonas Thern. Hearts captain Gary Locke, who was carried off injured after just seven minutes during the 1996 final, missed the 1998 final because of a hamstring injury and, being a Hearts-daft youngster, his anguish was felt by every Hearts supporter.

Rangers v Hearts Scottish Cup finals have a history of having remarkable beginnings. The 1976 final between the pair began at two minutes to three, Rangers scored within 80 seconds, so Hearts were a goal behind before the official kick-off time! Astonishingly, the 1996 final kicked off at a minute to three and Hearts lost their captain within seven minutes. The fans wondered what the 1998 final would have in store – they got their answer after just 33 seconds!

From the kick-off, Hearts stormed upfield. Stand-in captain Steve Fulton burst into the Rangers penalty box only to be halted by Ferguson. Halted illegally said referee Young and he awarded a penalty to Hearts. It looked initially like the foul had been committed outside the box but, tellingly, few Rangers players protested. Colin Cameron stepped up to slot the penalty beyond goalkeeper Goram and Hearts had a sensational lead after just 80 seconds. Maroon-clad supporters erupted in the Celtic Park cauldron and it was certainly a start to the match few people – even in Edinburgh – had predicted.

Rangers, although stung by such an early setback, responded. Gattuso embarked on a powerful run from midfield, which ended with a shot which was comfortably saved by Rousset. Then Laudrup had an effort that was blocked by 19-year-old Gary Naysmith.

Hearts, however, weren't just sitting back. Despite a significant change in tactics by manager Jefferies that saw the team adopt a more rigid 4-4-2 formation, rather than their normal swashbuckling style of 4-3-3, the Maroons were still capable of lightning raids on the break, epitomised by young Naysmith who was having an outstanding game at full-back. The Scotland Under-21 star had just been named Young Player of the Year and his assured defending and attacking abilities were there for all to see at Celtic Park.

After half an hour, Rangers' Ferguson – a veteran of St Mirren's cup triumph in 1987 – was put through by Laudrup but pulled his effort wide. Then came Rangers' best effort thus far. Taking a short free kick some 35 yards out, Lorenzo Amoruso fired in a magnificent shot that appeared to be heading for the top-left corner of the net. However, as Rangers prepared to celebrate the equaliser, Hearts keeper Gilles Rousset leapt majestically to palm the ball past the post. It was a fantastic save and a defining moment.

In the 1996 final, the big Frenchman let a shot slip through his fingers to give Rangers a two-goal advantage from which they never looked back. It was a schoolboy error and Rousset hid his face behind his hands at the realisation of what he had done. Now, two years later, he produced one of the great stops in cup final history and 23,000 Hearts supporters stood to acclaim the moment. Half-time arrived with Hearts still ahead and one wondered if history was about to be made.

At the start of the second half, Rangers replaced the unhappy Stensaas with the veteran campaigner Ally McCoist. It signalled an all-out attacking policy by Walter Smith and, for the opening five minutes of the second period, Hearts were pinned back in their own half.

Within minutes, McCoist received a pass from the tireless Laudrup but his effort went into the side net. Urged on by captain Gough – playing his last game for the Ibrox club – Rangers swept forward and one wondered if Hearts could hold out. However, after 52 minutes, the Hearts support erupted once more.

Rousset launched a long ball downfield from a free kick and it seemed that Amoruso would clear the danger. However, the Italian dithered as he went to strike the ball and Frenchman Stephane Adam nipped in behind him and took the ball from his toes. Racing into the penalty box, Adam fired in a powerful shot which goalkeeper Goram could only parry into the net and the score became 2-0 to Hearts. Adam ran with outstretched arms to an ecstatic Jambos support to milk the celebrations.

The noise from the Hearts end was deafening. Was the dream about to come true? Were 36 years of anguish about to end? The supporters, so often kicked in the teeth by countless near misses from their side, could scarcely believe it. However, there were still 38 minutes to go and a wounded Rangers side is when they are at their most dangerous.

Seconds later, Hearts almost ended the argument when Thomas Flogel headed a Steve Fulton free kick powerfully towards goal but his effort was well saved by Goram. Then, inevitably, Rangers stormed back.

McCoist, despite being written off by some people at 35 years of age, was proving a real handful for the youthful Hearts defence. A snap-shot from the striker from just six yards out was well saved by Rousset before the former Sunderland player was thwarted by Dave McPherson. Time was running out for Rangers but, with nine minutes to go, McCoist finally got the goal both he and his side deserved. Ferguson played the ball forward to Gattuso. The Italian slipped it to McCoist who drove the ball past Rousset and into the net from 18 yards.

The last few minutes of the 1998 Scottish Cup final were tense, nervous and fraught for supporters of both clubs. Rangers threw everything at the Hearts defence but Jefferies' side scented glory. Nevertheless, there was still time for more drama in this epic cup final.

With two minutes to go, McCoist went down in the penalty box after a foul by David Weir. Referee Young immediately blew his whistle. For a moment, it looked like a penalty to Rangers and Hearts' hopes appeared to be cruelly dashed once more. However, after a nod from the linesman, Young awarded a free-kick to Rangers on the edge of the penalty box, much to the disgust of McCoist. Laudrup's shot was deflected wide and Hearts and their supporters breathed a huge sigh of relief.

The period of injury time seemed to last forever. Fully four minutes of stoppage time had been played when, at last, Young blew for the end of the match. The Hearts support roared themselves hoarse and danced for joy. Jim Jefferies almost crushed his assistant Billy Brown with a hug of delight. Hearts had won the Scottish Cup for the first time since 1956 and decades of heartbreak had ended.

The scenes that followed at Celtic Park were remarkable. Grown men wept and the tide of emotion that washed over those in maroon seemed almost to overpower them. Veteran striker John Robertson, a substitute who never came on, was clearly overcome. Robertson had been at Hearts for 17 years but had yet to win a medal with the club he loved. Now, in his last season at Tynecastle, his dream had come true, as it had for the thousands of jubilant supporters who found it difficult to comprehend just what had happened.

When Steve Fulton went to collect the trophy, he invited injured club captain Gary Locke to go up with him. Locke – wearing his cup final suit – didn't need to be asked twice and the two players held the cup aloft to a huge ovation from the Hearts support.

Edinburgh partied all weekend as the players paraded the cup through the streets of the famous old city and on to Tynecastle Stadium for a truly emotional homecoming. An estimated 100,000 people welcomed them home and Edinburgh let down its collective hair. Manager Jefferies had said before the game that the players could become legends if they won the cup and there's little doubt that the Hearts support treated their heroes in a way befitting such a status.

It was an emotional end to an emotional season. In the last quarter of the league season, Hearts' championship challenge, admirable though it was, faded as the side dropped points to Kilmarnock and Motherwell. The final nail in their title coffin was, ironically, driven in by city rivals Hibernian, who recorded a rare win in the Edinburgh derby, 2-1 at Easter Road in April. It was, however, Hibernian's last hurrah – they were relegated at the end of the season.

Such upheavals meant little to those connected with Heart of Midlothian, however. It's true to say that the club had become something of a laughing stock in Scottish football because of their lack of success and their almost constant failure to produce the goods when it really mattered. The 1997/98 season changed all that. Throughout the campaign, Hearts had consistently produced a sparkling brand of fluent, attacking football that delighted the purists. They had given the Old Firm the fright of their lives in the race for the league title.

Their last piece of silverware was the League Cup in 1962. Now, after 36 years of hurt, Hearts had finally brought a trophy back to Tynecastle. They were winners once more. It was a dream come true for thousands of Hearts supporters.

v Aberdeen 5-2

Bank of Scotland SPL
23rd May 1999. Pittodrie

Hearts:	Aberdeen:
McKenzie	Warner
Naysmith	Perry
Ritchie	Whyte
Murray	Smith
Pressley	Jess
Jackson	Mayer
Flogel	Dow
Cameron	Anderson
Adam	Buchan
Severin	Hart
McSwegan	Winters

Referee: J Rowbotham (Kirkcaldy)

IT IS SAID that a week can be a long time in politics. A year must be an eternity – it certainly can be in football, as the period between May 1998 and May 1999 proved for Heart of Midlothian.

I have followed Hearts since my father took me to my first game in 1968 – I still vividly remember Hearts' 3-1 win at Falkirk – and in over four decades, the happiest I have felt as a Jambo was during the summer of 1998.

Hearts had finally shaken off their nearly men tag of Scottish football by winning the Scottish Cup on a memorable afternoon in May. Disbelief on the afternoon turned to drunken glee on the Saturday evening and tear-stained hangovers on seeing the team parade the cup through the streets of Edinburgh on the Sunday. It was what Hearts fans of my generation had waited decades for and, for long enough, thought we would never see.

1998 was the last year Scotland reached the finals of a major tournament and they played Brazil in the opening game of the World Cup finals in France. When John Collins swept home a penalty to equalise seven minutes before half-time, I turned to my mate in a pub in Dalkeith – having left work early to watch the game – and embraced him. Hearts were Scottish Cup holders. Hibs had just been relegated to the First Division. Now Scotland were – briefly at any rate – on parity with the world champions. Football for this Hearts fan just did not get any better than this.

As a glass half-empty kind of fella, I had always lowered my expectation levels where Hearts were concerned. Usually, optimism was seldom in short supply among some of my fellow Jambos at the beginning of the season, whereas I would simply point to the fact Hearts hadn't won anything in decades and, therefore, would likely revert to type and fall at the last hurdle. 1998 changed all that.

Now, Hearts were winners and the media predicted big things for Jim Jefferies' team, suggesting they would run the Old Firm close for the league championship once more. The opening game of the 1998/99 season simply enhanced that view. This was the season where the newly-created Bank of Scotland-sponsored Scottish Premier League – SPL for short – kicked off, with promises being made of a new era for Scotland's top clubs.

SPL officials had looked at the hugely successful FA Premiership in England and the vast sums of television money being paid by Sky. SPL chiefs thought the same would happen north of the border. As history would tell, things didn't quite work out that way.

However, the SPL did strike a deal with Sky to cover league games for the 1998/99 season and with the opening day fixtures including Hearts against Rangers at Tynecastle, all roads led to Gorgie. Sky, though, were committed to the English game, with the biggest games down south kicking off at 4pm on a Sunday. The problem was where to fit the SPL's top game of the weekend.

Sky thought they had the answer – Sunday evenings. Therefore, Hearts kicked off against Rangers at the frankly ridiculous time of 6.05pm on a Sunday. Small wonder then, that Hearts didn't have to use the full house signs. Chairman Chris Robinson opined that if a Scottish Cup-winning Hearts team couldn't sell out the opening league game of the season against Rangers, then questions had to be asked. The question both Hearts and Rangers fans were asking that Sunday evening was – why the hell did the SPL clubs agree to a 6.05pm kick-off time?

Hearts manager Jefferies had added to his cup-winning squad by recruiting Motherwell midfielder Rab McKinnon and Dundee United centre-half Steven Pressley. The latter was seen as a real coup for Hearts, as "Elvis" had been mighty impressive for United and the former Rangers player had stated his reason for moving to Tynecastle was to be successful. It was just what the Hearts fans wanted to hear.

That said, neither Pressley nor McKinnon featured against Rangers in the opening game because of injury, but this didn't stop Hearts beginning season 1998/99 the way they had ended 1997/98 – by defeating Rangers 2-1. Sunday night or not, the Hearts fans left Tynecastle in ecstatic mood – would their team now go one better and become league champions of Scotland for the first time since 1960?

After drawing with Dundee United and defeating Aberdeen, hopes were high, but whenever Hearts fans get too high, they are inevitably brought down to earth with a resounding thump. This happened when Hearts lost 3-0 at Kilmarnock at the end of August – Kille's new signing Ally McCoist hitting a hat-trick – and the hissing noise heard in Ayrshire that Sunday afternoon could well have been the sound of the Hearts balloon bursting. Hearts then lost 2-0 to Dundee at Tynecastle, before being held to a draw by Dunfermline Athletic. By now, the Maroons had dropped to sixth place in the SPL.

Hearts then lost hugely influential midfielder Colin Cameron to an injury serious enough to keep him out until March. With other players suffering from injury and loss of form, Jefferies moved to strengthen the squad. He turned to France and Spain for midfielders Vincent Guerin and Juanjo respectively and signed former Rangers striker Gary McSwegan on a free transfer from Dundee United.

Midfielder Lee Makel, signed the previous season from Blackburn Rovers as cover for Cameron, was given the chance to make the midfield position his own. No one was harder working than the Englishman, but he lacked the goalscoring prowess of Cameron, and with John Robertson now having left Tynecastle for pastures new and Jim Hamilton and Stephane Adam beginning to lose form, there became a real concern about where the goals would come from.

In December, Hearts lost four games in succession. Worse still, fans' favourite, the mercurial winger that was Neil McCann, was sold to Rangers for £2m ten days before Christmas. As is the way of these things, he made his Rangers debut five days later – in a 3-2 win over Hearts at Tynecastle. It stuck in the throat of many Hearts fans to see McCann come on as a late substitute – he had been idolised by those same supporters for four years and was an integral part of the Scottish Cup winning team. Hearts were now 14 points behind SPL leaders Rangers and hopes of a challenge for the league were like McCann – gone.

Where 1998 had begun with Hearts fans full of optimism, 1999 could not have started worse. Hearts lost five SPL games in a row – and failed to score in any of them. In early February, another of the cup-winning team departed when defender Davie Weir was sold to Everton. Poor Gary McSwegan bore the brunt of the Hearts supporters' criticism as he went on one of those goalless runs all strikers dread.

Hearts' nadir came on 20th March 1999 with a 2-0 loss at Dundee. Jim Jefferies tried desperately to stop the rot but the introduction of Frenchman Mohammed Berthe just seemed like desperation full stop. The midfield man was woeful against Dundee and was replaced by another recent signing who hadn't inspired confidence among the fans – Leigh Jenkinson. The result at Dens Park saw Hearts slump to the bottom of the SPL. Eleven months after Scottish Cup glory, Hearts were staring relegation in the face. Then, three things happened that turned Hearts' season around.

Firstly, Jefferies did make an inspired signing by bringing Celtic's attacking midfielder Darren Jackson to Tynecastle for £300,000. Secondly, after weeks without even coming close to hitting a barn door, McSwegan scored Hearts' first competitive goal for eight weeks in a 2-2 draw against Kilmarnock – and then couldn't stop scoring. Thirdly, midfield maestro Cameron returned from injury.

Hearts travelled to Tannadice to face Dundee United on a Tuesday evening in early April, knowing victory would lift them off the bottom of the SPL. McSwegan hit a wonder goal from 25 yards, and then added a second, before Cameron added a superb third for a 3-1 win. The season had turned.

Confidence flowed through the veins of the Hearts players and they put four goals past Motherwell at Fir Park and Dundee United at Tynecastle. By the time Hearts headed to Aberdeen for the final game of the season they were safe from relegation – and proceeded to put on a five-star show at Pittodrie.

Aberdeen themselves had suffered a slump in form in the second half of the season, to the extent they had dispensed with the services of manager Alex Miller and put Paul Hegarty in temporary charge. Indeed, Hearts boss Jim Jefferies was one of the names linked with the Aberdeen post.

Hearts were buoyed by their recent return to form while the Dons just wanted the season to end. Just two minutes were played, when McSwegan fired a low right-foot shot past keeper Warner to give the visitors the lead. However, Aberdeen equalised five minutes later, when Buchan unleashed an effort from 25 yards that whistled past Roddy McKenzie in the Hearts goal. This was the cue for Aberdeen to have a period of dominance, with Mayer and Jess coming close, although Hearts always looked dangerous when McSwegan had the ball.

Half-time came with the teams level – but that was a situation that didn't last long when the second half got underway. And it was a carbon copy of the first half, when McSwegan was given all the time in the world to control the ball, turn and hit a magnificent effort past Warner to restore Hearts' lead. Two minutes later, McSwegan completed his hat-trick when he tapped home from close range following a fine sweeping move that involved Darren Jackson and Colin Cameron. Hearts were 3-1 ahead.

Three minutes later, a now rampant Hearts surged forward again with Jackson and McSwegan this time providing the link-up play for Cameron to make a trademark run into the visitors' penalty box. Cameron was tripped by Buchan but dusted himself down before sending keeper Warner the wrong way to slot home the penalty to put Hearts 4-1 ahead – with just seven minutes played in the second half.

Jess did pull a goal back for the Dons with half an hour to go, but two minutes later, Hearts' French striker Stephane Adam – the cup final hero from 12 months and a week earlier – delivered a superb cross into the Aberdeen penalty box where Thomas Flogel nonchalantly flicked the ball past the despairing Warner. There were still 35 minutes left and Hearts were, astonishingly, 5-2 ahead and looking hungry for more.

It was only a combination of good luck and fine goalkeeping by Warner – this might seem a strange thing to say given he conceded five goals – that kept Hearts to five. Nonetheless, the final score of Aberdeen 2 Hearts 5 was the Tynecastle side's biggest win at Pittodrie for 49 years.

It had been a magnificent end to a rollercoaster season that began on a high, dipped alarmingly midway through, but ended with Hearts climbing again, with performances that made one think what might have been had Colin Cameron not suffered serious injury and Davie Weir and Neil McCann not been sold.

Moreover, what might have been, had Cameron not returned, Darren Jackson remained at Celtic and Gary McSwegan gave up on hitting barn doors!

v Celtic **3-2**
Bank of Scotland SPL
5th February 2000. Celtic Park

Hearts:	Celtic:
Niemi	Gould
Murray	Riseth
Naysmith	Stubbs
Petric	Boyd
Pressley	Mahe
Cameron	Petrov
Flogel	Healy
Jackson	Mjallby
Simpson	Berkovic
Tomaschek	Viduka
Wales	Moravcik

Referee: J Rowbotham (Kirkcaldy)

AS THE new millennium began, it had been less than two years since Hearts had lifted the Scottish Cup in such memorable fashion, but the intervening period had been, at times, traumatic as the club fell from challenging the Old Firm for the league championship to flirting with relegation in the space of 12 rollercoaster months.

The 1999/2000 season had seen manager Jim Jefferies try to steady the ship however, and with a substantial transfer kitty available thanks to a multi-million pound "investment" from media group SMG, some serious money was shelled out to "try and take Hearts to the next level" (© all newspapers). Hearts began the season with just two additions – striker Gary Wales from Hamilton Academical and former Rangers and Dundee United defender Gordan Petric – but as the campaign progressed, more new faces would arrive.

Having ended the previous season impressively, Hearts began 1999/00 in the same manner, a 4-1 hammering of St Johnstone in Perth heralding a brilliant start to the SPL. A week later, however, Rangers won 4-0 at Tynecastle and Hearts fans were on the emotional rollercoaster again. When Hearts were good, they were very good – striker Gary McSwegan repeated his feat at Pittodrie in May by scoring a hat-trick against Aberdeen in a 3-0 win at Tynecastle. However, when Hearts were not so good, they were awful as witnessed in a 4-0 reversal at Celtic Park a week later.

Jim Jefferies strove for the consistency his team needed. The festive period proved the manager needed an influx of fresh faces. Two weeks before Christmas, Hearts lost 3-1 at bottom of the table Aberdeen before, ten days later, succumbing 3-0 to a Kenny Miller-inspired Hibs at Tynecastle. As you would expect, this last defeat was hard to take for Hearts supporters and, astonishingly, questions were being asked about the manager and his tactics.

Jefferies fielded two more new faces against Hibs – goalkeeper Antti Niemi and midfielder Fitzroy Simpson. When the league season took a brief winter break after Christmas, Hearts were in sixth place in the SPL. Unlike the previous season, they weren't in any danger of relegation but, defensively, Hearts were far from convincing.

Jefferies tried to address this by spending £500,000 on Slovakian international midfielder Robert Tomaschek. However, Hearts were some distance away from the Old Firm and as Jim Jefferies brought his side to Parkhead on Saturday 5th February 2000, few people outside the hardy band of travelling fans thought the result would be anything other than another convincing Celtic victory.

Nearly 60,000 fans packed into Celtic Park, most in their usual expectant mood. Hearts' Darren Jackson was making a return to the arena where he had strutted his stuff in the green and white hoops before serious illness threatened a lot more than his footballing career. He was given a warm welcome from the Celtic hordes, but there was little sentimentality in the opening 20 minutes as the Bhoys almost set up camp in the Hearts half.

As the best Hearts goalkeeper this writer has had the privilege to see – Antti Niemi – and centre-half Steven Pressley tried manfully to stem the tide, it seemed only a matter of time before Celtic would make the breakthrough. They did after 18 minutes, when Moravcik fired them into the lead, a lead that was doubled only ten minutes later when Viduka shot past Niemi. Celtic 2 Hearts 0 and the Hearts support folded their arms in disgust and wore furrowed brows – we had seen this all too often in Glasgow, as the Maroons yet again paid the price for showing the Glasgow giants just too much respect.

However, as the Jambo following contemplated heading for a pie and a cup of tea – anything to take their eyes off what was happening on the pitch – the game turned just three minutes later. Colin Cameron latched on to a through ball and with just Gould to beat, coolly slipped the ball past the Celtic keeper to make it Celtic 2 Hearts 1.

It was the immediate response that Jefferies demanded and, more importantly as things were to turn out, it planted the first seeds of doubt in the minds of the Celtic players. Managed by former Liverpool legend John Barnes, there had been increasing speculation in the press that all was not well behind the scenes at Celtic Park and the events that followed were to prove there was more than a grain of truth in the rumours.

Jefferies certainly believed Celtic were there for the taking and he fired belief into the bellies of his Hearts players at half-time. Hearts began the second half like a maroon swarm around the Celtic goal.

Fitzroy Simpson didn't enjoy a particularly productive period at Tynecastle, but he produced arguably his finest performance in a maroon shirt that afternoon. Simpson was given plenty of space to spray passes to the all too eager Jackson and Cameron but one of his passes, ten minutes after the restart, was to the unlikely figure of Gary Naysmith.

The Midlothian youngster was scarcely noted for his goalscoring exploits but the full-back collected Simpson's incisive pass, galloped into the penalty box and rifled an unstoppable shot into the roof of the net, leaving keeper Gould grasping thin air.

Remarkably, Hearts had levelled the game at 2-2 – but Jefferies' marauders weren't finished yet!

Barnes' response was to replace Mjallby and the ineffectual Berkovic with youngster Burchill and the experienced Johnson, but it was Hearts who were now in the ascendancy, with Jackson causing havoc for the Celtic rearguard and the home support's dismay turned to fury with just seven minutes to go.

Jackson was bundled unceremoniously off the ball inside the Celtic penalty box. Referee John Rowbotham immediately pointed to the spot. Cameron did his usual expert job with the kick and Hearts had come back from the dead to lead 3-2. To a cacophony of boos and jeers from a disbelieving home support, the final whistle blew minutes later and Hearts had secured a famous and unlikely victory.

Hearts had often been accused of lacking the belief to take on the Old Firm, particularly in Glasgow, but once Cameron had pulled a goal back just after the half-hour, they had belief in bucketfuls.

Celtic's misery was compounded four days later, when First Division side Inverness Caledonian Thistle surpassed Hearts' memorable triumph by knocking the Hoops out of the Scottish Cup, winning 3-1 at Celtic Park. It was to prove the final nail in John Barnes' managerial coffin in Glasgow.

Hearts were just happy to savour a rare victory in Glasgow's east end. Not even *auld yins* like myself could remember the last time Hearts had come back from two goals down to defeat Celtic in Glasgow and it was a result and a performance which would become part of Gorgie folklore.

However, as if to prove the point about inconsistency, Hearts were then held to a goalless draw by Kilmarnock at Tynecastle, before Jim Jefferies' men recorded more impressive away victories at Motherwell, Dundee United and St Johnstone. It was with some relish, therefore, that Hearts headed to Easter Road in March for the next instalment of the Edinburgh derby.

When former Hibee Darren Jackson gave Hearts the lead midway through the first half, things looked promising. However, newly promoted Hibs, under manager Alex McLeish, were a different proposition to the team that was relegated two years earlier and, inspired by Frenchman Franck Sauzee, they stormed back to win 3-1 to leave disconsolate Jambos shaking their collective heads once more.

Hearts entertained both halves of the Old Firm within four days in April and the two results seemed to reflect the inconsistency of the Maroons. A Gary McSwegan goal was enough to give Hearts all three points and a second win in succession against Celtic. Hearts then eagerly awaited the visit of Rangers the following Wednesday evening, in the hope of doing an Old Firm double.

When McSwegan opened the scoring early on – the little striker just could not stop scoring this season – Tynecastle was ready to celebrate once more. Then, not for the first time, controversy struck when Rangers' Turkish midfielder Tugay clearly handled the ball before half-time only for referee Willie Young, inexplicably, to wave play on – and Rangers immediately equalised. They then snatched a scarcely deserved winner midway through the second half.

Hearts, though, remained in the hunt for a third place finish in the SPL and the Indian sign they held over Aberdeen continued when a Darren Jackson screamer from 25 yards flew into the net to secure a priceless 2-1 win at Pittodrie.

The final day of the SPL season came on 21st May 2000 – with an Edinburgh derby at Tynecastle. This would rule out any lacklustre end of the season approach but, in any case, Hearts still had work to do to secure third place in the league and the place in the following season's Uefa Cup that came with it.

Jefferies' side were in charge of their own destiny – three points against their city rivals would mean mission accomplished, no matter what fourth placed Motherwell did. A magnificent strike from Spanish winger Juanjo after half an hour had the Hearts fans on their feet. The wee man appeared to be moving away from the Hibs goal as he ran across the field before turning deftly and striking a brilliant long-range effort past Hibs keeper Colgan.

When Hibs' Paatelainen equalised early in the second half, nerves were jangling, particularly as news was coming through from Fir Park that Motherwell were ahead against Rangers. However, just five minutes later, that man McSwegan – who else – nodded home Hearts' second and the Maroons hung on for the win that saw them finish the best of the rest behind the Old Firm – and have more European football to look forward to.

Hearts' form in the cup competitions in the 1999/2000 season saw them reach the quarter-finals of both the League Cup and Scottish Cup. Queen of the South and East Fife were despatched early on in the League Cup, before Hearts lost the quarter-final 1-0 at Kilmarnock.

In the Scottish Cup, Second Division side Stenhousemuir visited Tynecastle and had the audacity to storm into a two-goal lead. It took all of Hearts' resolve to rescue the tie and a Colin Cameron penalty, added to two goals from McSwegan – his second coming two minutes from the end – spared Hearts' blushes. The Maroons then headed to Cumbernauld to face more Second Division opposition in Clyde and scored twice in the opening seven minutes to avoid a similar scare to the one they had in the previous round.

Hearts were then paired with Rangers in the quarter-final at Ibrox. It was another occasion when television dictated the kick-off time so we headed for Govan on a Sunday evening – and wished we hadn't bothered. I took my 14-year-old daughter Laura and she was subjected to some appalling behaviour from some Rangers fans in the adjacent stand. When I complained to the police, I was told "you shouldn't have taken her, then". To this day, I have not been back to Ibrox. Despite a spirited showing, Hearts lost 4-1 that evening, to end hopes of another Scottish Cup success.

It had been a strange season for Hearts, one where you could never predict with any accuracy what was going to happen. And what was about to happen six months later, was something few Hearts fans saw coming…

v VfB Stuttgart 3-2
Uefa Cup First Round Second Leg
28th September 2000. Tynecastle

Hearts:	VfB Stuttgart:
Niemi	Hildebrand
Murray	Meissner
Naysmith	Bordon
James	Schneider
Pressley	Carnell
Petric	Thiam
Locke	Balakov
Cameron	Seitz
Juanjo	Lisztes
Flogel	Hosny
Kirk	Dundee

Referee: B Derrien (Luxembourg)

WITH EUROPEAN football again on the horizon for Hearts, manager Jim Jefferies had hoped to strengthen his squad accordingly before the 2000/01 season commenced. However, money was tight at Tynecastle – wasn't it always – and the investment from SMG the previous season had been spent.

Rumours circulated that Jefferies wasn't made aware that the £4m given to him for new players also included salaries/signing-on fees etc. Therefore, the manager had to start the new season with virtually the same squad that had clinched third place in the SPL the previous campaign – and frustration enveloped Tynecastle. Whether this had an effect on the players' less than convincing start to the new season is unclear.

The SPL computer that produced the fixture list seemed to have its memory stuck. Hearts' opening game was the same fixture they had ended 1999/2000 with – namely Hibs at Tynecastle. A tousy game ended goalless. In fact, Hearts had to wait until 9th September before recording their first league win of the season, a 2-0 win over Dunfermline Athletic at Tynecastle. They had only lost one game – a 4-2 defeat by Celtic – but a succession of draws had meant Hearts were at the wrong end of the table. There was success, though, on the European front – albeit moderate success, as Hearts overcame Icelandic opposition IBV Vestmannaeyjar 5-0 on aggregate in the preliminary qualifying round of the Uefa Cup.

Hearts' next European opponents were a different proposition altogether – Bundesliga club VfB Stuttgart. The Germans were one of the top sides in the competition and they faced Hearts in the first leg in Germany on the back of a win over giants Bayern Munich. Jim Jefferies knew it would be a tough ask for his team and set his players out accordingly, in a formation that was designed to frustrate the hosts. Hearts began with Thomas Flogel as the lone striker and packed the midfield with experienced players Darren Jackson, Fitzroy Simpson, Juanjo and Colin Cameron.

It was a backs to the wall performance by Hearts and it took the Germans 35 minutes to breach the visitors' defence when Gordan Petric gave away a needless foul and Balakov's subsequent free kick sailed over the head of keeper Antti Niemi to open the scoring. Those of us who feared the floodgates might open were, thankfully, proved wrong as Hearts defended manfully and by the end of the game the Germans had resorted to speculative long-range efforts. Hearts' 1-0 loss meant they had a good chance of progressing when Stuttgart came to Tynecastle for the return leg a fortnight later.

Chairman Chris Robinson's predecessor Wallace Mercer had upset Hearts fans in European campaigns years before by increasing admission prices. When VfB Stuttgart came to Edinburgh, there was again anger among many of the faithful. Not so much at the ticket prices, which, for season ticket holders, were kept to the same admission as they were for SPL games – but more to do with the time the game kicked off.

Robinson had done a deal with a German television company to provide live transmission of the tie over in Germany. However, as this may have clashed with other European ties involving German teams that evening – and mindful of the trouble Hearts got into when they agreed to television coverage of the tie against Bayern Munich more than a decade earlier – Robinson agreed to delay the kick-off time to 9pm.

It was an unprecedented move and many Hearts fans were outraged. Hearts were always trying to impress that they were now a family club. The fans were asking how this fitted in with a game that would finish just before 11pm on a Thursday evening. For Hearts fans like me, who lived on the outskirts of Edinburgh, it would be well past midnight before we got home. Yet again, it seemed the consideration of the supporters was at the bottom of the list of priorities.

Jefferies had asked the supporters to be the team's "12th man" but the unique kick-off time meant there were fewer than 15,000 fans inside Tynecastle. Nonetheless, those Hearts fans in attendance roared their team on to the pitch. With injuries affecting his preparations, Jefferies had to field something of a patched-up team, with the likes of Gary McSwegan, Darren Jackson and Stephane Adam only fit enough to take their places on the substitutes' bench.

VfB Stuttgart had made some less than respectful utterances after the first leg and had promised to kill the game off as a contest as quickly as possible at Tynecastle. They did threaten early on as Hearts, fearful of losing a goal that would mean they would have to score three to progress, began rather nervously. Bordon missed a couple of early chances for the Germans before Hearts' Gary Locke made a late challenge on Carnell on the edge of the penalty box that resulted in the Bonnyrigg player becoming the first player to be booked and a real chance for the Germans from the free kick – which they wasted.

Jefferies urged his players forward and they were rewarded in the 17th minute. Gary Naysmith delivered a corner to the near post, which the towering figure of Kevin James met with his head. James flicked the ball towards fellow defender Steven Pressley who out-jumped Schneider to head home and give Hearts the lead on the night. Tynecastle erupted in a cacophony of noise.

After Seitz came close to equalising for Stuttgart following good build-up play from Lisztes and Dundee, Hearts suffered a blow when defender Locke succumbed to the injury he appeared to have sustained early on and was replaced by youngster Robbie Neilson after just 25 minutes. Neilson, however, showed he wasn't overawed by the occasion and he forced a fine save from Hildebrand, much to the delight of the home support.

The game swung from end to end and eight minutes before half-time came the goal Hearts dreaded. Stuttgart broke quickly from defence to attack and Seitz fired in an effort that Niemi did well to block – but the ball fell to Dundee who hooked it past the Finnish goalkeeper to level the scores on the night, but put the Germans 2-1 ahead on aggregate – and, crucially, they had scored an away goal that would count as double in the event of the aggregate score being tied at the end of the game.

In fact, Seitz came close to putting Stuttgart in front three minutes before half-time, only to be denied by a brilliant save from Niemi to keep it 1-1 at the interval with Hearts knowing they had to score twice in the second half or face elimination.

The Germans took control of the game as the second half began, with Meissner coming close to putting his side ahead. Thirteen minutes into the second period came the goal that had been threatening, when a corner from the ever-dangerous Seitz was flicked on by Hosny to Bordon who headed home, much to the delight of the noisy travelling German fans.

That looked like it for Hearts, who now needed three goals to rescue the tie. Heroically, they got one goal back just four minutes later when, after a move similar to the opening goal, James flicked on Naysmith's corner and there was Gordan Petric to apply the finishing touch to level the score at 2-2 – but with Hearts still behind 3-2 on aggregate.

Balakov could, and perhaps should, have finished the game shortly afterwards, but he smashed the ball high into the Roseburn Stand from 15 yards when it seemed easier to score.

With 14 minutes to go and Hearts still needing two goals, Jefferies threw on a half-fit Gary McSwegan to replace the tiring Andy Kirk. Urged on by the home support, Hearts kept coming forward and with just seven minutes left, McSwegan turned Meissner inside the Stuttgart penalty box – only for the German defender to pull him back. Referee Derrien awarded a penalty kick to Hearts before sending off the wrong player in Thiam, much to the anger of the Stuttgart players.

After consulting with his assistant, the referee then told Thiam he could remain on the park – before sending off the original offender Meissner. After the mayhem, Colin Cameron was coolness personified as he slotted home the penalty to give Hearts the lead on the night and now they were just one goal away from completing a sensational comeback.

With just four minutes left and Hearts pouring men forward, Stuttgart's frustration boiled over when Schneider became the second player to be sent off, leaving the Germans down to nine men. This signalled something akin to the assault on the Alamo from the home side and with just a minute to go, it seemed Hearts' prayers had been answered.

Neilson, surging forward, chipped a superb pass into the Stuttgart penalty box. There, in acres of room and with only goalkeeper Hildebrand to beat, was centre-half Petric. The Belgrade-born defender controlled the ball with his chest and unleashed a ferocious strike on goal. Agonisingly for the Hearts support, players and management team, Petric's effort didn't go into the net to put Heart into the next round – it flew high into the Gorgie Stand as 14,000 Hearts fans held their heads in their hands. The final whistle blew seconds later. Hearts had won 3-2 on the night to draw 3-3 on aggregate and went out on the away goals rule.

Hearts had come so close and yet were so far. Domestically, in an attempt to increase his attacking options, Jefferies brought in former Rangers and Scotland striker Gordon Durie and he made an immediate impact by scoring twice on his debut in a 3-0 win over Motherwell at Tynecastle. The Maroons then dismantled Dundee United 4-0 at Tannadice a week later, before the season turned on a sorry Sunday evening at Easter Road.

Despite Andy Kirk giving Hearts an early lead, this was to prove to be Hibs' night and they won 6-2. The less said about this game the better. When Hearts lost 3-0 at home to St Johnstone the week after, and then lost 5-2 to Celtic in the quarter-final of the League Cup at Tynecastle – although this was after extra time – some fans began to turn against the club. After the St Johnstone loss, there was a demonstration at the back of the old stand at Tynecastle calling for Robinson to go. Some also called for Jefferies to go.

Within a couple of weeks, Jefferies was gone – he had accepted an offer from English FA Premiership side Bradford City to become their manager, charged with keeping the Yorkshire team in the top flight of English football. When Hearts, under caretaker boss Peter Houston, conceded another six goals – this time at Celtic Park – as well as losing to Dunfermline Athletic, it seemed the season was falling apart.

Hearts knew they had to make a permanent appointment to the manager's position – and fast. The story of this appointment and his first season in charge at Tynecastle is described in the next chapter.

With Jim Jefferies' departure, it was a case of the King is Dead – Long Live the King. It was also a case, however, of wondering if he might have gone at all had Gordan Petric converted that last-minute chance against Stuttgart.

v **Dunfermline Ath 7-1**

Bank of Scotland SPL
24th February 2001. Tynecastle

Hearts:	Dunfermline Athletic:
Niemi	Ruitenbeek
Neilson	McGroarty
Flogel	Doesburg
Severin	Ferguson
Pressley	Skinner
Boyack	Skerla
Tomaschek	Crawford
Cameron	Thomson
Makel	Dair
Adam	Nicholson
Kirk	Tod

Referee: A Freeland (Aberdeen)

JIM JEFFERIES' departure from Tynecastle sent shockwaves through not just Gorgie, but the whole of Scottish football. His love for all things Heart of Midlothian was renowned and while one could understand his ambition to manage a club in the English FA Premiership – this league was being touted, particularly by those down south as being the best in the world – the fact it was perhaps the least fashionable club in the top flight, and one that was already among the favourites to be relegated, Bradford City, raised more than a few eyebrows.

When JJ left Tynecastle, the club put on a public display to indicate it was a very amicable departure. Chairman Chris Robinson said Jefferies would always be remembered as the man who brought the Scottish Cup back to Tynecastle and Jefferies himself said he would never rule out the possibility of returning to the Gorgie hot seat one day – words that would be prophetic indeed.

The question on everyone's lips was who would replace Jefferies? Ideally, it would be someone with a Hearts connection, someone who knew the club and how much it meant to its army of supporters. Someone who was young, ambitious and looking to make a name for himself as a manager. Someone who had some experience of managing a club, even if it was at a lower level. An obvious candidate ticked all of those boxes. Former Hearts and Scotland centre-half Craig Levein had been doing a fine job as manager of Cowdenbeath and was duly appointed Jim Jefferies' successor.

Levein's first game in charge of the club he had served so well as a player in the 1980s and early 1990s was against Rangers at Tynecastle on 3rd December 2000. Naturally, he was given a hero's reception as he made his way to the dug out in front of a crowd just short of 17,000. It's fair to say that, while many Hearts fans were upset at the departure of Jefferies, there were those who thought a change was needed and that Levein, very much his own man, would be the ideal person to establish Hearts as the main challengers to Celtic and Rangers once again.

Even in that first game against Rangers, there were signs of Levein's influence. There seemed to be more of an emphasis on passing the ball, and while Rangers won the game thanks to an early penalty from Jorg Albertz, Hearts should have taken something, given the visitors had two players sent off in the second half. Six days later, Hearts won 3-0 at Kilmarnock and hopes rose that Levein would be as big a success as Hearts manager as his predecessor.

The SPL fixture list was giving scant regard for tradition, as witness the fact that the traditional New Year Edinburgh derby was to be played – on Boxing Day. Hibs came to Tynecastle, their fans still goading their city rivals about the 6-2 drubbing handed out at Easter Road in October. Levein was determined there would be no such embarrassment this time around and even indulged in some managerial mind games before the game when he said that, as a Hearts player, his record against Hibs was pretty good – only two defeats in 14 years. Although Hibs did take a first-half lead, their festive cheer was soon doused when Gary McSwegan equalised with half an hour to go for a share of the spoils.

Levein knew he had to bring in fresh blood to the squad and he did this with a combination of bringing in youngsters impressing in the reserves and players who wouldn't cost much in transfer fees – a necessity, given Hearts had little money to spend in any case – but whom he knew could do a job. Former Rangers midfielder Steven Boyack arrived from Dundee for a modest fee of £50,000, while full-back Kieran McAnespie came on loan from Fulham. Another defender, Austin McCann, arrived from Airdrieonians, as Levein began to make his mark on an evolving Hearts team.

He also gave first-team debuts to youngsters Stephen Simmons and Darren Goldie and while Hearts had tightened up defensively, there remained a concern about the lack of goals. However, this was addressed in spectacular fashion when Dunfermline Athletic visited Tynecastle on SPL business at the end of February.

The Pars, managed by the ebullient Jimmy Calderwood, were enjoying a fine season and were in fifth place in the SPL, one ahead of Hearts. Levein made three changes to the team that was held to a draw by Dundee in the Scottish Cup a week earlier and if he was hoping his team would make a good start, his wish was granted within five minutes.

Full-back Robbie Neilson would become renowned for his long throw-ins during his time at Tynecastle, and one of his trademark throws found French striker Stephane Adam, who quickly controlled the ball from 12 yards out before shooting high into the net to give Hearts an early lead. It was Adam's first goal since December 1999, after a period during which he was blighted with injury, and the hero of the 1998 Scottish Cup final could not contain his delight.

Hearts looked in the mood to add to their lead, although the visitors should have equalised after 20 minutes. Crawford raced on to a pass by Ferguson – only for Hearts' Scott Severin to produce a magnificent blocking challenge. Five minutes later, Dunfermline manager Calderwood decided to make a double substitution. He took off Ferguson and Tod and replaced them with Dijkhuizen and Bullen. Neither Ferguson nor Tod looked injured, so one assumed the Pars boss was making a bold tactical substitution in a bid to outfox his young rival in the Hearts dugout. A move that backfired badly.

Four minutes later, Hearts scored again. Andy Kirk, whose work-rate caused the Pars defence no end of trouble, passed to Adam on the edge of the Dunfermline penalty box. The Frenchman's attempt on goal was parried by goalkeeper Ruitenbeek and appeared to be trundling over the line but the ever-alert Kirk raced in to make sure. Two minutes later, Calderwood's master plan was in tatters when Hearts scored a third goal. Steven Pressley delivered a superb pass towards Colin Cameron and the skipper ran through on goal, before brilliantly chipping the ball over Ruitenbeek to put Hearts 3-0 ahead.

Dunfermline looked shell-shocked but their ordeal was far from over. Six minutes before half-time, the impressive Boyack outpaced the Pars defence and left them trailing in his wake. The former Rangers player cut the ball back to Adam who brilliantly volleyed in Hearts' fourth goal of the afternoon. Adam would have completed his hat-trick before half-time had it not been for a fine save from the Dunfermline goalkeeper.

If the Pars thought the second half couldn't be any worse, such feelings were abandoned just a minute after the restart. Defender Skinner gave the ball away on the edge of his own penalty box and Adam fired in an effort that Ruitenbeek could only deflect into the path of Cameron, who gleefully knocked the ball home for his second and Hearts' fifth. Hearts five goals ahead with most of the second half still to play – we Jambos were just not accustomed to being in such a comfort zone!

As if to prove this point, Dunfermline duly pulled a goal back when Dair was given far too much space to fire home a shot past Antti Niemi who, until that point, must have been feeling rather left out of things. This merely irked the home team who scored a sixth goal on the hour mark. Kirk played a one-two with Robert Tomaschek on the edge of the penalty box and eased the ball past Ruitenbeek for the simplest of goals. That made it 6-1 with still half an hour to play and we wondered if Hearts might reach double figures. After Crawford almost grabbed a second for the visitors – denied by a brilliant save from Niemi – Hearts scored again in the 67th minute. Another defensive blunder by Dunfermline, this time Thomson was dispossessed by Tomaschek, allowed the Slovakian international to race in on goal and bury the ball into the net beyond a now thoroughly depressed Ruitenbeek. Hearts 7 Dunfermline Athletic 1 – with still more than 20 minutes to play.

Hearts did continue to attack, but they were dealt a blow when hero Adam limped off the field with what appeared to be a hamstring injury. The Frenchman looked to be close to tears as he left the field to a standing ovation from the adoring Hearts support. He had been blighted with injury far too often since his heroics in the Scottish Cup final of 1998 and, having just returned to the Hearts team, it looked like another spell on the sidelines for the great man.

Whether Adam's departure had an effect on the players, it wasn't clear but there was no further scoring and the game ended at 7-1 for the home team – Hearts' biggest league win for 15 years. More importantly, it was clear evidence that Craig Levein was on the way to making Hearts a force to be reckoned with once again.

It had been a difficult season for those of the maroon persuasion. Hammerings from Hibs and Celtic; the departure of Jim Jefferies and noises from the boardroom about Hearts moving out of Tynecastle to an out-of-city location – Straiton in Midlothian had been mentioned as a ground sharing possibility with Hibs, although no one at Easter Road seemed to know anything about this proposal – meant these were unsettling times for Hearts supporters. They did, however, put their faith in Craig Levein.

Hearts' league form continued to blow hot and cold for the rest of the 2000/01 season. A week after demolishing Dunfermline, the Maroons lost 2-0 to Rangers at Ibrox, although it has to be said both Rangers goals were scored by a player who cost £12m – Tore Andre Flo. Hearts scored convincing wins over Kilmarnock and Motherwell at Tynecastle and ended the season in fifth place in the SPL – an astonishing 45 points behind runaway champions Celtic. More worrying was the fact that Hearts were 14 points behind a certain other Edinburgh team.

Hearts' progress in the cup competitions took on a depressingly familiar tale. I mentioned in the previous chapter that Hearts reached the quarter-final of the League Cup this season, before losing to Celtic. In the Scottish Cup, Hearts needed replays to get past Berwick Rangers and Dundee – the latter was one of Hearts' better performances of the season, a 1-0 replay victory at Dens Park before, yet again, Celtic were quarter-final cup opponents. Craig Levein opted for a cautious approach at Celtic Park, but still Hearts lost to a goal from the home side's Henrik Larsson.

Levein's rebuilding of Hearts would continue apace with players such as Stephane Mahe, Kevin McKenna and Alan Maybury arriving at Tynecastle. There would also be a six-month loan appearance of Jamaican striker Ricardo Fuller, who would score one of the greatest goals ever scored at Tynecastle. Against Motherwell in December 2001, Fuller set off on a mazy 50-yard run that began in his own half and ended with him skipping past a couple of Motherwell defenders before slotting the ball home in a 3-1 win.

It was the work of a genius – sadly, one who Craig Levein couldn't keep at Tynecastle. However, another goal scoring hero wasn't far away.

v **Hibernian** 5-1
Bank of Scotland SPL
11th August 2002. Tynecastle

Hearts:	Hibernian:
Niemi	Caig
Maybury	Orman
Pressley	Smith
McKenna	Dempsie
Mahe	Murray
Simmons	O'Neil
Severin	Townsley
Boyack	Jack
Valois	Arpinon
De Vries	Luna
Kirk	O'Connor

Referee: M McCurry (Glasgow)

IT'S FAIR to say Craig Levein was making a name for himself in football management. Here was a young, articulate scholar of the game who, at the height of his playing career, was a brilliant defender in the Franz Beckenbauer mould. He suffered two serious knee injuries, which meant he had to give up the game prematurely – his decision to do so was announced at a tearful Tynecastle press conference in the autumn of 1997. Now, he was back at the club he served so well and where he made his name.

By the time the 2002/03 season started, Levein had rebuilt the Hearts team to his specification. Just a little over four years had passed since his predecessor Jim Jefferies had led Hearts to Scottish Cup glory, but most of that team had now left Gorgie for pastures new. This was now Levein's team.

One of his first signings was Andy Webster, a stylish centre-half very much in the Levein mould. Levein paid a handsome sum of £70,000 in March 2001 to Arbroath for the services of the 19-year-old Dundonian. Like Levein, Webster would go on to play for Scotland. He would be a crucial component of Levein's side that would go on to produce some memorable results, both domestically and in Europe, in the years that followed.

Hearts began 2002/03 with a steady, if unspectacular, 1-1 draw at Dundee, before welcoming Hibernian for the first Edinburgh derby of the season. The BBC had switched the game to a Sunday afternoon for live television transmission and although it was early August and the Edinburgh Festival was in full swing, the weather was more like November. Torrential rain lashed the capital city all day but this didn't stop more than 15,000 fans heading to Tynecastle for a game always hugely anticipated.

The game began rather like the weather conditions of the day – with Hearts flooding the Hibernian half. One of Hearts' new signings, French winger Jean Louis

Valois, was clearly in the mood and took little time to display his obvious skill. Hearts' other significant signing of the summer, Dutch striker Mark de Vries, was making his first start of the season, having come off the substitutes' bench the previous week at Dundee and his big physical presence seemed to have an unsettling effect on the Hibs defence right from the start.

Valois, despite the monsoon like conditions, was revelling in the atmosphere and the Hibs defenders were clearly having trouble containing him. That said it was Hibernian who nearly opened the scoring when Townsley played a neat pass to O'Connor whose shot dipped over the crossbar. To say Hibs opening the scoring would have been against the run of play would be akin to saying there was a shower in Edinburgh that day.

However, Hearts finally got the goal their play so richly deserved after 18 minutes, when keeper Niemi launched a long ball forward that was nodded on by de Vries towards Andy Kirk. "Ulster Andy", as he was affectionately known, produced a lob of some quality over the Hibs keeper and immediately ran to the jubilant Hearts supporters in the Wheatfield Stand. Kirk really should have made it 2-0 a few moments later, when he headed a sublime cross from Steven Boyack over the crossbar.

In the 27th minute, Hearts thought they had scored a second goal when, following a corner, Valois found Scott Severin, but the midfield man's spectacular diving header crashed off the crossbar with the Hibs keeper beaten. As half-time approached, some Hearts fans felt edgy about only having a one-goal lead for all their team's dominance. However, four minutes before the break, that man Valois delivered another fine cross into the Hibs penalty area and de Vries poked the ball beyond Caig to give Hearts a 2-0 lead at the interval.

Hearts fans, of course, can never take anything for granted and a two-goal lead quite often isn't enough. Five minutes into the second half, Hibs' Ian Murray headed home a cross from Brebner and it was game on in the Edinburgh derby. The goal gave the visitors hope and the game developed into an end-to-end affair. Valois continued to torment the Hibs defence and he provided yet another inviting cross, only for Kirk to fail to accept the invitation – but only just. "Ulster Andy" then produced a ferocious effort from six yards out, which Hibs keeper Caig brilliantly tipped over the crossbar.

Hearts swarmed forward again on 64 minutes with Valois, inevitably, involved. The Frenchman struck a shot that Caig could only parry and de Vries slammed home the rebound to put Hearts 3-1 ahead to the ecstasy of the home support.

Hibernian brought on the old warhorse Mixu Paatelainen – who played a significant part in Hibs' 6-2 win over Hearts at Easter Road two years earlier – in an attempt to score the two goals needed to salvage a draw. Two further goals were indeed scored as the game entered its final stage – but not by those in green and white.

As the 90-minute mark approached, some of the home support began whistling for referee Mike McCurry to blow his whistle for full-time. However, the magnificent Maroons, and Mark de Vries in particular, weren't finished yet. As Hibs pressed for a lifeline, Hearts broke upfield in the final minute of regulation time. Good work by substitute Gary Wales set up de Vries, who buried the ball past Caig for Hearts' fourth.

With the Roseburn Stand emptying quicker than a pint of 80 shillings ale at The Diggers on match day, three quarters of Tynecastle was rocking. Deep in injury time, Boyack delivered a deep cross into the Hibs penalty box, which the inevitable figure of de Vries met with his head and the ball bounced over the flailing Caig to make the final score an incredible Heart of Midlothian 5 Hibernian 1. The big Surinamese striker had astonishingly scored four goals on his home debut. Being against Hibs, it was a performance that would place the name de Vries in Tynecastle folklore.

As the fans spilled out on to Gorgie Road, the rain was still hammering down in the capital city but the jubilant Hearts support did not care. They were in dreamland. They had waited years for a result like this over their city neighbours, who still referred to Hibs' 7-0 win at Tynecastle on New Year's Day 1973 and the aforementioned more recent 6-2 win at Easter Road. Now revenge was sweet indeed.

Few players have made such a debut in the Edinburgh derby as Mark de Vries did that day. The six feet four inches striker from Dordrecht 90 was sensational and, incredibly, Hearts manager Craig Levein said afterwards he expected even more from the big man – once he was fully fit! However, as impressive as de Vries' scoring exploits were that day, the man of the match was not the big striker but another new boy, winger Jean-Louis Valois. He simply destroyed the Hibs defence that rain-soaked afternoon and he was instrumental in Hearts' dominant performance.

The former Luton Town player, who began his career at Auxerre under the legendary Guy Roux, was signed by Levein on a free transfer and Hearts fans were wondering just how on earth any team could have simply allowed the gifted Frenchman to leave for nothing. The answer would become apparent in the months ahead. On his day, Valois was sublime, but there were other days when he was anonymous – almost the archetypal Scots winger!

He was brilliant in season 2002/03 and he enthralled the Hearts fans with his skilful displays. Sadly though, Valois became something of a one-season wonder. A regular in his first campaign at Tynecastle, something seemed to happen to the Frenchman in the summer of 2003 and he failed to reproduce his form in the 2003/04 season. After losing form, he fell out of favour with Levein and was released early from his contract in January 2004.

Following a brief spell in Spanish football, Valois returned to Scotland at the somewhat unlikely port of call that was Clyde. He then signed for Burnley and featured in their famous FA Cup victory over Liverpool in January 2005. Again though, he flattered to deceive and left Lancashire for the United Arab Emirates later that year. As for his Dutch colleague that day, it would not be the last time de Vries would feature prominently in a Hearts game – more of this later!

The next Edinburgh derby following the 5-1 thrashing of the hapless Hibees came at Easter Road in November and, in many ways, was as sweet as the August hammering. Hearts had struggled all afternoon and trailed 1-0 with just five minutes remaining. As Hibs eyed a small measure of revenge, they reckoned without Hearts substitute Neil Janczyk. Four minutes from the end, the young midfielder crossed for big Kevin McKenna to nod past Hibs keeper Colgan to give Hearts an unlikely equaliser.

Two minutes into stoppage time, Janczyk provided a sweet pass to Phil Stamp who darted into the Hibs penalty box, before stroking the ball past Colgan to give

Hearts an even more unlikely winner. Even when Hearts played poorly, as they had done that afternoon, they were still good enough to beat Hibs! Craig Levein's men ended the season in third place in the SPL and qualified for the Uefa Cup.

Hearts had a decent run in the League Cup, reaching the semi-final before they lost to a solitary goal by Rangers' Dutch star Ronald de Boer at Hampden on a cold, miserable February evening. However, Hearts reserved their worst performance of the season for the competition that means so much to the fans as it's the one we all think Hearts – unlike other teams from Edinburgh – have a realistic chance of winning. Namely, the Scottish Cup.

Hearts were drawn away to Falkirk in the third round (the first round that included the top-flight clubs). The Bairns were in the First Division at the time and Hearts had prepared for the game with a midwinter break in Portugal. Perhaps the players were still thinking about this when they took to the field at ramshackle Brockville Park on a freezing cold January afternoon; it certainly wasn't the cup-tie they were thinking about in a shambolic first half in which they found themselves four goals down to their lower league opponents, thanks to a hat-trick from Colin Samuel and a goal from Owen Coyle.

There were shades of a 6-0 hammering at the same ground a decade earlier. Small wonder few Hearts supporters mourned the passing of Brockville when it was demolished to make way for a supermarket a few years later (OK, perhaps I felt a tinge of sadness, given Brockville was where I saw my first Hearts game in 1968).

Such thoughts, however, could not have been further from the minds of celebrating Hearts supporters as they left Tynecastle in August 2002 after hammering the Hibs. We were too busy asking our Hibby supporting associates what the time was – as we made it five past!

v Celtic 2-1

Bank of Scotland SPL
19th April 2003. Tynecastle

Hearts:	Celtic:
Moilanen	Douglas
Maybury	Mjallby
Pressley	Balde
Webster	Valgaeran
McCann	Agathe
MacFarlane	Lennon
Stamp	Petrov
Severin	Lambert
Valois	Thompson
Weir	Larsson
De Vries	Hartson

Referee: J Rowbotham (Kirkcaldy)

THE IMPACT of players such as Mark de Vries, Jean-Louis Valois and Phil Stamp was immediate, but Hearts knew the best they could realistically hope for in the SPL was a third-placed finish. Rangers and Celtic had built sizeable squads and were so far in front of the other teams in the league, one had to question the *raison d'etre* for the SPL – to make Scottish football more competitive.

After Hearts' late, late show against Hibs at Easter Road in November 2002, Craig Levein's side had climbed into third place in the SPL – but were 14 points behind second-placed Celtic and 15 behind league leaders Rangers. And this after just 13 games. The Old Firm had lost just one league game between them all season and when your team's hopes of winning the league, however small to begin with, have disappeared by the end of October, then it's small wonder some fans were asking what was the point in shelling out for ever-increasing prices for season tickets.

As ever, inconsistency was Hearts' bugbear. A week after winning at Easter Road, the Maroons were held to a goalless draw with Aberdeen at Tynecastle, before losing 3-1 at Dunfermline Athletic. December couldn't have started any worse. Rangers visited Tynecastle, and for 50 minutes Hearts gave as good as they got. However, Ricksen then scored for the visitors and shortly afterwards Hearts' Alan Maybury was sent off for a late tackle on former Hearts player Neil McCann and the home side's hopes of victory disappeared up the Tynecastle tunnel with the Irishman. Ten-man Hearts lost 4-0.

Worse was to follow three days later when Hearts, hit badly by injuries and suspensions, were hammered 6-1 at Motherwell by a team propping up the SPL and who had won just two league games all season. However, the sheer unpredictability of this Hearts team was demonstrated when the Maroons won their next three league games – including an impressive 3-0 win over Dundee United at Tannadice – to regain third place in the SPL. Then came the visit of Hibs on 2nd January 2003.

The first two Edinburgh derbies of the 2002/03 season were dramatic affairs, so we had no right to expect more of the same. Nevertheless, we got it in bucketfuls. A fantastic game swung from end to end right from kick-off. Hibs were two goals ahead after just 16 minutes and Hearts' 5-1 thrashing of their neighbours seemed an eternity ago. However, the Maroons fought back through captain Steven Pressley and the four-goal hero of the derby in August, Mark de Vries, and the game was tied at 2-2 with half an hour to go.

Both teams had chances, but when Hibs scored a third goal in the 89th minute it looked like revenge was on the cards. It appeared a damned certainty a minute into stoppage time, when Brebner converted a penalty to put Hibs 4-2 ahead. This was my cue to head for the exits – defeat is hard to take at any time but when it comes against your city rivals, it's particularly difficult to swallow.

However, straight from the kick-off Hearts substitute Graham Weir pulled a goal back to make it 4-3. Small consolation we thought, particularly as 94 minutes had been played. Then, incredibly, unbelievably, in the fifth minute of stoppage time, Weir scored again to level the game at 4-4 for arguably the most dramatic ending to an Edinburgh derby ever. Hearts celebrated every bit as much as they did in the 5-1 game five months earlier. Hibs looked crestfallen – just what did they have to do to get the better of their Edinburgh rivals?

Those 90 – or should I say 95 – minutes against Hibs seemed to sum up this Hearts team this season. You just did not know what to expect. After that incredible 4-4 draw, Hearts went on a winter break and, as I wrote in the previous chapter, probably wished they hadn't as they lost 4-0 to Falkirk in the Scottish Cup on their return. Typically, though, Hearts then defeated Aberdeen, Dunfermline Athletic and Kilmarnock.

By the time April came around – the so-called "business end" of the season – third-placed Hearts were four points clear of Kilmarnock, with these two well ahead of the chasing pack in the race for a place in the following season's Uefa Cup. Hearts were – whisper it – 25 points behind Celtic when Martin O'Neill's men visited Tynecastle on 19th April 2003. Celtic were playing catch-up with Rangers – the Hoops were eight points behind the league leaders but did have two games in hand – and knew three points in Gorgie were essential if they harboured hopes of overtaking their rivals at the top of the SPL.

Craig Levein, though, had his own agenda. Hearts had not managed to defeat Celtic in 13 attempts and a win was long overdue for the Gorgie faithful. Celtic were on the march to the Uefa Cup final, so a battle royale was promised on a sunny April afternoon in Edinburgh's west end.

Just 40 seconds after referee John Rowbotham blew his whistle to start the game, Hearts captain Steven Pressley brought down Thompson as the home side posted their intentions to Celtic that they weren't going to let the champions have things their own way. Minutes later, Phil Stamp did likewise to Valgaeren but with the Englishman having a reputation for "physical" challenges his name was the first to enter the referee's little black book that afternoon.

However, Hearts showed they weren't just about blood and thunder. Stamp's determination set up de Vries and the big striker was unfortunate to see his effort blocked by Celtic defender Balde. Seconds later, the unlikely figure of Alan Maybury saw his shot at goal deflected by Thompson, before a mistake by Valgaeren gave de Vries a chance that the big striker fired wide. Nonetheless, this was hugely encouraging from the home side and the Hearts support boomed out their raucous encouragement from the stands.

The industrious de Vries then fired in another effort that was deflected away from Graham Weir with the goal gaping. At the other end, Hearts' Finnish goalkeeper Tepi Moilanen saved well from Thompson and Hartson as play raged from end to end. It was nothing short of astonishing that an enthralling first half ended goalless.

The second half was just three minutes old, when it appeared Celtic had opened the scoring but Petrov's celebrations were cut short when his effort was disallowed for handball. Just before the hour mark, Hearts should have taken the lead when Stamp was through on Douglas, but his effort lacked conviction and the keeper tipped the ball over the crossbar – as he did moments later to a ferocious effort from Maybury.

This was undoubtedly one of the games of an already remarkable season and it seemed only a matter of time before such a pulsating match was graced with a goal. On the hour it was, when Celtic's Agathe cut down the right wing before cutting the ball back for Larsson who got the slightest of touches to ease the ball past Moilanen.

If you will excuse the pun, it was heartbreak for the home side but Craig Levein had built character in his team. After Jean-Louis Valois was inches away from converting a cross from de Vries, Hearts grabbed a richly deserved equaliser in the 73rd minute. Scott Severin got on the end of a free kick from Steven Pressley but the midfielder's effort was wayward – until Stamp galloped into the Celtic penalty box to drill the ball past Douglas. Tynecastle rocked!

Many teams might have settled for a share of the spoils against the league champions but Hearts weren't satisfied. Mjallby cleared away a goalbound header from de Vries before Valois struck the Celtic crossbar with a brilliant shot that looked a goal all the way. However, Celtic also knew a draw was of little use to them in their pursuit of Rangers and they pressed forward in desperate search of the winner.

Indeed, the visitors were camped deep in the Hearts half three minutes into injury time, with many Hearts fans whistling for the referee to end the game so their team could gain a vital point in the quest for European football. Then, Hearts broke from their own penalty box through the tireless Scott Severin.

Severin raced across the halfway line with the Celtic players chasing after him. With de Vries screaming for the ball, Severin saw a Hearts player to his left and passed the ball towards him. The player in question was full-back Austin McCann, not renowned for his goalscoring exploits. With the Hearts fans looking for a cross towards the towering figure of de Vries, McCann took the ball in his stride, looked up and, from 25 yards out, let rip with a screamer of a shot that flew high past keeper Douglas and into the roof of the net.

If I thought Tynecastle had rocked at Phil Stamp's equaliser, I thought the roof was about to be blown off the Wheatfield Stand and McCann fell to his knees to soak up the acclamation of his team-mates and scarcely believing supporters. The final whistle blew seconds later and Hearts had won a quite magnificent match 2-1. Hearts were now seven points ahead of Kilmarnock in third place in the SPL and the result all but secured a place in the Uefa Cup for 2003/04 – and pretty much ended Celtic's hopes of retaining their league championship.

Celtic manager Martin O'Neill was magnanimous in defeat afterwards and was mindful of the fact Rangers still had to head to Tynecastle before the end of the season, stating if Hearts played the way they did that afternoon, there would still be a few twists and turns yet in the race for the league title. Hearts played Celtic again three weeks later, but lost 1-0 at Celtic Park. Sadly, they couldn't repeat their Tynecastle showing, not only in the east end of Glasgow, but also when Rangers visited Gorgie for the penultimate league game of the season – and won 2-0.

However, after another rollercoaster of a season, Hearts did secure a third-placed finish in the SPL. Craig Levein was not only building his own team but also building a team that reflected his characteristics. As a player, Levein was a commanding, but stylish centre-half, similar in many ways to Scotland and Liverpool great Alan Hansen. Both Levein and Hansen had a never-say-die attitude to football and Hearts demonstrated this several times throughout season 2002/03. Those of us who witnessed the Maroons' stunning comebacks at Easter Road in November; Tynecastle on 2nd January; and against Celtic in April would certainly testify to that.

The challenge for Levein was to instil a consistency in his team so that performances and results – such as those against Celtic – were a regular feature of the season. Given the way he had already stamped his authority on the club he had served so well as a player, few were betting against the big man from Fife doing exactly that.

v Bordeaux 1-0

Uefa Cup Second Round First Leg
6th November 2003. Stade Chaban-Delmas

Hearts:	Bordeaux:
Gordon	Rame
Neilson	Alicarte
McKenna	Basto
Webster	Jemmali
Pressley	Jurietti
Kisnorbo	Pochettino
Maybury	E da Costa
Stamp	P da Costa
Wyness	Feindouno
Valois	Chamakh
De Vries	Darcheville

Referee: K Jacobson (Iceland)

A SIGNIFICANT feature of Craig Levein's time as manager of Hearts, was achieving some decent results in European competition – particularly away from Edinburgh. The 2003/04 season would see Hearts maintain their steady progress under the former Scotland centre-half even though money, as always, was tight at Tynecastle.

Chairman Chris Robinson had to tell Levein – like the majority of Hearts managers before him – that he would need to wheel and deal in the transfer market, as there would be no money for new players. However, Levein was proving more than adept at spotting attributes in players others couldn't see.

Levein recruited two attack-minded players in the summer of 2003. Dennis Wyness had a decent scoring record at Inverness Caledonian Thistle and Hearts faced a fight with Wyness' former team Aberdeen, who wanted him back at Pittodrie, for the Aberdonian's signature. The fact that Hearts were about to play in the Uefa Cup seemed to swing it for Wyness, who ventured south to Scotland's capital city and signed for Hearts.

Paul Hartley was a player who once played for Edinburgh's other team but saw the error of his ways. He had performed well for St Johnstone and Levein saw the Glaswegian as an integral part of the Hearts team – something Hartley would prove to be for some time after Levein's departure from Tynecastle. Both players, to the delight of chairman Robinson, cost nothing as they were at the end of their respective contracts.

Hearts had enjoyed a productive campaign in 2002/03 and a third-placed finish in the SPL meant participation in the Uefa Cup. Hearts awaited the draw for the first round knowing they would be sure to face tough opposition. They were paired with the Bosnian side Zeljeznicar Sarajevo and while the draw could have been tougher, they were grateful to have avoided the likes of Barcelona, Liverpool, Valencia and Borussia Dortmund.

The Bosnians, though, were no mugs and on their substitute bench was a 17-year-old striker who would go on to become a huge star in years to come. In January 2011, Edin Dzeko would move from German football to money-laden Manchester City for the not inconsiderable sum of £27m.

Hearts won the first leg 2-0 at Tynecastle, thanks to goals from Mark de Vries and Andy Webster. Crucially, they had avoided conceding an away goal, but those of us who recalled Hearts' Uefa Cup trip to neighbouring Velez Mostar in 1988, knew the return leg would be a tough affair.

The Bosnians weren't happy with their defeat in Edinburgh and sacked coach Amar Osmin afterwards. New coach Milomir Odovic told his players they not only still had a chance to progress, but they had to prove to him that they were good enough. It took a backs to the wall performance from Hearts to secure a goalless draw and progression to the second round on a 2-0 aggregate.

When the draw for the second round was made, Hearts fans clapped their hands with eager anticipation. No trip to the relative unknown this time. For Hearts were paired with one of the leading clubs in French football – FC Girondins de Bordeaux. The first leg was to be played in the south of France and the chance of heading to warmer climes seven weeks before Christmas to see their team take on one of Europe's top sides was not to be missed for Hearts supporters and 3,000 Jambos headed to the wine producing region of France.

Hearts arranged a special charter plane to take fans there and back on the same day. With hindsight, the events of Thursday 6th November 2003 meant that, perhaps, we should have stayed over to fully celebrate one of the most famous results in the history of Heart of Midlothian Football Club.

There were just over 15,000 fans at the Stade Chaban-Delmas in Bordeaux – a fifth of whom had made the journey from Scotland. Those of us who boarded Hearts' charter flight at 7am that day had been in the French city since 11am – and had spent much of the day sampling the delights of the city and French hospitality. It may have been early November but the temperature in the south of France was 72 degrees Fahrenheit and while some Hearts fans headed for open-air cafes, most congregated at an Irish bar (as you do when in France...) called The Connemara. It was a day when a copious amount of alcohol was consumed and it built up a magnificent atmosphere ahead of the match.

As for the game itself, the majority of Hearts supporters present may have been under various influences of alcohol but I suspect many of them were wondering if they had imbibed too much when they heard the team Craig Levein had selected for the game. Granted, several beers had been consumed during the course of the day but as I stood behind the goal with 3,000 other Jambos it seemed to me Levein had gone for a 4-3-3 option – as Dennis Wyness, Mark de Vries and Jean-Louis Valois were all named in the starting line-up. However, when the game kicked off, it soon became apparent that de Vries would plough a lone furrow up front. Wyness and Valois were part of a six-man midfield – with Kevin McKenna, Steven Pressley and Andy Webster forming a trio of centre-halves in front of young goalkeeper Craig Gordon, making his debut in European football at the age of 20.

Robbie Neilson, normally a full-back, was given one of the six midfield positions and the intent was clearly to stop the home side from producing anything approaching French flair. What's more – it worked.

Bordeaux struggled to produce a threat of any kind in the first 15 minutes. Hearts' six-man midfield snapped at the heels of any home player threatening to venture forward, with Bordeaux striker Jean-Claude Darcheville – who would later go on to play for Rangers in the SPL – hardly getting a touch of the ball.

The old adage in football in games like these is if the underdogs can survive the first 20 minutes, then anything is possible. After 20 minutes, came the first real chance of the game – but not at the end of the ground most expected. Neilson, of all people, had been fouled on the edge of the Bordeaux penalty box and while there were hopeful appeals from the less than sober visiting support, the resultant free kick taken by Valois, back in the country of his birth, went wide. Nevertheless, it added to the belief in the Hearts camp that a positive result was possible.

It did, however, alert the home team that they had a game on their hands. Jemmali fired in a ferocious shot that Gordon did well to save, before an effort from Feindouno went just over the crossbar. Moments later, a moment of carelessness from Valois presented another chance for Feindouno but again his effort was not on target.

The game was now taking on the pattern we all thought it would, with the French continuing to press, although Hearts threatened again just before half-time when Neilson – revelling in his midfield role – delivered a cross that caused consternation in the home defence. With both McKenna and de Vries lurking in the Bordeaux penalty area, the aforementioned Feindouno headed the ball towards his goalkeeper Rame – who had Wyness bearing down on him.

The Bordeaux number one managed to avert the danger but it was another encouraging sign for Hearts, roared on by their vociferous support who were showing their French counterparts just how to get behind your team. Those Jambos were happy to get the chance to ease their voices at half-time with the game still goalless – Craig Levein's master plan was, so far, working well.

Five minutes after the restart, Darcheville produced a chance out of nothing but fired his shot over the bar. Minutes later, the same player had a goalbound shot hooked off the line by Webster, before Gordon produced another fine save from Costa. It didn't help the now sobering Hearts support that Bordeaux were attacking the end behind which they stood anxiously and we constantly looked at our watches in the belief that time had stood still in the south of France.

Levein brought on fresh legs when Paul Hartley replaced Valois but Hearts suffered a blow when the magnificent Neilson had to go off injured, to be replaced by Austin McCann. Inevitably, it was Bordeaux who continued to make all the running and, at times, Gordon must have felt it was he against the French as the home team did everything but score. The young goalkeeper came of age that evening and one could see the frustration on the faces of the home players as the Hearts supporting goalie kept them at bay, one save in particular from Pochettino damn near taking the breath away.

Still the game remained goalless. Hearts supporters would have been delighted with that and the chance to complete the job at Tynecastle three weeks later. With just 12 minutes left, the deadlock was broken. On a rare foray into the Bordeaux half, Hearts were awarded a free kick for a foul on Phil Stamp that Hartley elected to take.

He was too far out to have a shot on goal but he expertly floated a long ball towards the far post, which the tall figure of McKenna met with his head. "Moose", as the big Canadian defender was known, headed the ball across the penalty box where Rame palmed his effort away – but only into the path of de Vries who slotted into the net for an incredible goal. Cue absolute bedlam in the Hearts end as 3,000 disbelieving maroon and white-clad supporters leapt for joy.

The home support was stunned. It has to be said the same feeling was prevalent among a nonetheless ecstatic travelling support. The game ended with an historic 1-0 win for Hearts, their first and, to date, only victory on French soil. Bordeaux were one of the leading clubs in France and for a young, inexperienced Hearts team – and manager – to come away with a victory was nothing short of sensational. At the end of the game, the Hearts players celebrated with those who had travelled to support them.

It was to Levein's credit that he said, immediately after the game had ended, that the tie had still to be won. Bordeaux weren't a top team in Europe for nothing and they would fancy their chances of overturning the deficit at Tynecastle in the return leg. Which, inevitably, as far as Hearts are concerned, they did. In front of a full house of close to 18,000 fans in Gorgie, the French team displayed their undoubted class with a performance of maturity and authority and won 2-0 on the night to progress 2-1 on aggregate.

Domestically, Hearts secured another third-placed finish in the SPL but lost to Dundee in the League Cup and Celtic in the Scottish Cup. Nonetheless, the disappointment of that cold November evening in Gorgie will never take away the jubilation felt by those of us who travelled to the south of France three weeks earlier.

Such trips take a fair degree of planning but it's doubtful if any of us could have made a better job if we had planned it in details ourselves. The weather, the hospitality, the magnificence of Bordeaux, the alcohol – and, of course, the result, meant it was just the perfect day to be a Hearts supporter.

In fact, I would say it was the best day I have had as a Hearts supporter outside of seeing the Jambos win the Scottish Cup. A day none of us who were there will ever forget.

v Sporting Braga 3-1
Uefa Cup First Round First Leg
16th September 2004. Murrayfield

Hearts:	Sporting Braga:
Gordon	Santos
Neilson	Gomes
Maybury	Dias
Webster	Loureiro
Pressley	Sergio Almeida
Hamill	Dos Santos
Kisnorbo	Wender-Said
Hartley	Ferreira
Stamp	Baha
McAllister	Nunes
De Vries	Vandinho Almeida

Referee: A Genov (Bulgaria)

HEARTS' HEROICS in the south of France in 2003 had whetted the appetite of many supporters for the taste of European football – despite the reversal to Bordeaux in the return leg at Tynecastle that stuck in the gullet somewhat.

Hearts had ended in third place in the SPL at the end of season 2003/04 – the second season in a row they had finished "the best of the rest" outside Glasgow's big two. Craig Levein had built a steady, workmanlike side that were difficult to beat, although a couple of heavy losses to the Old Firm during that season meant some people begged to differ. That said Hearts ended the season with a rare win at Ibrox, young midfielder Joe Hamill scoring the only goal.

With another European adventure on the horizon, Levein recruited to his Hearts squad and brought Spanish forward Ramon Pereira – from the not quite exotic location of Kirkcaldy, where the little man had been playing with Raith Rovers – and midfielder Michael Stewart to Tynecastle. Stewart had been a player of some promise at no less a place than Manchester United and he was given a brief chance in United's first team in 2000. However, he was to make just eight appearances for the Red Devils and Old Trafford manager Sir Alex Ferguson released the Edinburgh-born player in the summer of 2004.

Step forward Hearts chief Levein, who saw Stewart as a valuable addition to his team. Levein also brought in left-back Jamie McAllister from Livingston. Those in maroon looked upon the former Aberdeen player fondly. During his time at Livingston, he had scored in their momentous League Cup final triumph – over Hibernian at Hampden.

There was dissension in the ranks of the supporters even before the 2004/05 season began, though it was nothing to do with the team or coaching staff. Their anger was directed towards chairman Chris Robinson who, with Hearts' debt reaching crippling levels – over £21m – had announced the club would be selling Tynecastle Stadium and moving a few hundred yards along the road to Murrayfield Stadium. Tynecastle would be demolished to make way for new housing.

Hearts fans were horrified. Tynecastle was their home, their team's home and few wanted to leave. It wasn't as if Hearts were moving to a purpose-built stadium. They were moving to the home of Scottish rugby. Now, Murrayfield is a very impressive stadium with first-class facilities – no one can doubt that. However, its capacity is 67,500. Hearts faced the prospect of playing in front of at least 50,000 empty seats in a soulless arena that wasn't built for football.

Hearts fans began an impressive campaign to keep their club at Tynecastle. Robinson though, could see no other way out of Hearts' financial problems, a scenario that would take a bizarre twist as season 2004/05 progressed.

Hearts began the league campaign with a 1-0 win at Dundee but the opening weeks of the season were strangely flat as they struggled to score goals. The visit of Portuguese side Sporting Braga for the first round first leg of the Uefa Cup in September was a welcome respite. However, the tie had to be switched from Hearts' home, as Tynecastle wasn't deemed fit to meet Uefa requirements – and was to be played at Murrayfield Stadium.

The more cynical among the Hearts support suggested Chris Robinson didn't over exert himself in trying to make Tynecastle meet Uefa requirements. Switching the tie to Murrayfield was an ideal chance for a "trial run" – a taste of what might happen on a permanent basis. The game against Braga attracted an attendance of 18,769, larger than would have been at Tynecastle but still nearly 50,000 short of Murrayfield's capacity. Tynecastle was renowned for its special atmosphere – a crowd of less than 20,000 would be lost souls at Scottish rugby's HQ.

There was a bit of drama before the game even kicked off, as there was a delay in proceedings while one of the nets had to be fixed. This was comical ammunition to those who said the game should never have been played at Murrayfield in the first place. Sadly, that turned out to be the only major action the goalmouth saw in a rather drab opening period where Hearts were anxious not to concede an away goal and Braga seemed content to soak up pressure.

Jamie McAllister did have an effort on goal in the opening minutes, but his shot was wide of the post. Hearts looked the more impressive of the teams and had a great chance to score when de Vries set up Phil Stamp whose volley was saved by keeper Santos before the unfortunate McAllister fired the rebound well wide. The Maroons were enjoying plenty of possession but just couldn't find a way through a well-drilled Braga defence. They almost paid the price for their lack of firepower, when a mistake from Andy Webster allowed Said to set up substitute Junior, whose shot on target was well saved by Craig Gordon.

At half-time, the Portuguese visitors would have been pleased with a goalless scoreline, but within five minutes of the restart they were behind. Joe Hamill delivered a cross to the far post for big de Vries who nodded the ball into the path of Webster whose powerful header gave Santos not an earthly. Buoyed by this breakthrough, Hearts should have doubled their lead minutes later, when de Vries was again the provider for Stamp but the Englishman's effort smacked off the crossbar.

Hearts fans held their heads in their hands but a second goal did come in the 62nd minute when Paul Hartley found Robbie Neilson with an inch-perfect pass. The full-back sped down the right wing, fired the ball back to Hartley, who volleyed home superbly to put Hearts two goals ahead.

The Murrayfield crowd celebrated, but 60 seconds later calamity struck. Braga were awarded a somewhat dubious free kick that Junior took and found the head of Almeida whose header sailed past a helpless Gordon to make it 2-1 to Hearts and the loss of an away goal was a blow.

Braga now clearly fancied their chances of levelling the game but with just seconds left and the home support urging the referee to blow his whistle to ensure Hearts had a lead to take to Portugal for the return leg, another goal arrived. Joyously for the home fans, it was scored by Patrick Kisnorbo who headed home Hartley's corner to end the scoring at 3-1 to Hearts.

Having been enthralled by the experience in Bordeaux ten months earlier, hundreds of Hearts fans made the trip to Braga a fortnight later to watch their favourites defend their two-goal lead against one of the best teams in Portugal. The temperature in the city was in the 80s but thankfully, a shade cooler by the time the evening kick-off arrived.

When Braga took an early lead in their unique stadium – one of the ends behind the goal has no stand, just a huge rock face – we feared the worst and it looked like a backs-to-the-wall job for Hearts. However, Edinburgh's finest began to realise that Braga weren't too clever defensively and just before the half-hour mark, de Vries equalised. Joy among the visiting fans – Braga now needed to score twice even to force extra time. When de Vries scored again early in the second half the tie was all but over. Not even a late Braga equaliser could spoil the party and the game ended 2-2 on the night, Hearts progressing to the new group stage format of the Uefa Cup on a 5-3 aggregate.

Uefa wanted the competition to be like the successful Champions League with its groups of four or five clubs. Hearts' reward for overcoming Braga was to be drawn in a five-team group that included Dutch side Feyenoord, Swiss side Basel, Hungarians Ferencvaros and Germans Schalke 04. Hearts had a very tough opener – Feyenoord in Rotterdam. The Maroons were outclassed and lost 3-0.

A week later, there was even worse news as Craig Levein, suddenly and unexpectedly, departed for English Championship side Leicester City. Levein had done a fine job at Tynecastle, despite the lack of finance available to him to build the Hearts team he really wanted. His departure came at a time when Hearts were in the process of having a new owner.

Russian businessman Vladimir Romanov, based in the Baltic state of Lithuania, was in talks with Hearts chairman Chris Robinson about buying out his shares – and taking on the club's significant debt. Unconfirmed stories reported that Levein didn't fancy working under Romanov and headed south. Before long, he would take Alan Maybury, Patrick Kisnorbo and Mark de Vries with him.

Hearts' next opponents in the Uefa Cup were Schalke 04. Coach Peter Houston took temporary charge when Levein departed, but by the time the Germans arrived in Scotland's capital city, Hearts had another man in permanent charge. The legend that was former striker John Robertson had been doing a fine job managing Inverness

Caledonian Thistle and he was the obvious choice to succeed Levein as the man in charge of Hearts.

He took his place in the dugout for the first time on 4th November 2004 for the visit of Schalke 04 to Murrayfield. Sadly, there were little fireworks that night although a crowd of over 27,000 did try to give Hearts the support they needed. Despite dominating the game, yet again, it was Hearts' lack of firepower that let them down and they fell to a sucker punch when the Germans scored the only goal of the game with 15 minutes left.

The Gorgie men were not helped by the controversial dismissal of Kisnorbo just three minutes into the second half. The Australian had already been booked when he was adjudged by the Russian referee to have dived in order to win a penalty – and promptly received a second yellow and subsequently a red card. The irony was some of the German players had been falling over whenever a gust of wind hit them, a fact not lost on the irate Hearts support.

Even with three teams qualifying from the group, Hearts' Uefa Cup hopes were already hanging by a thread after two games. No points and no goals didn't fill those of us planning to head to the continent for Hearts' next fixture – against Swiss side Basel – with any great hope.

However, in John Robertson we trusted. If anyone could convince this group of Hearts players that they could secure the win that would keep their cup hopes alive it was wee 'Robbo'. Exactly a month before Christmas we boarded another chartered flight at Edinburgh Airport bound for the chilly climes of the Swiss/French border – and another all-day drinking session.

It was to prove to be another great story for the famous Heart of Midlothian!

v Basel 2-1
Uefa Cup Group Stage
25th November 2004. St Jakob Park

Hearts:	Basel:
Gordon	Zuberbuhler
Neilson	Zwyssig
Maybury	Huggel
Webster	Sterjovski
Pressley	Chipperfield
McAllister	Gimenez
Stewart	Correa
Hamill	Delgado
Wyness	Degan
De Vries	Smiljanic
Pereira	Rossi

Referee: K Jacobsson (Iceland)

HEARTS HAD become the first Scottish club to qualify for the group stages of the new-look Uefa Cup but their second defeat in the group meant their trip to Switzerland to face Basel at the end of November took on crucial status.

To have any chance of progressing in the competition, Hearts really had to win in the Swiss-French border city – something the likes of Inter Milan, Juventus, Liverpool and Valencia had all failed to achieve in recent years. Still, the Maroon Army were on the march again – given the club's impressive record in Europe in the preceding 12 months, they didn't have to look too far for their passports.

The Uefa Cup may have had its detractors but there was still a crowd of over 21,000 at St Jakob Park as the game kicked off. Again, there were a couple of thousand Hearts supporters present, many of whom had spent much of the preceding afternoon outside a pub in the centre of Basel.

Yes, you read that correctly dear reader – outside a pub. The cost of a pint in Switzerland rather prohibited the prospect of a gallon or two of foaming ale as part of the pre-match ritual. However, as Hearts fans discovered in no time at all, the cost of bottled beer from off-licences was on a par with that back home. So it was, that several hundred maroon clad Scots spent the afternoon scurrying from a city-centre off-licence and standing outside a licensed drinking establishment where many bottles of beer were consumed – and the gents inside the pub was, indeed, a much needed "convenience" to relieve the call of nature.

As for the game itself, Hearts manager John Robertson didn't have his problems to seek. Patrick Kisnorbo and Paul Hartley were suspended but, nonetheless, Robertson had declared his team would attack Basel at every opportunity – in truth, he didn't have much of a choice, as a third defeat would point Hearts towards the exit door, a little over a year since Bordeaux had done the same at Tynecastle. It was a team selection that would have, perhaps, given Robertson's predecessor palpitations – strikers de Vries, Pereira and Wyness all started the game, as did midfielder Michael Stewart.

The pre-match plan of Hearts having a go looked like it might go for a burton as early as the third minute, when the delightfully named Chipperfield delivered a free kick into the Hearts penalty box, from which Huggel brought out a fine save from keeper Craig Gordon.

However, after enduring a tricky opening few minutes, Hearts made a few attacking moves of their own and from a free kick given after young Joe Hamill was fouled, Jamie McAllister teed up Alan Maybury of all people, but Maybury's attempt on goal was typical for a full-back – his 30-yard effort almost made the top tier of the stand where the home support had congregated.

Basel, having played just one group game prior to the meeting with Hearts, were already a point better off than their Edinburgh opponents thanks to a goalless draw at Schalke 04 and were not as dependent on victory as Hearts. That said, they almost opened the scoring after 15 minutes, when Delgado's volley was well saved by Gordon, only for the ball to fall into the path of Rossi – but he headed tamely into the welcoming arms of Scotland's number one goalkeeper.

It was an open game, quite unlike a European game played by a Scots team away from home. Just before the half-hour mark, the best opportunity of the game thus far fell – to Hearts. They got a fortuitous break when the ball cannoned off referee Jakobsson to Stewart. The midfielder immediately picked out Dennis Wyness who fired in a shot that, agonisingly, went wide. It was a glorious opportunity spurned and John Robertson clutched his head, knowing there wouldn't be too many such chances that evening. Apart from the one that arrived two minutes later.

Fine build-up play from Hamill and Pereira set up the aforementioned Wyness on the edge of the penalty box. This time the Aberdonian's shot at goal was on target – but Pereira seemed to be in an offside position. As the ball nestled in the net beyond keeper Zuberbuhler, the home team claimed Hearts' Spanish striker had connected with Wyness' shot thereby making the goal offside.

However, the linesman deemed there had been no contact and, remarkably, Hearts were a goal to the good – their first goal in the group stages to date. Slightly inebriated Hearts supporters at the other end of the stadium danced for joy. Was this to be another episode in Hearts' recent glorious record in Europe?

Moments later, Andy Webster headed towards de Vries and the big centre-forward was inches away from connecting – and a chance to double Hearts' lead had gone. As half-time approached, de Vries and Basel keeper Zuberbuhler got "physical" and this enraged the home support, a section of whom directed racist abuse towards the Hearts man. A despicable incident on an otherwise enjoyable evening and when half-time arrived Hearts were a goal to the good.

Basel appeared to up the ante at the start of the second half and it looked as if Chipperfield had levelled the score minutes after the restart, when he produced a spectacular diving header only for Gordon to produce an equally spectacular save from almost point-blank range.

With 25 minutes left, Hearts were hanging on to their slender advantage and supporters began to believe victory was possible. Robertson also believed and he replaced an attacker, Pereira, with midfield man Phil Stamp before replacing Stewart with a more defensive midfielder in Neil McFarlane. And we all know what happens when Scots try to defend a lead.

Substitute Carignano almost equalised for the home side, only to be denied by Maybury, before Gordon saved from Zwyssig. Hearts fans anxiously looked at their watches. With 14 minutes left, the inevitable happened when Gordon, of all people, cleared the ball only as far as the feet of Carignano, who raced forward and duly stroked it past the horrified keeper and into the net. 1-1 much to the delight of the home support, and Hearts fans began to calculate if a draw would be enough to keep their heroes in the competition.

With less than a minute to go, Joe Hamill meandered down the wing with no one in the home defence really considering the youngster a threat. Hamill fired in a long cross towards the Basel penalty area more in hope, it must be said, than in expectation. After all, the Hearts players had given a supreme effort in the preceding 89 minutes and looked dead on their feet. However, substitute Stamp threw his diminutive frame to reach Hamill's cross and headed the ball down to a Hearts player haring forward at a fair rate of knots.

To the dismay of the Hearts fans behind the goal, this player wasn't striker Wyness or fellow forward Graham Weir, another substitute. The white-shirted Hearts player steaming forward was Robbie Neilson. Now there has never been a more committed player in a Hearts shirt than Robbie – more about him in the chapter about Hearts' Scottish Cup triumph of 2006. Nonetheless, his job as a full-back is not to score goals, his task is to help prevent them. Indeed, Neilson had never scored a goal for Hearts and there seemed a collective gasp from the on-looking Hearts support of "oh s**t it's Robbie Neilson" as they watched the ball bounce towards the galloping full-back.

However, what happened next was akin to Wayne Foster's famous winner against Hibernian in the Scottish Cup tie at Easter Road in 1994. Then, Gary Mackay's long through ball was finished with aplomb by Foster, a player not renowned for being a great goalscorer. More than a decade later, we watched through fingers partly covering our eyes as Neilson struck for goal. His shot was strong, low – and on target. In the midst of near disbelief among the 2,000 Hearts supporters behind the goal, Neilson's magnificent shot nestled in the left-hand corner of the net beyond keeper Zuberbuhler for a sensational winner.

Moments later, the final whistle sounded – Hearts had achieved yet another unlikely, but famous victory on foreign soil. FC Basel 1 Heart of Midlothian 2 was the final score, even to those of us who woke up bleary-eyed the following morning in the Swiss city to prepare for our flight home. It was another incredible night in Europe for Hearts and added to the superb results already achieved in a period of little over 12 months.

Bordeaux, Braga and now Basel. Un 'B' lievable!

Hearts now had high hopes of reaching the next round and it all hinged on their final group game against Hungarian side Ferencvaros at Murrayfield a week before Christmas. However, supporters of my vintage suspected what would happen next. As well as having to beat the Hungarians, Hearts were relying on Feyenoord to replicate Hearts' performance and defeat Basel in Switzerland. However, Basel won

1-0 – that meant Hearts could have defeated Ferencvaros 10-0 and still not have been able to qualify.

In the end, it was almost role-reversal for Hearts at Murrayfield. The Maroons dominated the game from start to finish but were caught on the break after half an hour, when Rosa scored the only goal of the game. Therefore, the evening – and Hearts' campaign in Europe – ended in disappointment for the crowd of over 26,000 at Murrayfield.

There was a curious incident during the game when John Robertson appeared to stamp on the foot of the Ferencvaros coach after a disputed decision. This didn't affect the Hungarian's opinion of Edinburgh though as less than four years later, Csaba Laszlo would be back in Scotland's capital city – as manager of Hearts.

The Jambos' next game after exiting the Uefa Cup was a 2-0 home defeat in the SPL to Celtic and it was clear Hearts were once again a team in transition. At the beginning of 2005, Vladimir Romanov had bought a controlling interest in Edinburgh's oldest and finest football club – and he immediately pledged to keep Hearts at Tynecastle. The dreaded move to Murrayfield was off – and Hearts fans celebrated. Romanov tried to bolster John Robertson's squad with the arrival of two Lithuanian internationals, Saulius Mikoliunas and Deividas Cesnauskis, both attacking players.

However, the 2004/05 season would end in disappointment for the maroon masses. A fifth-placed finish in the SPL was something of a letdown, given Hearts fans were now accustomed to finishing "the best of the rest" behind the Old Firm. Hearts tasted bitter defeat in the cups, reaching the semi-final of the League Cup where they lost 3-2 after extra time to Motherwell at Easter Road, while a 2-1 defeat in the Scottish Cup semi-final to Celtic at Hampden ended the season on a sour note. To make matters worse, manager Robertson left Tynecastle at the end of the campaign and Hearts were once again looking for a new man in charge.

A sad end to the season – the highlight of which undoubtedly came on a cold November evening on the Swiss/French border. When Robbie Neilson wrote his name into the Hearts history book!

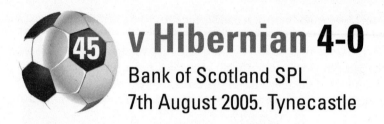

v Hibernian 4-0
Bank of Scotland SPL
7th August 2005. Tynecastle

Hearts:	Hibernian:
Gordon	Malkowski
Neilson	Whittaker
McAllister	Smith
Webster	Caldwell
Pressley	Murphy
Mikoliunas	Buezelin
Hartley	Stewart
Bednar	Thomson
Skacel	Glass
Brellier	O'Connor
Elliot	Konte

Referee: S Dougal (Bothwell)

JULY 2005. After a hard day at the office, I fancied a pint of refreshing ale as a perfect way to begin the weekend. As I entered The Diggers – one of Gorgie's finest drinking establishments – that Friday evening, another working week consigned to history, my mate Rob was at the bar and gesturing towards the corner of the pub. Sitting there, was Hearts' new chief executive Phil Anderton and newly appointed Hearts manager George Burley. We supped our pints and tried to act innocuously.

Hearts' new majority shareholder Vladimir Romanov had given money to the new manager to rebuild a team that had, despite a heroic result in Basel in the Uefa Cup, largely disappointed under John Robertson the previous season.

The appointment of Burley as Hearts manager was seen by many as something of a coup by Anderton. Burley, a former Scotland internationalist, had a fine managerial pedigree that began when he took over at Ayr United from former Scotland boss Ally MacLeod in 1991. After spells in charge of Motherwell and Colchester United, Burley took over at the club he played for with distinction in the 1970s – Ipswich Town. He led Ipswich to promotion from the First Division to a fifth-placed finish in the FA Premiership and a place in the Uefa Cup.

However, the following season, Town were relegated and Burley departed before taking over at Derby County. At Pride Park, Burley's relationship with the club's director of football was a stormy one and he left in the summer of 2005. He took over at Hearts in July and it's fair to say hopes were high among the fans.

Hearts embarked on a pre-season tour of the Irish Republic and I took my wife for a not quite romantic weekend to the fair city of Dublin. In the baking July heat, I left the missus for a Sunday afternoon trip to see St Patrick's Athletic take on Heart of Midlothian and witness the start of the George Burley era.

Hearts huffed and puffed in the heat and ground out a goalless draw. The consolation for the fans present was that Burley could see what was patently obvious – the Hearts team needed to be rebuilt. However, with the league season less than three weeks away, Burley faced a huge task.

Burley had many contacts in the game and it's fair to say his mobile phone bill for the month of July 2005 must have amounted to a considerable sum as new players began arriving at Tynecastle in rapid succession. Strikers Roman Bednar, Michal Pospisil and Edgaras Jankauskas, midfielders Rudi Skacel, Samuel Cammazola and Julien Brellier and defender Takis Fyssas all arrived at Tynecastle within days of each other. Moreover, these weren't ageing, half fit mercenaries – they were internationals.

Jankauskas was part of the FC Porto squad that won the Champions League in 2004, while Fyssas was part of the Greece team that unexpectedly won the European Championship in the same year. Some observers believed the new arrivals would take time to gel, Hearts would struggle and the Romanov Revolution would be struggling to take off. How wrong they were!

It's not unusual for Hearts to start the season slowly. Not this campaign. Hearts defeated Kilmarnock 4-2 at Rugby Park in their opening SPL game. What's more, Hearts were playing a swashbuckling style of football not seen since the cup-winning season of 1997/98 and were scoring goals aplenty. Hearts supporters eagerly looked forward to the first home game of the season – when Hibs visited Gorgie.

With the Edinburgh Festival in full swing and glorious August sunshine, the atmosphere was electric at Tynecastle. It was already at fever pitch, as chief executive Anderton had promised fireworks before the game. He was true to his word as a firework display erupted as the teams came on to the Tynecastle pitch – although its visual impact was lost somewhat in the blazing August sunshine.

Almost 16,500 fans were at Tynecastle to create a raucous atmosphere and the home team were the first to threaten when full-back Robbie Neilson floated a delightful cross from the right that Paul Hartley directed towards goal, but his agile effort was saved by Hibs keeper Malkowski.

At Kilmarnock the previous weekend, Hearts had begun the game in whirlwind fashion and it seemed like it was Burley's tactics to do the same against Hibs. Hearts were all over their Edinburgh rivals like a rash in the opening stages and after 13 minutes, they took the lead. Hartley, relishing playing against his old team, delivered a sublime pass to Bednar whose effort was well saved by Malkowski – only for Bednar's Czech compatriot Rudi Skacel to force the ball into the net. Hearts were a goal ahead and bedlam ensued at Tynecastle.

Hibs had a chance to equalise with a header from Caldwell that was saved by Craig Gordon with Buezelin regretting missing the rebound. Hearts, however, were in the ascendancy and the visitors' Polish goalkeeper looked nervous in his first Edinburgh derby.

Hearts captain Steven Pressley almost caught the Hibs number one out with a header but Smith cleared the effort as the Maroons continued to dominate. To add to Hibs' woes, their manager Tony Mowbray was sent to the stand by referee Stuart Dougal just before half-time, after disagreeing ever so slightly about a decision. When half-time arrived, it was nothing short of incredible that Hearts were just a single goal to the good.

Hibs came out for the second half with renewed effort and Thomson had an effort on goal that was just wide of Craig Gordon's post. However, this was to give the Hibs fans in the Roseburn Stand a degree of false hope as, in the 58th minute, Glass handled the ball in the Hibs penalty box after coming under pressure from Hartley. Penalty said referee Dougal and Hartley duly despatched the spot kick beyond the hapless Malkowski to double Hearts' advantage.

Hibs already looked like a beaten team and after Skacel and Bednar came close again, it was the home-grown Stephen Simmons who put Hearts in easy street in the 71st minute when he capitalised on a mistake from Hibs defender Buezelin, to rifle the ball past a helpless Malkowski.

Hearts were rampant now. Skacel and Hartley were almost teasing the Hibs defence – Skacel fired in a vicious effort that shaved the post while Hartley went inches wide with a free kick, as the home team turned the screw. With just seven minutes remaining and the home support baying for another goal, a fourth goal duly arrived when Saulius Mikoliunas got on the end of a corner.

The Lithuanian had no right to score from the position he was in, but spotting the now forlorn figure of Malkowski out of position, he fired in a shot that flew into the net to complete the scoring at 4-0 to Hearts. It had very nearly been a repeat of the 5-1 drubbing Hearts handed out to their neighbours on the same ground exactly three years earlier. It had been the most one-sided Edinburgh derby in years. Even the 5-1 game had Hibs well in contention at 3-1. However, this latest drubbing could have been six or, dare I say it, seven nil to the home team.

Having scored four goals in both their opening SPL games, Hearts were on fire. A week later, they headed to Tannadice and a difficult fixture with Dundee United. Few expected Hearts to maintain their four-goal salvo and in the end they didn't – they only won 3-0, with skipper Pressley taking great delight in scoring the opening goal against his former team.

Hearts then entertained Aberdeen, whose manager Jimmy Calderwood cited Burley's team as long ball merchants, stating he was preparing his players for an "aerial bombardment". This angered the Hearts management team and the Maroons duly outplayed the Dons, although the 2-0 scoreline probably didn't reflect the pattern of play.

Hearts defeated Motherwell 2-1 at Tynecastle before thumping Livingston 4-1 in West Lothian, where Vladimir Romanov sat among the Hearts supporters, much to the delight of those in maroon and white. Hearts then headed for the difficult venue of Inverness Caledonian Thistle and won thanks to a goal from Skacel.

It had been a phenomenal start to the season. Hearts had won their first seven SPL games and were, astonishingly, five points clear of Celtic at the top of the SPL. They were the SPL's top scorers – 20 goals, thus far – and midfielder Skacel had scored in all seven games, a feat that was threatening that of Hearts' legendary striker from the 1930s, Barney Battles, who scored in nine successive games.

The critics sniped that Hearts' real test would come when they played the Old Firm – none of their seven games so far had been against the "big two" from Glasgow. However, Hearts' next SPL opponents were Rangers who visited Tynecastle on 24th September. An early Roman Bednar goal was enough for Hearts to make it an incredible eight league wins in a row, although the win was tempered by an injury to the Czech striker who had to leave the field before half an hour was played.

Hearts dropped their first league points of the season at Falkirk, a place the Maroons regularly struggled. On the face of it, a 2-2 draw was disappointing, but scratch beneath the surface of the result and you will find that Hearts goalkeeper Craig Gordon was sent off after just 25 minutes after he denied Falkirk's Duffy a goalscoring opportunity. When the Bairns went 2-0 ahead with just 20 minutes left after Pressley scored an own goal, it looked like Hearts' magnificent unbeaten run was about to come to an end. However, Captain Courageous dragged his team back into the game. Pressley scored twice – the second goal coming deep into stoppage time – as Hearts showed incredible character to level the game at 2-2.

Hearts then headed to Celtic Park a fortnight later after a break for the international weekend and another acid test. Inevitably, Skacel scored Hearts' goal to level the game after the home side took an early lead and it ended 1-1. Hearts remained top of the SPL, three points clear of Celtic and seven ahead of Rangers who had played a game less.

There was now serious talk of Hearts mounting a title challenge to the Old Firm. Bankrolled by the ambitious Vladimir Romanov and marshalled by George Burley, in the first quarter of the season, Hearts' opponents simply could not live with them. Ten games into the SPL season, Hearts were not only top of the league but also unbeaten. They were scoring goals galore and had taken on and succeeded against Celtic and Rangers.

Disbelieving Hearts fans had to pinch themselves to make sure this was really happening. Life just couldn't have got any better. Until the morning of 22nd October 2005 …

46 v Hibernian 4-0

Tennents Scottish Cup Semi-Final
2nd April 2006. Hampden

Hearts:	Hibernian:
Gordon	Malkowski
Neilson	Whittaker
Pressley	Smith
Webster	Caldwell
Goncalves	Murphy
Cesnauskis	Sproule
Aguiar	Hogg
Hartley	Thomson
Skacel	Glass
Elliot	Fletcher
Jankauskas	Benjelloun

Referee: S Dougal (Bothwell)

TWO HOURS before kick-off on the afternoon Hearts were due to play Dunfermline Athletic at Tynecastle at the end of October 2005, came a devastating blow for Hearts fans. Manager George Burley had left Tynecastle. When news of his departure broke, the feel-good factor that had enveloped Gorgie for three months drifted away.

The reasons for Burley's departure from Hearts have never fully been explained. His replacement was a name no one had even remotely considered – Englishman Graham Rix. Rix's appointment was controversial. The former Arsenal and England player had been involved in a physical relationship with a girl who was under the legal age and, as such, he had a criminal record.

Roman Romanov – Vladimir's son and club chairman – had spoken about men being given a second chance and this was his. As things turned out, it wasn't much of a second chance – Romanov senior sacked him after three months and replaced him with Lithuanian Valdas Ivanauskas.

The story of Hearts' league campaign this season is detailed in the next chapter. Suffice to say, a season that promised so much threatened to turn to ruin. However, in the early part of 2006, Hearts rallied as they sought a second-place finish in the SPL that would not only split the Old Firm, but would mean entry for the qualifying stages of the following season's Champions League.

When the Scottish Cup came round, there was real belief that Hearts could lift this particular trophy for the second time in eight years. Hearts began their quest by defeating Kilmarnock 2-1 in a tight affair at Tynecastle, thanks to goals from Steven Pressley and Jamie McAllister. Hearts were then drawn against one of McAllister's former teams, Aberdeen, in the next round and a large travelling support contributed to a tremendous atmosphere at Tynecastle.

Hearts had made several new signings during the newly created January transfer window – one of two opportunities in the calendar year for clubs to buy and sell players – including a player who became something of an enigma in Gorgie. Belgian club Racing Genk's winger Mirsad Beslija was signed for a club record fee of £850,000, a move that astounded Scottish football and was seen by many as Hearts announcing their declaration to Celtic and Rangers that they were going to be challenging their domination of Scottish football.

The word on the street was that Hearts had beaten off several European clubs, as well as some in the English FA Premiership who were keen to add Beslija to their ranks. The Bosnian made his Hearts debut against Aberdeen but, in a sign of things to come, was largely subdued. It mattered little, as Hearts had the game sewn up by half-time when they were 3-0 ahead thanks to goals from Pospisil, youngster Calum Elliot and a penalty from captain Steven Pressley. Hearts' cause was helped by the sending off of Aberdeen's Alexander Diamond just on half-time for a foul that led to Hearts' penalty.

Hearts were, by now, the favourites for the trophy. Celtic had suffered an embarrassing third round exit to Clyde, while on the same day Hearts were trouncing Aberdeen, Hibernian produced one of the shocks of the season by knocking out Rangers 3-0 at Ibrox. The line-up for the quarter-finals of the Scottish Cup was, therefore, that rare beast indeed – one that did not include Celtic or Rangers.

For once, Hearts were paired with opponents from outside the SPL for the quarter-final – but, again, the tie against Partick Thistle would take place at Tynecastle. Typically, Hearts reserved their worst performance of the season against their First Division opponents and Thistle dominated large periods of the game.

Jankauskas gave Hearts an early lead, scoring after just six minutes. Whether complacency set in among the home players is unclear, but Thistle took charge of the game thereafter. It was something of a surprise when Deividas Cesnauskis, one of the Lithuanian contingent at Tynecastle, doubled Hearts' lead midway through the second half. However, Thistle pulled a goal back late on and for the final 15 minutes, Hearts were hanging on, trying to avoid the prospect of being taken to Firhill for a replay.

However, hang on they did – and the unlikely Scottish Cup semi-final line-up consisted of Hearts, Hibs, First Division side Dundee and Gretna of the Second Division. Would there be the first all-Edinburgh Scottish Cup final since 1896? The answer was no – because the old Edinburgh rivals were paired with each other for the semi-final.

There was much debate before the game, which was switched to Sunday lunchtime to suit the needs of satellite television, as to where it should be played. The obvious choice for an Edinburgh derby would have been Murrayfield Stadium in the capital city. This was a far bigger arena that the traditional venue for cup semi-finals – Glasgow's Hampden Park – meaning more fans would get to the game and would avoid the necessity of thousands of Hearts and Hibs fans travelling west on a Sunday morning. However, the fans' wishes, as is so often the case, were ignored and the game went ahead with a 12.15pm kick-off at Hampden Park on Sunday 2nd April 2006.

The four-week build-up to the biggest Edinburgh derby in decades was fraught. One of the worst experiences in football is losing a cup semi-final. To lose one to

189

your city rivals simply didn't bear thinking about. Moreover, Hearts supporters had taunted their neighbours with the oft-stated statistic that Hibernian had not won the Scottish Cup in over 100 years.

They knew that if Hibs won at Hampden, they would be red-hot favourites to break that hoodoo, particularly as Gretna had upset the odds by defeating Dundee in the other semi-final played the day before. More than 40,000 fans from Scotland's capital city made their way to Scotland's national football stadium for the clash of the titans.

Hearts manager Valdas Ivanauskas was forced into making changes, although the Hearts team changed so frequently this season it was difficult to say who was injured or who had been dropped. However, Julien Brellier and Roman Bednar were suspended, which meant recalls for Portuguese midfielder Bruno Aguiar and young forward Calum Elliot, making a rare starting appearance.

Hibernian also had their share of suspensions and injuries but this took nothing away from what would be the Edinburgh derby to end all Edinburgh derbies. Hearts, not unnaturally, had sold out their ticket allocation in double quick time. Curiously, the same could not be said of Hibs and there were large gaps in the green and white end.

Under George Burley, Hearts' tactic was usually to try to blow away their opponents in the opening minutes. Following Burley and Rix's departures, Ivanauskas was Hearts' third manager in six months, but the Lithuanian used the same approach. Hearts leapt out the starting blocks and Skacel sprinted past Hibs' Gary Caldwell in the opening minute but Jankauskas could not direct the Czech star's cross and the Hibernian alarm bells stopped – momentarily at least.

Hearts continued to look the more threatening, but keeper Craig Gordon had to keep alert, as was proved after 14 minutes when he tipped an effort from Hibs' Whittaker over the bar. Minutes later, Paul Hartley fired in a 30-yard effort that Malkowski palmed round the post for a corner as Hearts further increased the tempo.

They were rewarded in the 27th minute. Hibernian's Benjelloun was dispossessed by Hartley inside the Hearts half. The former Hibee raced forward with Jankauskas haring down the flank. Hartley played a sublime one-two with the Lithuanian, before getting the merest of flicks to the return pass to divert the ball past Malkowski and into the corner of the net. 1-0 to Hearts and one half of Hampden Park erupted.

Hearts suffered a blow when Steven Pressley picked up a head injury after showing total commitment in an aerial joust with Benjelloun and the former Rangers and Dundee United defender did not appear for the second half, his place taken by Takis Fyssas. It was a worry for we older Hearts supporters, given our penchant for thinking the worst. Hearts had dominated the game but held the slenderest of leads. Now our inspirational captain was off the field.

When another free kick from Hartley was deflected by Hibs defender Glass, it was heading for the net and the doubling of Hearts' lead – until Malkowski leapt superbly to turn the ball round the post. In the 57th minute, Elliot was bundled off the ball by Hogg, between the corner flag and the penalty box. Yet another free kick for Hearts and yet again Hartley stepped up to take it.

Hibs' defenders and Hearts' attacking players crowded the penalty box waiting for Hartley's usual expert delivery. He stepped back, looked up – and curled a magnificent shot between Malkowski and his near post. Hearts were 2-0 up and Hartley, Skacel et al celebrated at the corner flag in front of the dancing Hearts support. Yes, the Hibernian goalkeeper was badly at fault but you had to admire the skill of the scorer.

Hearts suffered another injury blow when Goncalves had to retire from the game, the Portuguese defender never recovering from a blow earlier that required lengthy treatment and incurred the wrath of referee Stuart Dougal who booked Hearts keeper Gordon for time wasting at the incident – a ridiculous decision.

Mikoliunas replaced Goncalves and he didn't take long to make an impact. The Lithuanian winger showed total commitment to take the ball off Hibs' Ivan Sproule before the Hibee fouled the Hearts man – and stamped on the player as he lay on the ground. It could be nothing other than a straight red card for the Hibs player, and with him went Hibs' chances of reaching the Scottish Cup final.

With nine minutes left, any lingering doubt held even by pessimists like me disappeared, when Hibs keeper Malkowski compounded his team's misery by trying to dribble the ball past Jankauskas on the edge of his penalty area – only for the big striker to take it off his toes, skip past him into the penalty box and stroke home for Hearts' third.

With just three minutes left, Hearts substitute Michal Pospisil raced through on goal, eager to get in on the scoring act. Hibs defender Smith pulled down the Czech striker on what appeared to be the edge of the box. Referee Dougal decreed it a penalty – and gave Smith a straight red card. Hartley – who else – duly dispatched the spot kick to complete a memorable hat-trick and he ran towards the joyous Hearts support with three fingers in the air. 4-0 to Hearts, Hibs down to nine men – we wanted the game to go on forever but it ended a couple of minutes later. This was just as well as there was serious drinking to be done when we arrived back in Edinburgh a couple of hours later. The Tynecastle Arms was rocking that Sunday evening!

Hearts would face Gretna in one of the most unlikely Scottish Cup finals ever on 13th May 2006. More of this in the next chapter. For, on that memorable April afternoon in Glasgow of all places, one thing was settled once and for all.

Hibs fans of a certain vintage still recall the Edinburgh derby of New Year's Day 1973 when their team scored seven fortuitous goals without reply at Tynecastle. They also mention a more recent occasion when their team beat Edinburgh's finest 6-2 at Easter Road. Hearts fans prefer to talk about four-goal debutant Mark de Vries and the 5-1 hammering of the Hibees at Tynecastle in 2002.

The Edinburgh derby of April 2006, however, blew all those previous games away. An Edinburgh derby that wasn't even played in Edinburgh. Nevertheless, it was the most important Edinburgh derby in over a century. And Edinburgh's biggest team won it – by the length of the M8 motorway.

It was the greatest Edinburgh derby triumph of them all – at least for now!

v **Aberdeen** 1-0
Bank of Scotland SPL
3rd May 2006. Tynecastle

Hearts:	Aberdeen:
Gordon	Langfield
Neilson	McNaughton
Fyssas	Anderson
Tall	Diamond
Pressley	Byrne
Cesnauskis	Nicholson
Hartley	Severin
Aguiar	Foster
Skacel	Smith
Bednar	Lovell
Jankauskas	Crawford

Referee: S Dougal (Bothwall)

IT MAY seem unusual for three of my list of Hearts' 50 greatest games to occur in the same season. However, the 2005/06 season was one of the most memorable in the long and proud history of Heart of Midlothian FC.

While Hearts progressed to the Scottish Cup final, there was disappointment that their challenge for the SPL title, that had began so strongly at the beginning of the season, had faded in 2006.

The day of George Burley's departure was a difficult one for everyone of the maroon persuasion to take. Captain Steven Pressley spoke of the players' shock and disbelief at the turn of events – apparently, the first the players knew of Burley's departure was at 10am of the day of the match against Dunfermline Athletic at Tynecastle.

As he had done when John Robertson and Craig Levein left the managerial position, coach John McGlynn stepped into the breach and picked the team to face the Pars. There was an understandably muted atmosphere in Gorgie but goals from Rudi Skacel and fellow Czech Michal Pospisil were enough to record a 2-0 win and keep Hearts top of the SPL. Nonetheless, the frustrations of the day were evident when Pressley was sent off in the final minute and when the final whistle blew, Skacel and Paul Hartley pulled off their Hearts shirts to reveal tee shirts that read "For the Gaffer". Clearly, Hearts had gone from plain sailing to troubled waters in less than 24 hours.

McGlynn was to be in charge of just four games. Hearts won three of those but also suffered their first league defeat of the season in circumstances that couldn't have been more painful – a 2-0 loss to Hibs at Easter Road, although they weren't helped by yet another red card when Lithuanian striker Edgaras Jankauskas was sent off with half an hour to go and the game still goalless. The home team scored two late goals and to rub salt into substantial wounds, Hearts' defeat allowed Celtic to claim top spot in the SPL on goal difference 24 hours later.

As detailed in an earlier chapter, Englishman Graham Rix was the shock choice to replace Burley as manager and his appointment received a mixed response from the Hearts support. His first game in charge saw another two points dropped in a 1-1 draw at Aberdeen, before two more points were lost in another 1-1 draw at Motherwell. Thanks to Dunfermline Athletic's shock 1-0 win at Celtic Park, Hearts were just one point behind the leaders but the early season panache that had characterised their play had disappeared along with Burley. Further points went to Inverness Caledonian Thistle and a second league loss of the season occurred at Ibrox – another red card for Hearts, this time Salius Mikoliunas.

On Boxing Day 2005, Hearts at last recaptured some form when they thrashed Falkirk 5-0 at Tynecastle to relieve some of the pressure already building on Rix. The visit of league leaders Celtic to Tynecastle on New Year's Day was to prove the acid test of Hearts' championship credentials. The Hoops were now four points clear of the Maroons going into the first game of 2006 and the well-worn cliche of "last chance saloon" appeared in many newspapers.

The match had an incredible start – Hearts posted their intentions by racing into a two-goal lead after only eight minutes, thanks to Jankauskas and Pressley. Hearts dominated the first half and could well have added to their lead. They didn't – and ten minutes into the second half, Celtic pulled a goal back through Pearson.

With 13 minutes left Hearts were still ahead 2-1 when, not for the first time that season, calamity struck. Takis Fyssas made what appeared to be a brilliant tackle on Celtic's Maloney, who fell to the ground a tad theatrically. Referee Iain Brines raced over and Hearts fans expected him to flash a yellow card for "simulation" (diving to you and me). Brines reached into his pocket and pulled out, not a yellow card, but a red one – and showed it to the Hearts player.

Bedlam ensued as the Greek full-back had to be persuaded to leave the field, while the Hearts players and supporters were enraged. With just three minutes left, the inevitable happened and Celtic equalised through McManus. Two more points spilt we thought, as we sat disbelievingly in the Wheatfield Stand – the roof of which, metaphorically, fell in during injury time when McManus scored again to steal all three points for Celtic. Hearts had turned a 2-0 lead into an agonising 3-2 defeat. They had now slipped seven points behind Celtic at the top of the SPL, a position from which they – and Graham Rix – would never recover. Such was Hearts' fury at the sending off of Fysass, Paul Hartley was also shown a red card after the game as the disciplinary record fell to a new low.

By now, the newly-created transfer window was in operation. Hearts reacted to the defeat from Celtic in astonishing fashion by wafting the chequebook to all and sundry in an attempt to make up the lost ground. Jose Goncalves, Bruno Aguiar, Nerijus Barasa, Lee Johnson, Juho Makela, Martin Petras, Ludek Straceny and Chris Hackett all arrived at Tynecastle to bolster the squad.

The most astonishing arrival of all, however, was winger Mirsad Beslija who arrived from Belgian side Racing Genk for a club record transfer fee of £850,000. Hearts fans were gobsmacked as few had heard of the Bosnian winger. Although Beslija tried his best, it wasn't long before his signing was being questioned.

At the end of January, Hearts put another four goals past the hapless Hibees at Tynecastle but the 4-1 win was notable for the absence of most of the players who had arrived during the month. When Hearts drew 1-1 with Rangers in mid-March, it was seen as a decent result but the mixed bag of results and lack of convincing performances since Rix's arrival had seen the Maroons fall 15 points behind league leaders Celtic. With the loss of another two points to Rangers, the end was nigh for Rix who was dismissed and replaced by Lithuanian coach Valdas Ivanauskas.

More turmoil for Hearts, who were now fighting off Rangers for second place in the SPL – a position that would mean qualification for the following season's Champions League. Hearts had not played in Europe's premier cup competition since 1960, under its former guise of the European Cup, and while owner Vladimir Romanov knew the league title was now beyond the Maroons, a second-placed finish and the chance to sit at European football's top table was now a necessity.

Ivanauskas was an affable character and, importantly, he knew how Romanov worked. The cynics suggested Ivanauskas would be little more than Romanov's 'puppet' but results and performances – another defeat at Easter Road aside – picked up. At the end of April, Hearts gained revenge on Celtic by defeating the newly crowned champions 3-0 at Tynecastle, meaning a win against Aberdeen in Gorgie on Wednesday 3rd May would clinch second spot in the SPL and a chance for Champions League football.

More than 17,000 squeezed into Tynecastle on a fine May evening to witness history being made. The atmosphere was the best I have ever experienced at the old ground and as the game kicked off I could feel the hairs on the back of my neck stand up, such was the intensity of the occasion. Aberdeen still harboured hopes of playing in the following season's Uefa Cup so would prove difficult opponents.

Hearts, as they had done so often that season, began the game at lightning pace and were soon camped in the Aberdeen half. Paul Hartley made the first chance when he dispossessed Smith and passed to Roman Bednar. The Czech Republic striker laid the ball into the path of Deividas Cesnauskis who seemed set to score – but the Lithuanian lacked the composure required and his shot on goal was woefully wide. An early sign of nerves from the home team.

The Dons were content to soak up the considerable pressure from the home side and to hit on the break, something they did midway through the first half when Foster raced down the left wing, before his dangerous cross was collected well by Hearts goalkeeper Craig Gordon.

Big Edgaras Jankauskas had experienced something of a tempestuous relationship with the Hearts support. The Lithuanian striker quite often demonstrated a lackadaisical approach in certain games but against Aberdeen that evening, he was immense. Clearly, he knew what this meant to Hearts and was eager to play once again in the Champions League.

Chances were becoming rare as the enormity of what was at stake began to take its toll. A huge sigh blew around Tynecastle when Lovell seemed set to score for the visitors, but the striker was offside. Just before half-time, Paul Hartley delivered one of his now trademark free kicks that found the head of Steven Pressley and the captain's header came within a whisker of finding the net.

Bednar then set up Rudi Skacel with a chance and it was in keeping with the evening that the high-scoring midfielder screwed his effort on goal wide of the target, when earlier in the season he would have buried such an attempt with his eyes closed. At 0-0, half-time was one of the tensest intervals I could recall in nearly 40 years of going to Tynecastle.

The second period was just seven minutes old when Hearts, at last, made the breakthrough. Robbie Neilson delivered one of his famous long throws into the Aberdeen penalty box. Bednar rose high to head the ball on, but Dons defender Diamond used a hand to try to prevent further damage. "Penalty!" screamed 17,000 Hearts fans – and referee Stuart Dougal agreed. The official saw fit to only book the Aberdeen man, which was an odd decision given he had clearly denied Hearts a goalscoring opportunity. With the eyes of the huge Hearts support upon him, Hartley stepped forward. He handled the pressure magnificently as he stroked the ball past Langfield in the Aberdeen goal to put Hearts ahead.

Hearts, to their enormous credit, weren't content to sit back and defend their precious lead and Hartley and Jankauskas both came close to scoring a second goal that would have put the game beyond the visitors. It was only in the final few minutes that Hearts defended en masse, as Aberdeen tried to spoil the party. They couldn't – the game ended 1-0 to Hearts.

The emotional scenes that followed at Tynecastle will remain with me for the rest of my days. Some fans – and indeed players – were overcome with emotion. For the first time in 46 years, Hearts were back in the European Cup. Although they would have to face two qualifying rounds to reach the financially lucrative group stages, the fact they had an opportunity to do so was beyond the wildest dreams of many.

The Champions League anthem was belted out at Tynecastle at the end of a hugely emotional – and successful – evening. Hearts had one last SPL game to play, at Ibrox, but the result was immaterial. Hearts had split the Old Firm. And they would join – albeit briefly – Europe's football elite.

48 v Gretna 1-1 (AET, Hearts win 4-2 on penalties)
Tennents Scottish Cup Final
13th May 2006. Hampden

Hearts:	Gretna:
Gordon	Main
Neilson	Birch
Fyssas	Townsley
Tall	Innes
Pressley	Nicholls
Cesnauskis	McGuffie
Aguiar	Tosh
Hartley	O'Neil
Skacel	Skelton
Bednar	Grady
Jankauskas	Deuchar

Referee: D McDonald (Edinburgh)

ARLIER IN this book, I chronicled Hearts' Scottish Cup triumph in 1998. A highly emotive occasion, ending 36 long years without Hearts supporters seeing a trophy of any note being delivered to Tynecastle.

Despite Hearts playing some sparkling football that year, few of us had any great expectation of Hearts defeating Rangers in the final at Celtic Park. We had hope, certainly – to quote from one of my favourite films, *The Shawshank Redemption*, hope is a good thing, maybe the best of things and no good thing ever dies. However, Hearts fans know never to expect anything as the fortunes of this great club has an unfortunate knack of kicking one in the teeth when you get even an inkling of glory. The events at Dens Park, Dundee in May 1986 and Hampden Park in April 1988 and May 1996 are testament to that. The build-up to the Scottish Cup final of 2006, however, was different.

At the beginning of 2006, you might have got fair odds for Hearts reaching the Scottish Cup final. The odds you would have got for Gretna also being in the final, well you could have named your own price. Hearts' memorable semi-final victory over city rivals Hibernian was, many people observed, the final before the final, which was quite disrespectful to Gretna who, to use a cliche used by most newspapers, were Scottish football's fairy story.

Under ebullient owner Brook Mileson, the Borders club rose from non-league football, through the Scottish Leagues, and had just been promoted to Division One of the SFL. Mileson had pumped several hundred thousand pounds into the club and they could afford to bring decent seasoned professionals to Rydale Park. Their rapid success was no fluke and Gretna fans were, to use another cliche, "living the dream".

A year after their cup final with Hearts, Gretna secured promotion to the Scottish Premier League and the dream had come true. However, it was a dream that would ultimately quickly turn into a nightmare when Mileson died and the club were left with crippling debts. Gretna were relegated at the end of their first and what would prove to be only season in the top flight of Scottish football – the tragedy of Brook Mileson became a tragedy of Gretna football club and they folded at the end of the 2007/08 season. Although Gretna 2008 was rescued from the ashes, it meant a return to non-league football.

Having secured a place in the qualifying stages of the Champions League for the 2006/07 season, Hearts were confident of seeing off their lower league opponents and claiming their second Scottish Cup in eight years. Hearts fans, even those of us who have been through the mire on more occasions than we care to remember, were supremely confident – a trait that doesn't sit easily on Gorgie Road.

Hearts don't get to that many Scottish Cup finals but there was a nagging feeling in my mind that they could do the ultimate disservice and defeat themselves in the final. By that, I mean complacency could set in and many of the Hearts players – the overseas contingent in particular – might believe all they had to do to lift the famous old trophy was turn up at Hampden on Saturday 13th May 2006. After all, surely the hard work had already been done. I'm sure I wasn't the only Hearts supporter feeling uneasy while reading on the internet about victory parades being planned in some detail days before the event by fans who reckoned Hearts winning the cup was a mere formality. Some of us knew better.

Some of the Glasgow-based media declared their fears about the showcase of the Scottish football season being something of a damp squib and hoped the anticipated rows of empty seats wouldn't devalue the occasion. No Old Firm in the final would be bad news for the sponsors, they opined. Having a Second Division team in the final made a mockery of Scottish football, some suggested. Such a game would be something of an embarrassment, others declared. They were all proved wrong in so many ways. More than 51,000 fans headed for Hampden Park for an occasion that brought excitement aplenty.

Tynecastle captain Steven Pressley had often spoken of his desire to lift silverware in a maroon shirt and he cut an almost Braveheart-type figure as he led his team out in the Hampden sun. He knew, more than anyone, he might not get such an opportunity to get a cup winners' medal again.

Hearts began the game as many predicted – in the ascendancy. After just five minutes, Paul Hartley delivered a cross into the Gretna penalty box but Pressley headed the ball wide and an early chance to settle the nerves had gone. Two minutes later, Takis Fyssas's attempt on goal fell kindly to Deividas Cesnauskis and the Lithuanian's shot from the edge of the penalty area crashed off the crossbar with Gretna goalkeeper Main beaten.

The 40,000 Hearts supporters who had virtually taken over the national stadium roared their approval and sensed an early goal might open the floodgates. Rudi Skacel and Edgaras Jankauskas brought out fine saves from Main and it seemed only a matter of the time before the Maroons opened the scoring. However, as the first half wore on, Hearts had nothing to show for their domination of the game.

Full-back Robbie Neilson was keen to get forward and help his colleagues find the breakthrough and his fine cross found Roman Bednar from eight yards out. However, the Czech Republic striker headed over the bar. Worryingly, the afternoon was beginning to take on a look of "one of those days", a feeling enhanced when Hearts goalkeeper Craig Gordon, a virtual spectator, tried to launch a long ball upfield only to see his effort charged down by Gretna attacker Grady but thankfully, the danger came to nothing.

Hearts resumed on the offensive and Bruno Aguiar came agonisingly close with an effort that was deflected wide, before Hartley had an opportunity but was denied by the alertness of goalkeeper Main. After just over half an hour, Bednar had another chance but while his header was on target, it was directed straight at Main and with just ten minutes until half-time, Hearts fans began to anxiously check their watches. Their team had had little difficulty in scoring goals all season but it was typical of Hearts to fall short against a side they were expected to beat easily – even if it was a cup final.

Gretna didn't venture up the park too often but they went close with a free kick that Gordon was happy to tip over the crossbar. This gave encouragement to the 10,000 Gretna fans in the national stadium and increased the tension among the maroon hordes. However, with five minutes to go before half-time, Hearts fans erupted in a cacophony of joy – and relief. All except my mate, Gordon, who chose that moment to head for the toilet, the result of the consumption of a pint too many pre-match.

Neilson launched a throw towards the Gretna penalty box. The Gretna defence, who had performed heroics up to this point, inexplicably let the ball run through to Skacel who seized the opportunity to drill home a low shot past Main and into the corner of the net. Skacel ran to the Hearts support and lifted his shirt to revel a tee shirt that read "Thanks Jambos I Will Never Forget" – an action that incurred the wrath of referee Dougie McDonald who promptly booked the Czech star. At last, the Maroon Army could relax and contemplate celebrating. Or could they?

Just four minutes of the second half had elapsed when Gretna should have drawn level. Deuchar's header fell to Tosh but the former Aberdeen player pulled his shot at goal wide and Hearts breathed again.

With the score refusing to budge from 1-0, Bednar was sent through by Jankauskas. The striker had made an impressive start to the season but had suffered an injury that had kept him out for several weeks and, it's fair to say, he had not been quite the same player since his return. Not for the first time that afternoon, he screwed his shot wide and Gretna survived.

Hearts really needed a second goal to kill off the challenge. A feeling underlined when the game produced what Hearts supporters have referred to ever since, as "that tackle". Gretna's David Graham went past a couple of half-hearted challenges and was through on Gordon. He rounded the Scotland keeper and seemed set to draw parity when Robbie Neilson made a tackle comparable with England's Bobby Moore on Pele during the 1970 World Cup finals in Mexico (ask your parents, younger readers). Neilson's heroics kept Hearts ahead but it gave their opponents belief that winning the cup was not the impossible dream many considered it to be.

The out-of-sorts Bednar was replaced by his compatriot Michal Pospisil as Hearts sought to regain the initiative. With 15 minutes to go, Cesnauskis, an attacking player, made a challenge on O'Neil inside the Hearts penalty box. It was a forward's challenge and resulted in the inevitable, a penalty to Gretna. Hearts supporters urged

Gordon to save McGuffie's kick. He did – but the ball went straight back to the Gretna player who slotted it into the empty net. 1-1 and the small band of Gretna fans celebrated wildly.

Hartley and Skacel came close to giving Hearts the lead again but extra time loomed – thankfully, as it turned out as Gretna's McGuffie had the chance to write himself into the history books but Gordon produced a superb save to avoid one of the biggest Scottish Cup upsets of all time.

There was the feeling of slight embarrassment as extra time got underway. A team that would be hoping to play in next season's Champions League were being held by a Second Division team. The game had still to be won. Skacel hit a post before Jankauskas missed a glorious opportunity, as the seriousness of the situation finally seemed to hit the Hearts players.

The clock ticked inexorably towards the dreaded penalty shoot-out. Just five minutes remained when Skacel found himself clean through on Alan Main. The Czech rounded the keeper and was set to score the winner when Main brought him down. "Penalty!" screamed 40,000 Hearts supporters. Nothing doing said referee McDonald who immediately booked Fyssas for protesting and a clearly angered Hartley for dissent seconds later.

In the dying moments, Hartley let his anger get the better of him and kicked Gretna's Townsley on the touchline. A second yellow card meant red for the former St Johnstone player and while the numerical advantage for Gretna meant nothing with just seconds remaining, it meant one of Hearts' principal penalty takers would not be able to participate in the dreaded shoot-out that followed.

More than 50,000 fans collectively held their breath as the cup final was settled on penalties. Pressley converted the first kick and was followed by Neilson, Skacel and Pospisil. For Gretna, Townsley missed his effort and when Skelton stepped up, he knew he had to score to keep Gretna's dream alive. He blazed his effort against the crossbar – and Hearts had won the Scottish Cup for the seventh time.

For the second time in eight years, a weekend of huge celebrations would take place in Scotland's capital city. Well, one half of it anyway. Open top buses don't tend to travel down Leith Walk.

The cup triumph was a fitting end to an unforgettable season. Vladimir Romanov attended the final at Hampden and while the majority shareholder may have presided over some controversial decisions that season, his money had not only kept Hearts at Tynecastle but had helped deliver silverware, not something that happens regularly in Gorgie.

When it does, as Hearts fans proved that memorable weekend, it's worth celebrating.

v Aberdeen 5-0
Clydesdale Bank SPL
11th December 2010. Tynecastle

Hearts:	Aberdeen:
Kello	Langfield
Jonsson	Robertson
Zaliukas	Diamond
Bouzid	Ifil
Palazuelos	Considine
Templeton	Young
Black	Hartley
Mrowiec	Folly
Skacel	Aluko
Kyle	Vernon
Elliott	Maguire

Referee: M Tumilty (Hartlepool)

THERE WAS a strange parallel between Hearts' Scottish Cup-winning team of 1998 and the one of 2006. As detailed earlier, ten months after winning the Scottish Cup in 1998, Hearts flirted dangerously with relegation before recovering sufficiently. Eight years later, Hearts started the 2006/07 season with a Champions League qualifier – and ended it in disarray, with yet another change of manager.

More than 28,000 fans headed to Murrayfield Stadium to see Hearts play their Champions League qualifying round first leg against Bosnian side NK Siroki Brijeg and after struggling in the first half, three second-half goals without reply meant a goalless draw in the return in Bosnia was more than sufficient to reach the final qualifying round – and to be two games away from the lucrative group stages.

However, the quality of the opposition rose considerably and AEK Athens won 2-1 in the first leg at Murrayfield – watched by Hearts' largest home attendance for 30 years, 32,459. Hearts lost the return in Greece 3-0 a fortnight later and the Champions League dream was over – although there was the consolation of dropping into the Uefa Cup.

Hearts made a decent start to their 2006/07 SPL campaign and defeated Dunfermline Athletic and reigning champions Celtic in their opening two games. However, they dropped points to their nemesis Falkirk before losing to Rangers and the glorious football of 12 months earlier was becoming a fading memory.

Manager Valdas Ivanauskas had brought in several new players with a view to Hearts playing in Europe. Hristos Karipidis, Mauricio Pinilla, Tiago Costa, Marius Zaliukas, Andrius Velicka and Eggert Jonsson were just some of the new arrivals, although the acrimonious departures of Andy Webster and Rudi Skacel were serious blows.

After a decent start to the SPL, Hearts began to struggle and home losses to St Mirren, Kilmarnock and Aberdeen were not what owner Vladimir Romanov expected. He placed manager Ivanauskas on 'gardening leave' and brought in the little-known Eduard Malofeev as interim manager – a move that perplexed fans and players alike. A month later Ivanauskas was back in charge.

Hearts did defeat Hibs 3-2 on Boxing Day but this only partly made up for elimination from the League Cup by their Edinburgh rivals at Easter Road six weeks earlier. Despite having a large squad, Hearts were struggling to score goals. The arrival of Ghanaian attacking midfielder Laryea Kingston at the end of the January transfer window would help, but this wasn't enough to prevent Hearts relinquishing their hold on the Scottish Cup by exiting the 2007 competition in the fourth round, following a 1-0 defeat at Dunfermline Athletic.

A 1-1 draw at home to St Mirren was the last straw for Romanov, who again relieved Ivanauskas of his duties and replaced him with Anatoly Korobochka. The Russian, who was already at Tynecastle in his role as sporting director, didn't speak a lot of English, which clearly didn't help, although he relied on his assistant Stephen Frail to deliver the message to the media.

Hearts lost at Aberdeen and then heavily to Dundee United at Tynecastle, as a season that promised so much at the beginning slowly fizzled out, although there was a flourishing end to the campaign with two wins over Hibs and an impressive 3-1 win at Celtic Park against the SPL champions. However, a fourth-placed finish in the SPL was hugely disappointing and meant the club missed out on European football altogether the following season.

Korobochka remained in charge for the beginning of season 2007/08 that began with a glamour friendly against probably the best club side in the world. The visit of FC Barcelona at the end of July attracted just under 58,000 fans to Murrayfield – thus making it Hearts' largest ever home attendance. The Catalan superstars won 3-1 but it was a magnificent occasion.

Sadly, this proved to be the highlight of an awful season that ended with Hearts failing to even make the top six of the SPL. Korobochka was relieved of his duties on the last day of 2007 and his assistant Frail took charge. Hearts ended an awful season in eighth place in the SPL and while they did reach the semi-final of the League Cup they were beaten by Rangers 2-0 at Hampden while in the Scottish Cup, the Maroons contrived to throw away a two-goal lead in the fourth round against Motherwell at Tynecastle – and lost the replay 1-0 at Fir Park. The appointment of Hungarian Csaba Laszlo as manager in the summer of 2008 was another move from Vladimir Romanov that took everyone by surprise and Laszlo's first season in charge was a relatively successful one with a third-placed finish in the SPL, although a home defeat from Airdrie United in the League Cup wasn't in the script.

The highlight of the season was knocking Hibs out of the Scottish Cup with a 2-0 win at Easter Road with a rare goal from a player who attracted much criticism during his time at Tynecastle, striker Christian Nade. The Frenchman once scored a wonderful goal for Sheffield United against Arsenal and this seemed enough to persuade Anatoly Korobochka to convince Romanov to part with £500,000 for his services. Nade would prove to be the archetypal enigma – he scored a good goal once and we're all waiting for him to do it again.

His laissez-faire approach would infuriate Hearts fans and he clearly wasn't overly concerned about his weight or fitness. Nade would become the object of ridicule, initially from opposition fans, but it wasn't long before Hearts fans joined in.

After knocking Hibs out of the Scottish Cup, Hearts' next opponents were Falkirk at Tynecastle. Therefore, when I mention the name Falkirk, perhaps you can guess what happened next.

The 2009/10 season saw Hearts struggle to achieve the consistency of the previous campaign. Their sojourn into Europe in the now re-named Europa League was short-lived, as a 4-0 hammering in the play-off first leg by Dinamo Zagreb in Croatia rendered the return at Tynecastle meaningless, although the Maroons did win 2-0.

With the bumbling Nade up front, Hearts were struggling to score goals and by Christmas 2009, they were fifth in the SPL but had scored just 16 times in 17 league games. When Hearts exited the Scottish Cup at the first time of asking with a 2-0 defeat at Aberdeen, the writing was on the wall for Csaba Laszlo. Less than a week later, he was shown the exit door at Tynecastle.

Yet again, Romanov pulled off a shock by announcing Laszlo's replacement within a couple of hours of his departure – Jim Jefferies. The man who led Hearts to Scottish Cup glory in 1998 had left the manager's position at Kilmarnock earlier in the season and, thus, was a free agent. His return to Tynecastle was greeted enthusiastically by the majority of Hearts supporters, starved as they were of the attacking flair for which Jefferies was renowned.

Jefferies knew things had changed at Tynecastle in the near decade since he had left but he vowed to work with Romanov and the two men seemed to strike up an immediate trust and respect. Jefferies took the rest of 2009/10 to assess the squad he had inherited and Hearts at least managed to finish in the top six of the SPL, albeit in sixth position.

One of the few highlights of a curious season was the defeat of Celtic in Glasgow in the quarter-final of the League Cup, although not even the presence of the newly-appointed Jefferies could prevent another semi-final disappointment when Hearts lost 1-0 to St Mirren at Fir Park.

It didn't take Jefferies long to assess what needed to be done to resuscitate Hearts. Players such as Kingston and Nade were shown the door and new players such as Republic of Ireland striker Stephen Elliott and former Scotland striker Kevin Kyle were drafted in, as was defender Darren Barr from Falkirk.

As the 2010/11 season began, Hearts were playing much better football even if, perhaps, results didn't always demonstrate this. The return of 2006 Scottish Cup hero Rudi Skacel at the end of September was acclaimed by an adoring Hearts support. After losing 3-0 at home to Kilmarnock, Hearts then embarked on an astonishing winning streak and a fortnight before Christmas entertained Aberdeen.

The Dons had endured an awful season. A month earlier, they had been hammered 9-0 by Celtic, a result that ultimately cost their manager Mark McGhee his job. By the time the Dons arrived at Tynecastle, they had a new man in charge, former Scotland manager Craig Brown. Over 13,000 fans headed for Gorgie on a cold afternoon, not only to escape Christmas shopping but also to see if Hearts could make it five SPL wins in a row.

With young winger David Templeton in fine form, Hearts made a flying start, although it was the visitors who had the first chance but defender Diamond headed wide of goal. It was the only time the Dons were seriously in the game as Hearts raced to a two-goal lead after just nine minutes. First, Templeton linked up well with Skacel before racing into the Aberdeen penalty box.

Maguire lunged in and while the fans screamed for a penalty kick, young Templeton didn't wait for the referee's decision and squeezed the ball past two Dons defenders to give Hearts the lead. Four minutes later, Templeton was again involved and he sprinted down the left wing before delivering a cross that gave Skacel the easiest of chances to make it 2-0. After their mauling at Celtic, one could almost see the visitors fearing the worst. However, despite totally dominating possession, Hearts couldn't add to their lead in an embarrassingly one-sided first half in which Ian Black, Kyle and Elliott all had chances.

Six minutes into the second half, Hearts made it 3-0. Centre-half Marius Zaliukas fended off the overly physical challenge from former Hearts team-mate Paul Hartley – now captain of Aberdeen – before ambling forward. The Lithuanian passed to Ruben Palazuelos, whose perfectly timed cross was headed home by Elliott.

Hearts were rampant and seven minutes later, they made it 4-0. Good work from Adrian Mrowiec on the right set Templeton free and the young winger unselfishly passed to Skacel who had the easiest of tap-ins from barely two yards. Minutes later, Skacel could have completed his hat-trick after he moved on to a header from Kyle but Dons keeper Langfield saved well.

A fifth goal did arrive 13 minutes from the end, when Lithuanian substitute Arvydas Novikovas drifted in from the wing before curling a magnificent effort beyond the flailing arms of Langfield. The gamed ended at 5-0 to Hearts, although substitute Calum Elliott should have made it six, but his lob over Langfield also cleared the crossbar.

After hammering Aberdeen, Hearts rather carelessly dropped two points to Inverness Caledonian Thistle at Tynecastle the following week but then won their next four SPL games to pick up a remarkable 31 points out of a possible 33. However, Hearts were then affected by an injury to striker Kevin Kyle who would miss the rest of the season. Without his presence – and that of goalkeeper Marian Kello who was also injured and then left out the team for "personal reasons" – Hearts began to run out of steam, as was evident in a 4-0 thrashing by Celtic which put paid to any league title ambitions.

Indeed, Jim Jefferies' side won only one of their last 12 SPL fixtures, and that was when they scored two late goals to defeat St Mirren 3-2 at Tynecastle. Nonetheless, Hearts' mid-season form was sufficient to secure third place in the SPL and a place in the following season's Europa League.

There was disappointment in the domestic cups when Hearts lost 4-3 at First Division side Falkirk in the League Cup and stumbled out of the Scottish Cup at the first attempt, 1-0 to St Johnstone on a night of crushing disappointment at Tynecastle.

However, that hammering of Aberdeen – and the promise of youngsters such as David Templeton – gave Hearts fans hope that their side would once again be challenging Celtic and Rangers.

v Hibernian 5-1
William Hill Scottish Cup Final
19th May 2012. Hampden

Hearts:	Hibernian:
MacDonald	Brown
Grainger	Doherty
Barr	Hanlon
Webster	McPake
McGowan	Kujabi
Zaliukas	Claros
Santana	Soares
Black	Stevenson
Driver	Osbourne
Skacel	O'Connor
Elliott	Griffiths

Referee: C Thomson (Paisley)

YOU MAY have noticed, dear reader, a recurring theme throughout this book. Namely, that whenever Hearts look like they are on the verge of sustained success – the glorious decade that was the 1950s apart – the roof metaphorically falls in at Tynecastle and the club dips from the heights of glory to the depths of despair.

Hearts ended the 2010/11 season in third place in the Clydesdale Bank SPL. However, in the end they were clinging on to their position, despite being 13 points ahead at one stage. At the beginning of 2011, their nearest challengers for third and entry into the following season's Europa League were Kilmarnock, Motherwell and Inverness Caledonian Thistle.

All three were too inconsistent to offer a serious challenge although Hearts, having gone on an impressive run during which they took 31 out of a possible 33 points, then somewhat inevitably pressed the self-destruct button. One win out of 12 in the final stage of the season suggested Jim Jefferies' side had taken their feet off the gas, so to speak.

It was Dundee United – at one stage 20 points behind Hearts – who threatened to steal third place in the SPL but, in the end, Hearts clinched it by two points. However, it was a worrying end to the season and those concerns surfaced again as the 2011/12 season began.

Manager Jefferies brought new faces to Tynecastle in the summer of 2011. On one memorable day towards the end of May, Jefferies wasted no time in putting his plans in place for the new season by recruiting defender Danny Grainger, midfielder Jamie Hamill and centre-forward John Sutton. He almost added a fourth player that day but the move to bring Aberdeen's Zander Diamond to Tynecastle ultimately fell through.

It was a day to take the breath away and when Jefferies signed the hugely talented Kilmarnock midfielder Mehdi Taouil it signalled Hearts' intention of building on last season's success and challenging Rangers for their league championship. When Hearts opened their Clydesdale Bank SPL campaign for season 2011/12 with an encouraging 1-1 draw at Ibrox, some supporters were as optimistic as Hearts fans can ever be.

However, despite that result, there was some criticism of Jefferies' tactical approach that Saturday lunchtime at Ibrox. Hearts dominated the first half and led at half-time through David Obua's goal. After the break, however, Hearts seemed content to sit back and not capitalise on their dominance – not the wisest thing to do at Ibrox. Rangers duly equalised and could well have snatched victory at the end. Some people may have thought it was a sign of progress that Hearts were disappointed at leaving Govan with a draw but the feeling persisted that the champions were there for the taking and Hearts should have won the game – if only they carried the conviction to do so.

When, eight days later, Hearts lost their first home league game of the season, 1-0 to Dundee United, the notoriously threadbare patience of Vladimir Romanov snapped. He sacked Jefferies and replaced him with former Sporting Lisbon manager Paulo Sergio. The cynics sniped that sacking Jefferies was a move similar to when George Burley was dismissed six years earlier and that appointing a foreign manager who lost his job as a result of getting knocked out of Europe by Rangers – as Sporting Lisbon had been – was hardly a sign of ambition.

And the early days of Sergio's tutelage were hardly inspiring. Hearts did defeat Hungarian side Paksi 5-2 on aggregate in the second qualifying round of the Europa League but perhaps wished they hadn't bothered when they were drawn against English giants Tottenham Hotspur in the final qualifying round.

Tynecastle was packed for the first leg as Spurs brought their big guns to Scotland's capital city. It took the English side just four minutes to show their class when van der Vaart opened the scoring and there began a master class from the FA Premiership side. Hearts were chasing shadows and Spurs won 5-0 on the night although it could have been seven or eight.

Sergio said afterwards his team had shown far too much respect and although a bit of pride was salvaged when a young Hearts team secured a goalless draw in the second leg at White Hart Lane a week later, the affect on morale was substantial.

A 2-0 win over an even more struggling Hibernian side at Tynecastle helped the mood but Hearts were still struggling with form and results. Sergio had a different football philosophy to his predecessor and it seemed some Hearts players struggled with the concept of keeping possession and probing for openings rather than the more direct style of Jefferies.

Sergio tinkered with the team for the trip to Somerset Park to face First Division side Ayr United in the Scottish Communities League Cup. Youngster Scott Robinson had given Hearts the lead and Eggert Jonsson appeared to have added a second but the goal was controversially chalked off for handball by the Icelandic international. Inevitably, the home team equalised with just under half an hour to go. With no further scoring, even after extra time, Hearts lost after a penalty shoot-out. Missing penalties was to be an unwelcome feature of Hearts' season.

The visit of Celtic to Gorgie in October was a sign progress was being made, however, as Hearts won 2-0 and when the Maroons won by a similar scoreline at Dunfermline six days later, we hoped the corner had been turned. But Hearts then went four games in succession without scoring and defeats by St Johnstone and Celtic at the beginning of December caused concern among the fans – as did the fact stories emerged that Hearts were late in paying their first-team players, a situation that dragged on for three months over the festive period. The Hearts players took their grievance to the Scottish Premier League who threatened Hearts with an unnamed punishment if they didn't pay their players what they were due.

Whether this created a siege mentality isn't wholly certain but Hearts embarked on an impressive run of results from mid-December to mid-January. Dunfermline Athletic were hammered 4-0 at Tynecastle, and Motherwell beaten 2-0 before Hearts endured a goalless draw in farcical gale force wind conditions at Aberdeen just after Christmas. On 2nd January 2012, Hearts first-footed Hibernian and won more easily than the 3-1 scoreline suggests. Add a missed penalty, David Templeton hitting the post and Andrew Driver missing a gilt-edged chance and it could well have been 6-1.

Hearts would continue to enjoy Edinburgh derby dominance this season – one that would culminate with the biggest capital derby of all in Glasgow. When the William Hill-sponsored Scottish Cup came around for the top-flight clubs in January, Hearts were given a home draw against junior side Auchinleck Talbot. History was made, as Hearts had never played a junior side in the Scottish Cup before – and history was almost made in an unwanted sense as the Ayrshire side defended furiously at Tynecastle and looked like leaving with a well-deserved replay until substitute Gordon Smith drove home a late winner for the Maroons.

Hearts then enacted two similar tales against the saints of Scottish football. Firstly, St Johnstone scored a late equaliser at Tynecastle to force a replay in Perth. However, an extra-time winner from Marius Zaliukas gave Hearts a 2-1 win to set up a quarter-final clash with St Mirren. Again, Hearts let slip a lead to allow the Paisley Saints to secure a replay. Again, though, Hearts came good in the replay, winning 2-0.

This set up a semi-final clash against cup holders Celtic at Hampden. After a dull first half, the game burst into life early in the second period when Rudi Skacel gave Hearts the lead. However, there was a horrible feeling of déjà vu when the Hoops equalised with three minutes to go and memories of the 1988 semi-final clash – when Celtic hit two goals in the final three minutes to knock Hearts out – came flooding back.

However, former Celtic striker Craig Beattie scored a last minute penalty – before racing off the field, bare-chested, to celebrate with the maroon hordes – to give Hearts a place in the William Hill Scottish Cup final. An historic final at that, for it was against their greatest rivals, Hibernian.

As was the case before the all-Edinburgh semi-final in 2006, the build-up to the first Scottish Cup final between Hearts and Hibs since 1896 was full of tension. Hearts were installed by the bookmakers as odds-on favourites but several players, including Ian Black and talisman Rudi Skacel, were looking unlikely to be continuing their careers at Tynecastle, as there were no offers of any new contracts on the table.

Semi final hero Craig Beattie had been nursing a hamstring injury and wasn't included in the starting 11. Hibernian, who had only just managed to avoid relegation, had several players who were on loan, including striker Leigh Griffiths who had scored their winner in the semi-final win over Aberdeen.

A crowd of over 51,000 packed into Hampden and the tension was palpable as the teams walked on to the field. It was Hearts, however, who made the brighter start and good work from Driver saw a cross for Skacel but the Czech Republic player could not direct his header on target.

If Hearts were nervous they certainly didn't show it during that opening period as they pinned their city rivals inside their own half and with 15 minutes gone, the breakthrough arrived. A corner from Danny Grainger seemed to bemuse the Hibs defence. Ryan McGowan showed commitment to get to the ball first and his attempt at goal fell at the feet of Darren Barr who stabbed the ball past Hibs goalkeeper Brown and into the net to give Hearts a deserved lead.

Already in the ascendancy, Hearts' confidence grew further. Shortly after the goal, Hibs defender Kujabi was booked for a foul on Santana – something that would have major implications later. Black was dominant for Hearts and it seemed astonishing that Hibs were allowing the former Inverness Caledonian Thistle player so much space to orchestrate the Hearts midfield.

It was from Black's pass that Skacel doubled the Maroons' lead after 27 minutes. Collecting the ball on the edge of the Hibs penalty box, Skacel produced a trademark turn past McPake before firing in a shot that took a deflection off the Hibs player before flying past Brown for 2-0 to Hearts and the Maroon Army erupted in anticipation of another Hearts cup triumph.

Hibs had barely been in the game and when striker O'Connor had a chance on the edge of the Hearts penalty box, his effort on goal soared over the bar and in among the goading Hearts fans in the West Stand.

Hearts nearly made it game over when Suso Santana's effort on goal was scrambled off the line by McPake. And, typical of Hearts, what should have been 3-0 turned into 2-1 as Hibs grabbed an unexpected lifeline a minute before half-time when McPake poked home Soares' cross. At half-time, there was slight irritation among the Hearts camp that the game was now on a knife-edge after dominating the game.

The second half had a spectacular start. In the 47th minute, Santana set off on a run down the right wing, skipping easily past a couple of Hibs challenges. He had his shirt pulled by the pursuing Kujabi who also clipped the Spaniard's heels as the winger danced into the penalty box. Penalty said referee Craig Thomson, who also booked the Hibs player for a second time meaning the Easter Road team were down to ten men. They also went 3-1 down when Danny Grainger stroked home the resultant spot kick and looked to the skies in tribute to his late grandfather.

Any lingering doubts that the Scottish Cup was heading back to Gorgie disappeared two minutes later when Hibs keeper Brown could only parry Stephen Elliott's header and Ryan McGowan leapt to head the ball home for 4-1 to Hearts – and it was game over, a fact the mass exodus of Hibs fans at this point clearly indicated.

Hearts seemed content to toy with their great rivals and sprayed passes all over the Hampden turf, much to the delight of the baying Jambo Army. With 15 minutes to go, Skacel collected the ball on the edge of the penalty box and fired in an effort that trundled past Brown to make it an astonishing 5-1 to Hearts.

Ecstatic Hearts supporters taunted those few Hibs fans who were still in the national stadium with chants of "ole", "we want six" and "there's only one Pat Fenlon". This was too much for the Hibernian manager who made an ill-judged salute with his arm to the Hearts support and was duly sent to the stand by referee Craig Thomson for his troubles.

The game ended at Heart of Midlothian 5 Hibernian 1. I had waited 30 years to see Hearts win a trophy before they won the Scottish Cup in 1998; this was Hearts' third Scottish Cup triumph in 14 years and was the sweetest of them all. Hearts had dominated the Edinburgh derby for nearly 30 years but this magnificent victory over an admittedly very poor Hibernian team took derby domination and humiliation of their city rivals to new levels.

As in 1998 and 2006, the west end of Edinburgh partied. As the Maroon Army bellowed throughout that glorious weekend, the Hearts were having a party – the Hibs were in their beds!